Technoscience in contemporary film

MANCHESTER
UNIVERSITY PRESS

Inside Popular Film

General editors Mark Jancovich and Eric Schaefer

Inside Popular Film is a forum for writers who are working to develop new ways of analysing popular film. Each book offers a critical introduction to existing debates while also exploring new approaches. In general, the books give historically informed accounts of popular film which present this area as altogether more complex than is commonly suggested by established film theories.

Developments over the past decade have led to a broader understanding of film which moves beyond the traditional oppositions between high and low culture, popular and avant-garde. The analysis of film has also moved beyond a concentration on the textual forms of films, to include an analysis of both the social situations within which films are consumed by audiences, and the relationship between film and other popular forms. The series therefore addresses issues such as the complex intertextual systems which link film, literature, art and music, as well as the production and consumption of film through a variety of hybrid media, including video, cable and satellite.

The authors take interdisciplinary approaches which bring together a variety of theoretical and critical debates that have developed in film, media and cultural studies. They neither embrace nor condemn popular film, but explore specific forms and genres within the contexts of their production and consumption.

Already published:

Thomas Austin *Hollywood, hype and audiences*
Harry M. Benshoff *Monsters in the closet: homosexuality and the horror film*
Julia Hallam and Margaret Marshment *Realism and popular cinema*
Joanne Hollows and Mark Jancovich (eds) *Approaches to popular film*
Nicole Matthews *Gender in Hollywood: comedy after the new right*
Jacinda Read *The new avengers: feminism, femininity and the rape-revenge cycle*

Technoscience in contemporary film

Beyond science fiction

Aylish Wood

Manchester University Press

Manchester and New York

distributed exclusively in the USA by Palgrave

Published by Manchester University Press
Oxford Road, Manchester M13 9NR, UK
and Room 400, 175 Fifth Avenue, New York, NY10010, USA
www.manchesteruniversitypress.co.uk

Distributed exclusively in the USA by
Palgrave, 175 Fifth Avenue, New York,
NY 10010, USA

Distributed exclusively in Canada by
UBC Press, University of British Columbia, 2029 West Mall,
Vancouver, BC, Canada V6T 1Z2

British Library Cataloguing-in-Publication Data
A catalogue record for this book is available from the British Library

Library of Congress Cataloging-in-Publication Data applied for

ISBN 0 7190 5772 8 *hardback*
      0 7190 5773 6 *paperback*

First published 2002

10 09 08 07 06 05 04 03 02   10 9 8 7 6 5 4 3 2 1

Typeset in Sabon with Frutiger
by Northern Phototypesetting Co Ltd, Bolton

Printed in Great Britain
by Bell & Bain Ltd, Glasgow

For Marjorie Mary Margaret

Contents

Acknowledgements

I would like to acknowledge Mark Jancovich's support during the early stages of this project, and also the University of Nottingham for its financial support through a postgraduate studentship. Sharon Monteith, Ben Marsden and Andrew Tudor provided helpful commentaries on an earlier draft of this manuscript.

Over the duration of this book many people have been generous both intellectually and with their friendship – thank you. I would like to specifically mention Michael Hoar and Alex MacDonald for their company at the 'bad' films we always seemed to see together, and more generally for talking about films. Emma Smith and Luci Squire for their many kindnesses. Anne-Marie Rafferty for the caffeine-care packages, and June McCombie for letting her home be overrun with videos. Nina Wakeford has been supportive throughout, and in many ways helped get things started. And finally, Susan Billingham for enduring more fictions of technoscience than any person should.

Introduction

You want to hear something really nutty? I heard of a couple of guys who want to build something called an aeroplane, you know you get people to go in, and fly around like birds, it's ridiculous, right? And what about breaking the sound barrier, or rockets to the moon? Atomic energy, or a mission to Mars? Science fiction, right? Look, all I'm asking is for you to just have the tiniest bit of vision. You know, to just sit back for one minute and look at the big picture. To take a chance on something that just might end up being the most profoundly impactful moment for humanity, for the history ... of history.[1]

Imagine the scene: an angry and frustrated scientist delivers the above outburst to an audience who have just suggested that her ideas are more based in fiction than reality. There is nothing particularly extraordinary about this speech; in fact, it is almost a staple of sci-ence-fiction rhetoric. The vibratingly angry and/or weary scientist confronts a sceptical group of onlookers and chastises them for their lack of vision. It is also a speech which resonates with that of Dr Frankenstein (as played by Colin Clive in the *Frankenstein* of 1931), but unlike that archetypal mad-scientist, Ellie Arroway (the scientist who makes the speech above) is a righteous figure who fights her way through the corruption and self-interest of all those who surround her. But the likes of Ellie Arroway do not really interest me; rather, the anonymous and grey but powerful people she is criticising, because they are the ones who impose the restrictions and whose influences have to be negotiated in order for a 'profound moment' in the history of humans and their technologies to occur. Images of science and technology from the late twentieth century have long left behind the idea of the gentleman scientist working away in splendid isolation on his grand idea in his castle, or cellar, or even occasionally his elite community. What can be found, instead, are a series of images in which the outcome of a scientist's work is that which emerges from a complex network of influences, some constricting, and others unexpectedly productive.

This book makes no claim to say anything about the everyday practices of actual scientists and technologists. Instead it draws out the ways that contemporary science and technology are imagined within fictions, and in this particular study, within American film fictions produced from 1980 onwards. For some, this may seem not seem relevant to anything in the world, because it contributes nothing to the practices of science and technology. But to dismiss a study of filmic images of science and technology as 'merely fictional' is to miss an important point. The cultural products of any given period both expose and explore the concerns of that period, and whilst they are certainly fictionalised and packaged to fit the conventions of different kinds of genres, these products nonetheless touch on very real questions. *Technoscience in contemporary film* addresses the ways in which images of science and technology explore and expose cultural perceptions of technoscience, with a particular emphasis on how such perceptions influence ideas about what it means to be human in the late twentieth century.

For anyone who frequently watches American films, especially those produced within Hollywood, the science-fiction genre forms a key source of images of science and technology. Throughout its history, the genre has been full of spectacular images of science and technologies. From high-budget to low-budget, from the esoteric or obscure to the downright banal, from the blockbuster to the cult film, heroes battle the forces of evil, alien invasions are triumphantly averted and a vast new world opens up for exploration – or more cynically, exploitation – by the human race. Within many of these films, as well as tales of 'derring-do', there is a wealth of stories about science and technologies in themselves. Take a relatively recent example: *Chain Reaction* (1996, US). The story is about a group of scientists who discover a way to make cheap fuel, and attempt to make the knowledge available throughout the world. But just at the moment of their success, the majority of the team are murdered. The two key survivors begin a battle of wits with the agencies that want to control the new knowledge. Like many SF films, *Chain Reaction* features a new technology and heroes who battle for good. The technology also forms the central spectacle of the film it opens with a display of the machine whose power is evident, somewhat ironically, in the vast explosion that signals its destruction (twice over). In addition to features common to the genre, *Chain Reaction* explores concerns specific to a particular historical and cultural context – in this instance, worries prevalent in the 1990s about the impact of technologies on the environment, as well as concerns about sustainable resources. *Chain Reaction*, then, combines generic conventions with a more historically located commentary on the effects of science and technology on the wider world.[2] It also raises questions about the effects of the wider world on the development of science and technology. The whole reason why the fusion-technology of the film gets dramatically blown into oblivion, is because of a battle to control both access to, and the development of, the technology.

This final point brings me to one of the key terms of this book: technoscience. The word technoscience has a specific usage within social studies of science and technology.[3] Very briefly, it refers to a whole variety of factors that influence the outcome of attempts to create knowledge or objects. The term technoscience encapsulates the processes through which any range of influences works on the practices of science and technology, and is not a shorthand collapse of the words science and technology.[4] For people looking at the everyday activities of scientists and technologists, these influences can include humans and non-human objects, economic and political decisions, accidental events, both disastrous and unexpectedly useful. Donna Haraway's comments on technoscience usefully indicate the diverse possibilities:

> Any interesting being in technoscience, such as a textbook, molecule, equation, mouse, pipette, bomb, fungus, technician, agitator, or scientist, can and often should – be teased open to show the sticky economic, technical, political, organic, historical, mythic, and textual threads that make up its tissues ... the threads are alive; they transform into each other; they move away from our categorical gaze. The relations among the technical, mythic, economic, political, formal, textual, historical, and organic are not causal. But the articulations are consequential; they matter.[5]

Knowledge here does not come about in either an isolated or a random way; rather, events and circumstances impact on the ways in which knowledges emerge, and furthermore, on what *kinds* of knowledge can emerge. In other words, the processes through which a knowledge or object comes into being are highly contingent.

The idea of technoscience as a complex and contingent process is central to my readings of the films in *Technoscience in contemporary film*. Many of the films discussed depict the ways in which science and technology emerge at the intersection of a number of influences, influences that can shape the outcomes of events. This is the case in *Small Soldiers* (1998, US) where a toy-making company is bought out, and the new management exerts pressure on the workers to make a high-profile toy in a short period of time. In order to develop a potentially lucrative range, the toy creators are given full access to the diverse materials held within the new company, a company that includes arms manufacturers. One of the toy creators finds a batch of cheap microchips that he incorporates into the microprocessors of the toys. These microchips, which were designed for military use, malfunction in such a way that the toys become fully functional, or at least functional within the parameters of their 'search and destroy' programming. In this set-up to the conflict between one range of toys, the action-oriented Commando Elite, and a second, the peaceful Gorgonites, the development of the toy technology progresses through a series of contingencies. A small company is taken over by a larger one, an event which expands the resources available to the toy makers. But the take-over also creates a more highly pressured system of work practice, as the new investor wants large returns on his money. The new toy technology develops within the coincidence of pressures exerted by the new investor, the partially finished toy, and the availability of a cheap batch of chips.

What technoscience brings to this study of images of science and technology is essentially an emphasis on the coincidence of elements that can both restrict and initiate parts of the process through which knowledge and objects come into the world. In the instance of *Small Soldiers* the coincidence of events leads almost to disaster. And in keeping with the monstrous creations of many a mad scientist horror film, the Commando Elite cause havoc until they are vanquished by the actions of the resourceful hero. The existence of numerous films whose outcomes follow a similar pattern – product of science runs amok and has to be brought back under control – has led to the accusation that SF films (and also horror) are frequently and simplistically anti-science or technophobic.[6] Whilst such films do exist, indeed the recent *Hollow Man* (2000, US) clearly plays on the set of conventions in which a scientist is driven over the edge by his discovery, there are many other films where the images of technoscience generate more complicated and nuanced stories about the place of science and technology in the contemporary world.

Before moving on to an introduction to the concerns of this book, I want first to indicate that *Technoscience in contemporary film* does not take a genre-based approach to images of technoscience. Typically discussions of such images have been focused through the SF and horror genres. And to a certain extent this makes sense, since images of science and technology are most frequently found within these genres. However, it is also true to say that these kinds of images are not *exclusively* found in the horror or SF genres. They are also evident in westerns, comedies, melodramas, thrillers and even occasionally musicals. One of the purposes of this study is to bring together films from a variety of different genres. In order to signal this, I use the term 'fiction of technoscience' not only to indicate the conceptual framework provided by technoscience, but also to designate a particular grouping of films. This grouping sets aside the more conventional boundaries of genre in order to bring together a variety of films which are frequently overlooked, but which make an equally vital contribution to a cultural narrative about technoscience.

As I have suggested, the purpose of this book is to generate readings of fictions of technoscience that reveal a sense of the complicated stories about the place of science and technology in the contemporary world. The trajectory of the book begins with how fictions of technoscience imagine science as a system of knowledge and as an institution; it then moves on to think about the effects of these institutions in the wider world. Chapter 1, First contact: introducing technoscience, works through ideas about the relationships between the practices of science and the subsequent generation of scientific knowledge. These are themes that emerge from the films themselves, and they do so in two particular ways. The first is a focus on slightly more abstract ideas about the processes linked with the generation of knowledge and institutions, and these are dealt with in Chapter 1. The second looks at the effects of these knowledges and institutions on the human figures of the films, issues that are dealt with in Chapter 2.

One way to begin thinking about how fictions of technoscience generate ideas about scientific knowledge is through stories that draw out impressions of what scientific knowledge can and cannot say about the world. In *The Nightmare Before Christmas* (1993,

US) Jack Skellington, the Pumpkin King, grinds up Christmas-tree baubles and mixes the powder into various solutions in a misguided attempt to extract the spirit of Christmas. The point being made in *The Nightmare Before Christmas* is that some kinds of knowledge are not open to understanding through the rationalising practices of science. A similar position can be seen in *Sleepy Hollow* (1998, US). Here, Constable Ichabod Crane appears ludicrous when his modern (within the time frame of the film) tools of scientific forensic enquiry do not fit in with the worldviews of either his superiors in New York, or the residents of Sleepy Hollow. Crane's use of instrumentation is mocked as he looks more than slightly absurd peering through his complex headwear of lenses and micrometers, and the witnesses to his investigations look on with increasing incredulity and twitching discomfort. However, this sense of absurdity should not necessarily be regarded as a rejection of science as a system of knowledge; rather, science is a system of knowledge of little use within the story-world. In the world view of *Sleepy Hollow*, the scientific explanations offered by Crane are filtered out because they serve no purpose, in that they have no capacity to explain the phenomenon that troubles the people of Sleepy Hollow.

Chapter 1 follows out this line of thought, using *Lorenzo's Oil* (1992, US), *Medicine Man* (1992, US), *The Lawnmower Man* (1992, US) and *Jurassic Park* (1992, US). Each of these films features a range of images of science and technology, but they go beyond the idea that scientific knowledge is fully formed prior to coming into contact, or conflict, with a social world. Instead of presenting such knowledge as something that emerged in a domain that is distinct from a social world, these films present it as being contingent on competing influences, in other words, as a technoscience. The influences that are depicted in these films vary from medical practices and research, through corporate concerns, including the pharmaceutical and entertainment industries, to the military. Not surprisingly, given this scope of influences, the films raise doubts about the neutrality of scientific research. The initial question, then, addressed in Chapter 1 is specifically around the idea of neutrality, or to use another associated word, the objectivity of science. *Lorenzo's Oil* and *Medicine Man* are discussed as films that critically examine the idea of objectivity, and I argue that these two films problematise the status of scientific knowledge as wholly objective. However, this does not mean that scientific or medical research is in any sense dismissed; rather, it is to argue that

Lorenzo's Oil and *Medicine Man* display an awareness of the *interestedness* of research. By interestedness I mean that the films make explicit the various demands and restrictions that exert pressures on the generation of knowledge – demands and restrictions which include economic and social factors. These factors also encompass pressing concerns around issues of race and gender. The idea of interestedness is also important to the second question addressed in Chapter 1. This revolves around the spectacle-based narratives of *The Lawnmower Man* and *Jurassic Park* and how they are concerned with the effects of corporate and military influences on the practices of science. Between *Lorenzo's Oil*, *Medicine Man*, *The Lawnmower Man* and *Jurassic Park*, it becomes clear that images of science and technology are far from simplistic or technophobic. Instead, such images imaginatively explore how knowledge comes into the social world because it has a value attached to it. Furthermore, there are systems in place which can both include and exclude potential knowledge on the basis of its value as a commodity.

Chapter 2 presents an alternative set of questions to those raised in Chapter 1. Rethinking the idea that science and technology are part of an institution, this chapter shifts the focus to the effects of technoscience on the human figures of the social worlds depicted in the films *12 Monkeys* (1995, US), *D.A.R.Y.L.* (1985, US), *Junior* (1994, US) and *sex, lies and videotape* (1989, US). Each of these four films presents a different kind of relationship between the human figures and the technoscience with which they come into contact. Variously they explore and imagine the different ways technoscience can influence the human (or equivalent to human) figures by modifying, to different degrees, the ways in which they lead their lives. Through *12 Monkeys*, *D.A.R.Y.L.*, *Junior* and *sex, lies and videotape* it is clear that the presence of technoscience in the social world is not straightforward. Instead it takes up a range of positions, some of which are restrictive and destructive, and some of which have the potential to generate new ways of being in the world.

As my discussion of *12 Monkeys*, *D.A.R.Y.L.*, *Junior* and *sex, lies and videotape* makes apparent, these fictions of technoscience suggest a move beyond the idea of science and technology as simply good or bad objects in the world. Instead, these objects accumulate multiple meanings around them. This idea of multiple meanings can be taken further. It is possible to talk about different knowledges and objects as representative of different kinds of meanings about technoscience:

for instance, Batman's fancy gadgets stand for ideas about fairness, whilst those of Mr Freeze or Poison Ivy in *Batman and Robin* (1997, US) represent two kinds of vendetta. This might lead to a pigeon-hole view of science and technology, where a particular knowledge or object is associated with a simple or singular meaning. It is also possible, however, to think about individual knowledges and objects as having more than one meaning in themselves. Or put in another way, the meaning of the same object can be transformed according to the different contexts in which it is found. For instance, in *The Bone Collector* (1999, US) a police officer, Lincoln Rhyme, becomes a quadriplegic as the result of an injury. Within the story-world of *The Bone Collector*, Rhyme is provided with a set of computer technologies that literally keep him alive, whilst at the same time trying to keep him interested in staying alive by providing access to the world outside his flat. As the plot progresses, however, he gradually becomes more and more involved in the central case of the narrative, the tracking down of a multiple murderer. As a part of this development, the computer technologies shift to being the means by which he analyses evidence and communicates with other law-enforcement officers. In a further shift, these technologies also make Rhyme vulnerable. When the murderer attacks him directly, he uses the technology of Rhyme's heart-pacing machine to try and bring on a catastrophic fit. Through these and other shifts within the plot of *The Bone Collector*, technology can be seen as an object whose meaning is not exclusively linked to its functionality.[7]

As this discussion of *The Bone Collector* demonstrates, the material construction of a technology is not altered by its location in the social world; rather, the meanings associated with the technologies undergo a transformation. Chapter 3, The gremlin effect, discusses *Gremlins* (1984, US), *Gremlins 2: The New Batch* (1990, US), *Strange Days* (1995, US) and *Fresh Kill* (1995, US) as films in which the meanings of technological objects undergo a series of such transformations. Each of these films has a plot in which the relationships between the human figures and the technologies shift, and then shift again. To take one example, the video-phones of Clamp Tower in *Gremlins 2* shift from a system for communication, to a means of attack, and then finally to a system for counterattack. As these shifts occur across the text, the potential fluidity of the meanings of the objects emerges, but the extent to which this fluidity is sustained varies from film to film. Within *Gremlins* and *Gremlins 2*, there is a playful reconfiguration of the relationship between the technologies and the animate beings (humans and Creatures), but the endings of the films tend to close down the range of possibilities. *Strange Days* and *Fresh Kill* similarly have plots in which a technology can be understood to have meanings that are contingent upon the particularities of its social and cultural space. However, unlike the two *Gremlin* films, the social and cultural spaces of *Strange Days* and *Fresh Kill* retain a greater potential for openness and on-going change, rather than closure.

In Chapter 3, then, I discuss the ways in which the meanings given to technological objects in the world are open to transformation. In Chapter 4 I extend this analysis to a particular version of images of technology, that of the android or cyborg. The android and cyborg in a sense represent a special case, as their appearance resembles that of a human. The very fact that these technological figures are played by human actors ensures that they are transformed from simply technological objects to more immediately humanised figures. Through *Android* (1982, US), *Making Mr Right* (1987, US) and *Alien: Resurrection* (1997, US) I consider how particular categories of humanness are used to stabilise the meanings of the technologies as human-like. Thinking about how these categories of humanness are used reveals two things. First, such categories reveal which codes of humanness are privileged through their ability to transform the meanings of the technological figures, and these include codes of gender, race and sexuality, as well as ideas about consciousness, emotions and a need for community. Secondly, thinking about these categories of humanness reveals how they are used to make technologies knowable through the dimensions of the social world. In effect, this amounts to giving technologies a 'friendly face'. But this face is not simply the superficial one provided the actor, as it is also linked to a range of needs and behaviours. The outcome of this, I argue, is a safe management of technology, as all its potential differences are displaced under the gloss of humanness.

The final chapter of this book reconsiders the question of the management of technologies by discussing a potential problem that arises from the assumption that technologies can be understood through categories associated with humanness. The films considered in Chapter 4 tend to utilise human behaviours to manage or package technologies, but in doing so leave unexplored those aspects of technology that cannot readily be given meaning within the terms of humanness. In Chapter 5, through *Wargames* (1983, US), *Edward Scissorhands* (1990, US), *RoboCop* (1987, US) and *GATTACA* (1997, US), I argue that there remains something unpredictable in technoscience. I take up this position *not* to reassert an essential distinction between humanness and technologies, but to suggest that constructions of technology retain a difference to humanness. By difference, I mean that the ways in which technoscientific objects are understood are open to possibilities beyond the aspects of humanness mobilised by the films discussed in this study. The cultural imaginings of technoscience created in America since the 1980s need not be seen as closed circuits that keep channelling the same stories. Many of them offer the potential for something different, even though the nature of that difference as yet remains uncertain. The purpose of this book is to start thinking through some of many possibilities explored in fictions of technoscience.

Notes

1 This is a speech delivered by the character Dr Eleanor Arroway in *Contact* (1997, US).

2 Whilst many SF films share similar sets of conventions, the stories that they tell vary with historical context. There have been a number of studies that consider the historical specificities of SF films, as well as the horror genre. For example, Andrew Tudor's *Monsters and Mad Scientists: A Cultural History of the Horror Movie* (Oxford: Blackwell, 1989) provides an overview of the genres between 1930 and 1980. J.P. Telotte's *A Distant Technology: Science Fiction Film and the Machine Age* (Hanover, NH: Wesleyan University Press, 1999) is a study of 1930s SF films. Both Mark Jancovich's *Rational Fears: American Horror in the 1950s* (Manchester: Manchester University Press, 1996) and David Seed's *American Science Fiction and the Cold War* (Edinburgh: Edinburgh University Press, 1999) consider the specificities of 1950s SF films. Scott Bukatman in *Terminal Identity: The Virtual Subject in Postmodern Science Fiction* (Durham, NC: Duke University Press, 1993) and Claudia Springer in *Electronic Eros: Bodies and Desire in the Postindustrial Age* (Austin: University of Texas Press, 1996) look at SF produced since the 1980s. Because it is not confined to particular genres, *Technoscience in Contemporary Film* goes beyond these studies.

3 An introduction to these ideas can be found in Bruno Latour, *Science in Action: How to Follow Scientists and Engineers through Society* (Milton Keynes: Open University Press, 1987); John Law (ed.), *A Sociology of Monsters: Essays on Power, Technology and Domination* (London and

New York: Routledge, 1991); Greg Myers, 'Out of the Laboratory and Down to the Bay: Writing in Science and Technology Studies,' *Written Communication*, 13:1 (January 1996) 5–43; Sharon Traweek, 'An Introduction to Cultural and Social Studies of Sciences and Technologies,' *Culture, Medicine and Psychiatry*, 17 (1993) 3–25.

4 Bruno Latour makes this point in the following way: 'I will use the word **technoscience** from now on, to describe all the elements tied to the scientific contents no matter how dirty, unexpected or foreign they seem, and the expression '**science and technology**', in quotation marks, to designate *what is kept of technoscience* once the trials of responsibility have been settled' (emphases in original), Latour, *Science in Action*, p. 174.

5 Donna J. Haraway, *Modest_Witness@ Second_Millenium.FemaleMan© _Meets OncoMouse,™:Feminism and Technoscience* (London and New York: Routledge, 1997) pp. 68–69.

6 A relatively early (in terms of SF film criticism) version of this argument can be found in Stanley Solomon, *Beyond Formula: American Film Genres* (New York: Harcourt Brace Jovanovich Publishers, 1976). See especially p. 117. A more recent version of a similar argument can be found in T.J. Matheson, 'Marcuse, Ellul, and the Science-Fiction Film,' *Science-Fiction Studies*, 19 (1992) 326–339.

7 For discussions of the diverse ways in which technologies can operate in the social world see: B. Ruby Rich, 'The Party Line: Gender and Technology in the Home,' in Jennifer Terry and Melodie Calvert (eds.), *Processed Lives: Gender and Technology in Everyday Life* (London and New York: Routledge, 1997) pp. 198–208; David F. Nye, *Narratives and Spaces: Technology and the Construction of American Culture* (Exeter: University of Exeter Press, 1997); and Stanley Aronowitz, Barbara Martinsons and Michael Menser (eds.), *Technoscience and Cyberculture: A Cultural Study* (London and New York: Routledge, 1996).

1

First contact:
introducing technoscience

The opening sequence of *Contact* (1997, US) depicts a journey through time and space. Beginning with a medium close-up view of the Earth, the Florida peninsula locating the landmass as Northern America, the image pulls back past the nine planets of the solar system to go deeper and deeper into space, taking us through meteor showers, gas clouds and nebulae. Following the silence of the minimal credit sequence, the initial image of the Earth comes as a shock as it is accompanied by noise, the white noise of transmissions so dense it is impossible to single out any one of them. As we are taken deeper into space, occasional sound segments become briefly discernible, and, in reverse chronology, each decade is marked out by television theme tunes and then radio through snippets of songs, as well as political speeches. These sounds get weaker, fade into silence, but the images continue, intimating a space so vast that even seven decades worth of transmissions have only partially covered the distance. The sequence ends with a gathering together of white light, light which coalesces into an image of a window reflected in the pupil of a young girl.

Having come back down to Earth via this visual device, the narrative of *Contact* revolves around an attempt to go back into space, as this young girl is to be the hero of the film. She will become Dr Ellie Arroway, a scientist who wants to find what is out there. In this first meeting with her, we find the young Ellie full of curiosity; encouraged by her father, she is learning about astronomy, and already attempting to make contact through a CB radio. Even here there are signs of her future ambitions to reach further: she indicates her need for a bigger radio antenna. As she says these words, a jump cut from the young Ellie seated in front of her radio set, to an older Ellie standing beside a vast radio-telescope dish high in a

South American mountain range, suggests that her needs have been met. However, this sense of achievement is rapidly dispersed as Ellie's scientific endeavours are threatened by a funding crisis. And the circumstances of this crisis reveal the realities of modern research in astronomy – dependent on expensive and sophisticated technology, success is not simply based on brilliance, instead it is contingent on gaining funding for access to facilities.

Although the narrative of *Contact* is finally more interested in the question of faith, whether it be faith in spirituality, faith in science, or the similarities between these apparently opposing positions, it is through Ellie's search for funding that the film touches on the processes of technoscience. In the debates surrounding funding sources and budgets, scientific research emerges as a process embedded in political and economic networks. Ellie has to work hard to convince people to fund her, and only succeeds because a millionaire-businessman decides she is a good commercial risk. When the alien message central to the narrative of *Contact* is received, the question of who has access to this information comes into play. Should it be under military jurisdiction, with access limited by the command of the president of the United States, or should the information be available to the whole of the human race? Who will benefit, either commercially or symbolically, from being involved in the project to build the machine encoded within the alien message?

Thinking through such questions opens up fictions of technoscience like *Contact* as texts which create meanings about people who are scientists, about the institutions to which they belong, and the types of knowledge which can be called scientific. It would simplistic to try to label *Contact* as either pro-science or anti-science; the film is more complex than that. It can be explored, instead, through a focus on how science and technology come to happen: how human operations and organisations place restraints on what can and cannot be scientific, and how the processes and practices of science can be seen in terms of a technoscience.

Scientists in context

Although this book moves beyond genre boundaries, it takes as its starting point writing on the SF and horror genres. Critical works have focused on the ways in which SF and horror films articulate an anxiety about progress, as well as social and cultural concerns contemporary to the text, such as Cold-War narratives, race and gender issues, and also the changing conceptions of humanness in a technological environment.[1] In contrast, this chapter will address the ways in which fictions of technoscience construct scientific knowledge and practice as a part of an institution embedded in economic, political and cultural practices. Whilst the primary focus of this book is on contemporary film, I want first briefly to suggest that the approach of technoscience is also of use when looking back over a history of fictions of technoscience. Andrew Tudor's *Monsters and Mad Scientists: A Cultural History of the Horror Movie* begins to address such questions. *Monsters and Mad Scientists* provides an extensive historical account of the horror genre, and it includes an analysis of the changing relationship between science and the social communities of the text. Indicating the shift from the shadowy and isolated figures of the 1930s horror film, towards a more socially located presence in the 1950s, Tudor states:

> No longer the special quasi-magical activity of thirties mad science tucked away in old houses and Gothic castles, science now is more prosaic and more all embracing. Penetrating into every corner of our lives, the science developed in fifties horror movies is a constitutive part of our everyday world, its admired and feared exponents harbingers of both progress and disaster, its most common threat – radiation – unseen, but a potential invader of any area of our activities.[2]

However, in arguing that the science of the 1950s is a part of the everyday world, Tudor is suggesting that the science of the 1930s and 1940s was isolated, 'tucked away'. This is a position also taken up by J.P. Telotte in *A Distant Technology*. In his analysis of US, French, British, German and Soviet SF cinemas of the 1920s and 1930s, Telotte suggests that science and technology are remote from social concerns 'in a tradition of isolated scientists depicted in the Machine Age'.[3]

In contrast, I argue that if the images of science that appear in the 1930s are not restricted to the SF and horror genres; that if, instead, the scientist is placed within a broader category of films, such as fictions of technoscience, even in the 1930s their context, their place within a social, and even rudimentary institutional location, becomes evident. *The Citadel* (1938, US/UK), based on A.J. Cronin's novel of the same name, narrates the journey of a young man, Andrew Manson, through the machinations of the medical profession. *Dark*

Victory (1939, US) is a film more usually noted for the performance by Bette Davis as Judith Traherne, the wilful young socialite who develops a cancer of the brain, but who falls in love with and marries her brain surgeon, Dr Frederick Steele. However, the wonderfully melodramatic ending of the film – Judith, her sight having failed, pretends to be able to see so that her husband can go and present his research to a potential funding body – locates the progress of science within a system that is dependent on access to funding.[4] In addition, both of these films draw on the archetype of the scientist as hero, something which is not usually associated with a period dominated by horror films such as *Frankenstein* (1931, US), *Dr Jekyll and Mr Hyde* (1932, US) and *Doctor X* (1932, US). This heroic scientist is equally evident in another body of films of the 1903s – the bio-pics such as *The Story of Louis Pasteur* (1936, US), *Edison, the Man* (1940, US) and *Dr Ehrlich's Magic Bullet* (1940, US). Another important, though slightly later, bio-pic was that of Marie and Pierre Curie, *Madame Curie* (1943, US).[5] Whilst telling the story of Marie and Pierre's love affair, it presents Marie Curie as a heroic scientist who devotes her life to science. *Madame Curie* is a rare example of an image of a woman scientist, since the majority of films in the 1930s and 1940s depicted women as assistants and/or daughters of male scientists. Interestingly, comedies of this period that feature scientists – such as *Bringing Up Baby* (1938, US) and *Vivacious Lady* (1938, US) – are very much about 'humanising' them by playing on the stereotype of the socially ineffectual male scientist.

Moving on from the 1930s, it is possible to trace the different ways in which scientists and science commonly appear in relation to an establishment, and from the 1940s onwards the influences of national, military or corporate concerns become more pronounced. This is not to say that all fictions of technoscience made since the 1940s have the same context, but that a repeating concern is the ways in which science and technology become caught up in various dynamics of power. One such dynamic is the relationship between science and the military, the details of which vary through the different decades. In the 1940s a number of spy narratives, such as *Junior G-men* (1940, US), *A Date with the Falcon* (1941, US), *The House on 92nd Street* (1945, US), *Cloak and Dagger* (1946, US) and *Notorious* (1946, US), present scientific knowledge as a valuable commodity over which the opposing factions battle to gain control. At stake is access to knowledge and technologies. In the context of the Second World War, the US authorities are promoted as not only right but also as *having* the right to make decisions about where, and to whom, knowledge can accrue. Science and technology in these spy-thriller films is clearly represented as operating within a military nexus of power, a component of the national war effort.

A number of SF genre films of the 1950s can be seen as extensions of this 1940s scenario. In these films, rather than the scientist being a figure who is often simply rescued by a military operation, the scientist is more actively a part of the military and/or government team. The scientist(s) in *Them!* (1954, US), *It Came from Beneath the Sea* (1953, US) and *The Monster that Challenged the World* (1957, US) share their knowledge with the government and the military, enabling and masterminding a solution to a problem.[6] The thriller *Panic in the Streets* (1950, US) follows a similar theme. Dr Clinton Reed is a Public Health Service doctor who works with the reluctant police authorities to track the source of the highly contagious 'pneumonic fever'.[7] Whilst many of the 1950s films present scientists and the military and/or police working as a team in conjunction with one another, *The Thing from Another World* (1951, US) depicts a more ambivalent relationship. Although the film follows the scenario of a military-science operation, in this instance the scientist is the primary difficulty, apart from the seven-foot alien creature, of course. This ambivalence can also be seen in a number of other films such as *Invasion of the Body Snatchers* (1956, US) and *The Incredible Shrinking Man* (1957, US). Both of these offer a view in which science and technology are unable to do anything to explain the phenomena presented within the films. In *The Incredible Shrinking Man* the doctors and scientists are unable to help Scott Carey when he begins to shrink, or even explain what is happening. Miles Binnell and Dan Kauffman are unable to find an explanation for, or a response to, the pods in *The Invasion of the Body Snatchers*. In neither film is this inability a result of incompetence; rather, the films suggest that science and technology are not capable of solving every problem.

When viewed through the theme of the relationship between the military and science, fictions of technoscience in the 1960s return to some of the issues raised within the 1940s scenarios; that is, the control of scientific knowledge takes on a nationalistic importance. In this decade the context is the Cold War rather than the Second World War, and so the enemy is often the 'Eastern Bloc'. Films as varied as *The Amazing Transparent Man* (1960, US), *Dr No* (1962,

UK) and the Bond series, *The Ipcress Files* (1965, UK), *Our Man Flint* (1965, US), *Torn Curtain* (1966, US), *Fantastic Voyage* (1966, US), *The Brides of Fu Manchu* (1966, US) and *Casino Royale* (1967, US) have narratives which revolve around the attempts by Western powers either to prevent knowledge going from the West to the East, or to gain knowledge from the East. Central to these films is the control of scientific knowledge and innovative technologies, especially those that have the potential to destabilise world peace, either directly through mass destruction or indirectly by affecting the economic base of the country. A distinctiveness of these 1960s narratives is the more explicit linkage made between the control of knowledge *and* power, whether this power be military, financial or political. Running parallel to such espionage narratives are some of the more famous SF films of the period – *Dr Strangelove: Or How I Learned to Stop Worrying and Love the Bomb* (1963, UK/US), *Fail-Safe* (1964, US), *2001: A Space Odyssey* (1968, UK/US) and *Colossus: The Forbin Project* (1969, US).[8] Like the spy-thriller films, each of these touches on the relationship between power and technology. Though often this occurs within a scenario where technologies have begun to behave in unexpected ways, malfunctioned or evolved into something not anticipated, the relationship is again located within an interplay of political, economic and cultural perspectives. Through the 1970s different kinds of connections between science and power emerge. Whilst the military presence is to some extent side-lined, the linkage between the control of technology and power remains. *Silent Running* (1971, US), *Soylent Green* (1973, US) and *Logan's Run* (1976, US), each of which expresses concerns about the environment, all have scenarios in which the control of technology is linked to an authoritarian power. *The China Syndrome* (1978, US) is similarly concerned with the effects of technologies on the environment, but the narrative addresses the sloppiness of the authorities of the nuclear plant, rather than their authoritarianism.

Even this very brief overview of fictions of technoscience from the 1930s onwards suggests that images of science and technology have been more complex than many commentators have allowed. They have neither been confined to the SF and horror genre, nor have they been simply anti-science or pro-science. Instead, these fictions of technoscience have increasingly placed the practices of science within the social and cultural concerns of a given period. Commenting on this, Andrew Tudor observes of 1960s horror and

SF films that: 'science has been assimilated into the institutional structure of capitalist society'.[9] Where for Tudor this location acts to diminish science, to domesticate the horror genre's tendency to question establishment views of the world, I believe that when thinking about images of technoscience more generally, such a location is invaluable as it reveals science to be part of a social/cultural framework. The remainder of this chapter moves into a discussion of more contemporary films as I consider *Lorenzo's Oil* (1992, US), *Medicine Man* (1992, US), *The Lawnmower Man* (1992, US) and *Jurassic Park* (1992, US), films which can variously be described as medical melodrama, eco-comedy, SF and action adventure. Each of these texts engages in different ways with how scientific knowledge is constructed, and with science as an institution; in other words, they explore the relationship between science and technology and social/cultural frameworks. In discussing these films I will re-examine the themes discussed above, but in the context of a particular dynamic. In these four films the dynamic that most often occurs is the commercialisation of the practices of science and technology, a concern which underlies a number of other films made since the 1980s, such as *Blade Runner* (1982, US), *Brainstorm* (1983, US), *RoboCop* (1987, US), *Eve of Destruction* (1991, US), *Extreme Measures* (1996, US), *The Nutty Professor* (1996, US), *Flubber* (1997, US) and the *Alien* series. The issue being raised here, however, is not simply the exploitation of science for profit; rather, it is that the potential for profit determines the practices of science.

Before moving into a discussion of the ways in which fictions of technoscience explore the social and cultural embeddedness of the practices of technoscience, I first of all consider how *Lorenzo's Oil* and *Medicine Man* explore the constructions of scientific knowledge. I do this to give some sense of how such films depict the processes by which scientific knowledge is understood to accumulate – or, to put it another way, what is allowed to become scientific knowledge.

Knowing knowledge

At one point in *Lorenzo's Oil*, a doctor says to the father of the sick child: 'Augusto, I am a scientist, and I am of absolutely no use to you whatsoever, unless I can retain my objectivity.' This comment reveals the anxiety at the heart of *Lorenzo's Oil*: that is, the desire of parents to do everything possible to help their child, versus the necessity for medical science to be cautious, so as to ensure that people are not subjected to unnecessary risks in the pursuit of research. Within *Lorenzo's Oil* the tension provoked by this anxiety often operates through the duality of objective versus subjective knowledge, a duality which has also historically informed constructions of scientific knowledge. Within the operations of science, objective knowledge is the privileged way of knowing. As a consequence, knowledges that are not constructed as objective become associated with subjective positions, positions which may variously take on the connotations of being too involved to have an impartial perspective, too emotional, or, more extremely, irrational. Such connotations often result in the invalidation of any subjective points of view.

In many of the debates about scientific knowledge and objectivity a second term, rationality, is often mobilised, where rationality can be understood as follows:

> The kind of rationality invoked by modern philosophers ... usually refers to logical rules, and to the constraints of 'consistency,' 'coherence,' 'non-contradiction,' as they are used to articulate or theorize in abstract terms from a disengaged perspective, or to spell out propositions and to specify the rules of inference, both deductive or inductive, or to judge the appropriateness of means used to reach stated objectives.[10]

The idea of a set of logical rules 'used to theorize in abstract terms from a disengaged perspective' is a familiar one, particularly when linked to the pursuit of scientific knowledge. But there are numerous texts, both fictional and non-fictional, which have challenged the apparent straightforwardness of this kind of argument.[11] These challenges have taken various forms, but the following irreverent quotation from W.H. Newton-Smith's *The Rationality of Science* reveals a particular concern, that of the apparent detachment of scientists as they go about their work:

> And in the noble (or perhaps it is Nobel) pursuit of some worthy aim (variously characterized as truth, knowledge, explanation, etc.) the members of the community dispassionately and disinterestedly apply their tools, the scientific method, each application of which takes us a further step on the royal road to the much esteemed goal.[12]

Newton-Smith's usage of the terms dispassionate and disinterested, which are often equated with an objective approach, is revealing, as they are both words that can take on double meanings. If a so-called independent viewpoint is demanded then both are positively valued

perspectives; if, on the contrary, a perspective informed by direct
and felt experience of an event is required, such a viewpoint can
appear as cold and unfeeling. One distinctive feature of images of
science and technology is the movement between the extremes of
these two potential outcomes.

In *Lorenzo's Oil* and *Medicine Man* the narratives lay out the ways
in which scientific research relies on 'logical rules' to validate its
findings. In doing so, both films call into question whether a
detached mode of operating is as dispassionate and disinterested as
it appears to be, and therefore whether there can be such a simple
opposition between objective and subjective. *Lorenzo's Oil* is a
fictionalised account of the successful efforts of the parents of a
six-year-old boy, Lorenzo, to understand the terminal illness ade-
noleukodystrophy (ALD), with which he has been diagnosed. The
telling of the story explicitly draws on melodramatic cinematic
conventions. Throughout there is a striking use of music, saturated
colour and oblique camera angles, all of which imbue an already
moving subject matter with emotional power. At the same time, in
Lorenzo's Oil medical and scientific knowledge are constructed as
something delineated by rationality. The combination of this melodramatic mode of narration with the examination of the procedures
of medical science creates a sense that the accumulation of knowledge is fraught with complexities.

One of the clearest articulations in *Lorenzo's Oil* of the research
practices of conventional medical science is the meeting of the ALD
Foundation attended by Michaela and Augusto Odone, Lorenzo's
parents. The ALD Foundation is a parent-sponsored support group
that raises funds and disseminates information about the disease.
Within the chronology of the narrative, by the time that the Odones
attend this meeting, Lorenzo has been diagnosed and has undergone
a series of medical texts and interventions. Throughout this period,
which in real time occurs over five months, Lorenzo has been shown
to have altered from the happy young child of the opening
sequences, to one who is debilitated and severely ill. The progression of Lorenzo's illness is made to seem all the more brutal as it is
juxtaposed with the helplessness of his parents and the inability of
medical science to do anything to combat the disease. At the point
at which the Odones visit the ALD Foundation meeting, Lorenzo is
taking part in an experimental dietary protocol, but the preliminary
results are poor.[13] At the meeting Michaela, frustrated with what she

perceives as the lack of attention being given to the children, asks a question about the counterintuitive effects of the experimental diet. By posing this critical question about the efficacy of the diet, Michaela attempts to break with the conventions of experimental procedure by asking the other parents to share information about their sons on the experimental diet. In the ensuing argument, the positions taken by the opposing groups lay out the processes by which medical research occurs. The chair of the meeting refuses to allow an informal sharing of information because it would be anecdotal and therefore meaningless to the doctors – only scientists are expert enough to make meanings from the results of the experiment. As another of the Foundation's organisers says: 'the interpretation of experiments is the solemn responsibility of the scientists'. Non-experts here are perceived as not only unable to grasp the meanings of a medical framework based on 'formal pilot studies', 'a strict protocol and statistical samples', but also their questions and concerns have no place within the medical discourse. At the end of this acrimonious exchange, the chair justifies her and her colleagues' position by simply stating 'this is the way that science works'.

Although the views of the Foundation's organisers seem to be presented within *Lorenzo's Oil* as quite naive and passive in the face of medical expertise, it is possible to be sympathetic to their views about the need for caution. But, given the positioning of this exchange within the plot, where medical science has been presented as unable to do anything to help either Lorenzo or the other boys who suffer from the illness, there is also a strong pull towards the more critical position taken up by the Odones. As such, the exchange outlined both reveals, and examines, the premise that objective medical knowledge, based on a process of systematic protocols, overseen and interpreted by experts, exists in an unproblematic opposition with anecdotal, or non-expert, knowledge. In the sequence discussed above, *Lorenzo's Oil* exposes a hierarchy between different ways of knowing in which objective knowledge is perceived as the most valid. The other, less valid knowledge invoked within the sequence is a subjective or anecdotal one. This clash between the two positions is also played out visually through a series of shot-reverse-shots between the Odones at the back of a school hall, and the Foundation Committee on the stage at the front. In the middle the majority of the audience sit, uncertain as the argument goes back and forth above their heads. Later in *Lorenzo's Oil*, at another meeting of the Foundation, when the

Odones have discovered a potential therapy, this clash is replayed, but with a different outcome. This second debate ends with the room in uproar, as the crowd of parents demand that the potential therapy should be tested as soon as possible. Unlike the first meeting in which these parents were either silenced or kept out of the picture – in many of the shot-reverse-shots they are either only just visible or absent because of the use of medium close-ups – in this second meeting they are visually and aurally demonstrating. In the transition between the two meetings, the parents have been given more agency, they have the power to question the processes of medical science. Their non-expert subjective position has been given a place, but as one that operates in conjunction with the expertise of the scientists.

The same opposition of rational versus emotional is central to the story of *Medicine Man*. This film, which could be described as an eco-comedy, revolves around the relationship between two scientists. One, Robert Campbell, is a researcher who has remained in the Amazonian Rainforest for years, seeking out natural cures for disease. The second, Rae Crane, is a younger generation of scientist, brilliant at research but also embedded within the commercial framework that provides financial support for research. The opening credit sequence represents Crane's journey to the Rainforest as a gradual leaving behind of comforts, a physical transition into a completely different kind of living. Whilst the purpose of this sequence seems to be to present the Rainforest as something unexpected and extraordinary to an outsider's point of view, it also serves to introduce the idea that the Rainforest is under threat. The sense of unexpectedness is conveyed problematically through a play on the way the conventions of native peoples are perceived as completely other, especially when first encountered by a person used to living in a large urban space, such as a Northern American city. When Crane arrives at the village she is left alone in the dark, and hearing sounds she moves closer to their origin, discovering a tribal ritual under way. The sequence attempts to make fun of her ignorance, as she stands staring open-mouthed at the performance, apparently unable to make sense of the bodies moving in the light of large central fire, until she is unexpectedly greeted by the scientist she has come to meet, Robert Campbell. This feeling of strangeness is dispersed in the next set of images, as in the daylight of the following morning Crane makes her way into the village. In this sequence, where there are glimpses of buildings and people through the foliage of the forest, the village simply appears to be a community of people, albeit a community which has a different set of conventions to those of an outsider such as Crane. The initial views of the peaceful community within the forest also act as an antidote to some of the earlier images encountered when Crane is driving through a section of forest. Here the destruction of the forest is foregrounded as it is chopped down, the timber driven away on huge trucks, and the remaining area burnt to allow the building of a road. The progress of the modern world, the same world that Crane represents, is here clearly destructive and avaricious. Although the scenes in the village initially make the images of destruction seem as though they belong to another more distant place, this illusion is shattered when Crane is taken by Campbell to see the forest. Here, the camera seems to move up and across the height and breadth of the forest, giving a sense of its vast proportions. The fluidity of these shots mimics the motion of the pulley and rope system used by the characters within the film to negotiate the huge trees. The tones of green of the foliage, and the light in these shots of the forest, create a sharp contrast with later shots of the same area once it has been burnt. The inevitability of this coming change is intimated when Crane, having broken through the canopy of the forest, sees the plume of black smoke not so far away into the distance. The transformation of the forest from a beautiful and unexpected place, to one decimated by the mechanics of road building, provides more than the location for the shooting of the film. It is also the context within which *Medicine Man* places its commentary on the practice of scientific research and its relationship to an exploitative version of progress.

The commentary on scientific research in *Medicine Man* begins with the meeting between Robert Campbell and Rae Crane. Throughout their first meeting, Crane and Campbell verbally fight with one another – Campbell, because he resents her intrusion; and Crane, because she correctly (at least in part) assumes his resentment to be based on his assumptions about her as a younger and inexperienced woman. In the midst of their argument, Campbell claims that he has found a serum that can cure lymphoma. When unable to substantiate his claim with appropriate documentation, he is accused by Crane of letting his personal problems get in the way of his clinical judgement. The implication of this exchange is that undocumented description is not only not expert enough, but is evidence of a lack of objectivity. Through the arguments between Crane and Campbell, the legitimate objective practice presented in

Medicine Man is, like that of *Lorenzo's Oil*, predicated on processes of systemisation. When Campbell challenges Crane to prove for herself that his serum works, she is depicted systematically carrying out biopsies, measuring and cataloguing rat tumours, making notes, looking down microscopes, and using the machines which discipline her objective relationship to the knowledge. Only when Crane has done all this, gone through the proper processes, can she emerge wide-eyed with anticipation that Campbell really has found a cure.

When read as explorations of the constructions of scientific knowledge, *Lorenzo's Oil* and *Medicine Man* both begin by clearly invalidating subjective positions. However, they do so only to pose a question about the validity of a stringent separation between objectivity and subjectivity. This questioning in *Lorenzo's Oil* accumulates through the shifting alignments between Michaela and Augusto Odone and processes of medical research. Initially, the Odones, who are trying every medical route to save Lorenzo, are visually caught in the confusion that surrounds their son's illness. Prior to diagnosis, high and low camera shots with disorienting angular framing are used to suggest the disorder and uncertainties caused by the onset of Lorenzo's illness. As Lorenzo climbs on a chair to capture a colourful bauble from the Christmas tree, he is framed at an angle, one that tilts even further as he falls, crashing to the ground in slowed-motion. The off-square framing of the subsequent sequence of a doctor speaking maintains the feeling of disorientation. In keeping with the confusion that surrounds Lorenzo's illness, during and immediately after the diagnosis the Odones are frequently shown in a two-shot, outside the domain of objective knowledge but trying to grasp what is going on around them. In the meeting with Lorenzo's specialist, when the diagnosis of ALD is given, the Odones sit together being spoken *to* by a doctor, with few shot-reverse-shot edits to locate them within a visual dialogue. They are also depicted watching together from behind a glass window whilst Lorenzo is pushed inside an enveloping body scanner; this latter scene shows Michaela and Augusto restrained by the window frame, their expressive faces behind the glass, their emotions outside the clinical space. In a pivotal scene, they sit on the margins of a lecture theatre separated from their son by the body of the speaking doctor, as the severely debilitated Lorenzo is the teaching aid in a medical research lecture. As the sequence continues, and the doctor speaks in medical terms to his assembled colleagues, he is interrupted by Lorenzo, who tells him to stop using 'those words'. Lorenzo's interjection can be seen as his voicing a rejection of the ways that medical language disempowers the individual when he/she becomes subject to that discourse.

These scenes with Lorenzo, marked by a series of anxious and helpless looks from Michaela and Augusto towards their son as he is being inscribed as a subject to study, seem to mark a turning point within *Lorenzo's Oil*. Subsequently, the Odones continue in the spirit of Lorenzo's interjection and begin to seek information and knowledge as they attempt to understand for themselves, and to learn the language of fatty acid metabolism in order to understand 'those words'. As piles of biochemistry textbooks and research papers overwhelm the *mise-en-scène* of their family room they become actively engaged, visually as well as verbally, in the discussions about the disease. No longer sitting on the edges, they are the ones who make events happen as they bring together a group of scientists from around the world to hold the first symposium on ALD, an event that leads to the first stage of Lorenzo's treatment.

As they accumulate the expertise to understand the medical discourses surrounding Lorenzo's disease, the Odones begin to make use of objective processes of medical science for themselves. Although, when they discover a possible treatment, they refuse to adhere to the ethical regulations concerning human testing, they do go ahead adhering to the objective processes of medical research by using a control subject (Michaela's sister) before trying out the treatment on Lorenzo. However, as they learn and move from being non-experts to experts, they do not completely refuse their former subjective positions. This refusal by the Odones to separate their subjective and objective positions causes a relocation of the terms of the central duality of objective and subjective, the duality that informs the construction of scientific knowledge in *Lorenzo's Oil*. And this relocation becomes one of the main critical points of the text. Whilst objectivity, as a mode of systematic acquisition of information which can then be formulated as knowledge, remains intact, it no longer simply operates as a privileged term against subjectivity. In the earlier sequences of *Lorenzo's Oil*, parental knowledge was excluded as non-expert, as were any questions that were not informed by medical discourses. All of these were associated, directly or indirectly, with too great an emotional attachment to the need to find a way of stopping the progression of the disease.

Towards the end of the film, these very same attachments have enabled the accretion of knowledge that prevents Lorenzo from dying. Since the Odones' love for their son has motivated their pursuit of knowledge, the objective and subjective terms of the duality no longer operate as separate elements. They have, instead, come together. The insistence on a logical set of rules to ensure a coherent approach to knowledge is no longer seen as simplistically dispassionate or disinterested. Whilst a central place for rigour remains, there is also a place alongside for a passionate interestedness. In the resolution of *Lorenzo's Oil*, this new position is celebrated, not only within the diegesis when Augusto Odone is given an honorary medical degree, but also by the end credit sequence that shows actual images of boys who have survived ALD because of Lorenzo's Oil.[14]

In *Medicine Man* there is a similar collapse of the opposition between objectivity and subjectivity. Like *Lorenzo's Oil*, it presents research as a method based on systematicity that requires logic and coherence; however, it similarly shows emotions to be a part of Campbell's research impetus – his desire to carry on with his research is strongly motivated by a sense of atonement. Within the narrative of *Medicine Man*, through his youthful lack of understanding of the potentially catastrophic effects of Western people's illnesses on an isolated Rainforest tribe, Campbell had inadvertently been the cause of the death of a whole village. Campbell's desire to find cures for disease, whilst remaining embedded in Western scientific methods, is motivated through his need for atonement. When read in this way, both *Lorenzo's Oil* and *Medicine Man* touch, albeit obliquely, on a paradox evident in discussions about the scientific method and objectivity. In constructions of objectivity, the dualities of objective and subjective and of rationality and emotion traditionally operate together, with rationality and objectivity both being the privileged and validated terms. That the striving for knowledge through objective study is a desire to know, and is therefore driven in part by emotion, rarely seems to trouble the opposition.[15] This reading of *Lorenzo's Oil* and *Medicine Man* suggests that there is, then, an instability in the dualisms that inform the foundations on which scientific knowledge is constructed.

The questioning of the construction of objectivity in *Lorenzo's Oil* and *Medicine Man* is not only apparent in the contradiction that an individual can desire objective knowledge, as both texts further suggest that what is privileged as scientific knowledge is not neutral but also operates through the categories of race and gender. Such a perspective within fictions of technoscience resonates with similar issues raised by recent studies of the history of science. Within this discipline, a number of critics have argued that what is presented as objective knowledge is embedded within a system that privileges as objective that knowledge which is associated with whiteness and masculinity.[16] In *Medicine Man*, expert knowledge is recognisable and granted legitimacy only within the domain of Western scientific knowledge. Visually, discussions about the cancer cure occur exclusively in the space occupied by the two white characters, that is the laboratory space. The anecdotal, the non-expert knowledge is associated with the spaces inhabited by the native Amazonian people. Whilst Campbell begins to tell his story of the cure of the first child in the village space, when Crane demands documentation the action moves back to the laboratory space, where the scientific proof is finally obtained through the regime of experimentation. Such a use of space is reiterated later in the film when Crane is forced into making a choice between curing an individual or keeping the serum for analysis. When a second child becomes ill, Crane initially refuses to allow Campbell to use the last of the serum to cure him. Taking up a dispassionate position, she claims that the serum must be kept for analysis, and that one child can be sacrificed to the greater good. In these scenes she appears trapped inside the laboratory space; framed inside the verticals of the wooden building, and unable to move beyond its boundaries, she can only look out towards the village and listen to the sounds coming from there. When Crane makes the decision to save the child she leaves the laboratory, goes into the village space and administers the injection that results in the child's survival. As if to underline the point more clearly, the laboratory space is subsequently destroyed; it becomes a place to which Crane, both literally and intellectually, cannot return.

The use of space is not the only way that exclusions in the constructions of knowledge become apparent in *Medicine Man*. They are also evident in the relationship between Campbell, Crane and the tribal Medicine Man. Initially, as Campbell himself tells the story, he discovered the serum because he followed and copied the Medicine Man – he simply collected the same plants he saw the Medicine Man collecting. Without consultation he appropriated the man's knowledge, and in so doing failed to engage with his expertise. When unable to repeat his extraction of the serum from the

plants, Campbell claims to have communicated with the Medicine
Man, but indicates that the latter would give him no information.
However, in a subsequent meeting between the Medicine Man and
Campbell, one that is directly narrated to viewers of *Medicine Man*,
an alternative possibility emerges. It is clear in this second meeting
that Campbell, the Western scientist, is unable to hear the information given to him by the Medicine Man.[17] In the clash of languages
and knowledge systems that occurs between the Westerners and the
Native people, the Western scientists are unable to see what is literally before their eyes – the ants in the plants, not the plants themselves, are the source of the cure. Versed as they are in the protocols
of clean laboratory work, Campbell and Crane consider the insects
in their samples to be an infestation, and it never occurs to them that
the ants may be important. Even when the Medicine Man's words
about the plants are translated by another villager: 'No juju in
skyflower, only house for bugs, Campbell is a fool', Campbell's dis-
appointment in the Medicine Man's apparent lack of useful knowledge causes him to miss the crucial word *bugs*. The two scientists
belatedly realise that the source of the cure is the ants after they
notice that the insects are the source of the contamination of a sugar
solution that is injected into one of their machines as a baseline control.[18] Only once the information is converted, via a piece of technology, into a language and convention that the Western scientists
have the expertise to interpret, do they finally understand. The
knowledge of the Native people remains excluded until it is translated, not simply verbally, but into a knowledge system which is
legitimated within the scientists' Western worldview. The resolution
of *Medicine Man* seems to want to suggest that the Westerners have
learnt from this mistake, and they decide to stay with the villagers so
that they can learn from the Medicine Man. However, this clearly
remains on their terms as a bargain is struck between Crane and
Campbell about whose name goes first on the scientific publication.

Whilst in *Medicine Man* the constructions of objective knowledge
occur through a privileging of the Western technological perspective, in *Lorenzo's Oil* such constructions operate in relation to
gender difference. This gender difference has traditionally operated
through a series of assumed alignments across the dualities of
masculine/feminine, men/women and rational/emotional. By this I
mean masculine=men=rational and feminine=women=emotional.
Typically, women as carers are positioned as emotional, whilst men

located outside of the domestic space are more aligned with rational. Although *Lorenzo's Oil* superficially might appear to reiterate such a simplistic construction, it can also be read as taking up a more complex position. Initially, Michaela and Augusto act as a tandem pair, and their status as parents makes them both too attached to Lorenzo to be anything other than emotionally involved in the process of finding a potential therapy. When they shift into a position of expertise they appear to do so together: they are both seen reading in the library, and participating in the ALD symposium. This alteration in Michaela and Augusto's relationship to expertise seems to run against the traditional construction of gendered roles, with men aligned with rational roles and women with emotional ones. Yet in spite of this transition, Michaela remains more strongly coded as Lorenzo's carer. In many of the most emotionally charged scenes of the film, it is an exhausted Michaela who holds Lorenzo in her arms, coaxing him through a prolonged fit, who reads him stories, or argues with the nurse who does not believe that Lorenzo is still a sentient human being. In contrast, Augusto becomes increasingly marginalised. He is either completely absent from the scenes, or on their periphery. In the very stylised hospital sequence in which Lorenzo is expected by the doctors to die, Michaela, centrally framed from a high angle, sits on a chair in the centre of the room holding Lorenzo in her arms. Augusto stands on the edges of the space, helpless and excluded. In spite, then, of the apparent gain of expertise by both parents, it would be easy argue that underlying this is a replaying of traditionally gendered perspectives – Michaela heroically battling with Lorenzo's needs in the home, whilst Augusto sits in the library thinking biochemistry; his heroic breakthrough coming when he is able to understand the enzyme mechanism, an event that ultimately prevents the progress of Lorenzo's disease.[19] This reading, however, seems too unsympathetic to the more complex turns in the narrative which, rather than simply depicting the parents' reactions to their child's illness, attempts to explore the different responses of the two. When Michaela understands that it is her family, and more especially herself, who is the source of Lorenzo's illness – ALD is transmitted from mother (as a genetic carrier) to son – Michaela becomes both guilty and angry. She withdraws from her family and church, refuses to eat and focuses all her energy on Lorenzo's care as a means of making amends. Such a position of guilt gives some sense to the motivation of her refusal to let

Augusto be involved in holding Lorenzo through the long night in the hospital.

Of the two parents' reactions to Lorenzo's illness, it is Augusto's which are the least resolved within the narrative of *Lorenzo's Oil*. In an early sequence, just after Lorenzo's diagnosis, Augusto sits with a book in a library where he reads about the progression of ALD. As the music increases in volume, the images consist of a series of ever-closer zoom-ins on the words written on the pages. These are stark, hard clinical words – dementia, optic atrophy, dysphasia, mute, blind, deaf, coma – words to which Augusto seems to lose his son. The sequence ends in high-melodramatic mode, the music combining with Augusto's howls as he lies weeping in a stairwell. Later in the narrative, when Michaela challenges Augusto, saying to him that he has lost sight of Lorenzo, that his son has merely become for him a 'biochemical conundrum' to be solved, Augusto's answer does not respond to her question. As he retreats into his native language, Italian, Augusto's anguished halting responses are given in subtitles. They reveal that Augusto does not know Lorenzo as he is now, and only wants him back as he was before. His defence, his way of coping with his emotions, is to fall back on the puzzle of Lorenzo's illness. The language of fatty acid metabolism becomes his way of communicating with Lorenzo, as he seems unable to comprehend him in the same way as Michaela.

By aligning Augusto's defensive response with his new expertise in biochemistry, and Michaela's with her role as carer, *Lorenzo's Oil* is in danger of simply reiterating the alignment of masculine=men=rational and feminine=women=emotional. However, by the end of its narrative it has done something more complex. It *has* paired Augusto with rationality and objectivity, but in a way that interrogates the possibilities open to male expressions of grief. That Augusto seems only able to channel his emotions into his study of the disease, that he is uncomfortably located on the periphery of the care-giving, creates an unresolved tension in the text. Here, Augusto's rational and objective approach to his son's illness is clearly validated, but there is a question mark over whether it is also an escape for him, a way of managing his emotions. By 'managing' here, I do not mean that Augusto is shown confronting and rationalising his feelings about Lorenzo's illness, but rather that he side-steps such questions by taking another route, the attempt to understand the biochemical problem posed by the illness. As such, this represents a retreat into rationality, a retreat that again constitutes a blurring of the opposition rational and emotional.

Shopping for knowledge

The section above discussed a number ways in which constructions of scientific knowledge in *Lorenzo's Oil* and *Medicine Man* complicate the use of the terms objective and rational. This argument was based on relatively abstract ideas about the relationship between practitioners of science or medicine and the objects which they study, revolving around the terms dispassionate and disinterested. But this is not the only route through which it is possible to address critically the notion that the practices of science and technology are necessarily objective and rational. Both dispassionate and disinterested imply a further term which has been associated with the practices of science – neutrality, which is usually taken to mean the transcendence of political, social and cultural moments and spaces. In science studies, critics of the view that science is a neutral practice take up two positions. In the first, they argue that science can never transcend the cultural moments and spaces in which it occurs, and therefore a rational approach is better served by taking a situated position in relation to knowledge. The implied outcome of this position is a reflective and located perspective on knowledge, a perspective that will somehow enable a better rationalism.[20] Such an approach, whilst making explicit the contingencies of rationalism, leaves in place the possibility of a fully rational and objective science. In the alternative view, rationality and objectivity are always limited. What they mean can only be understood from within a discourse. The possibility remains for the practice of science to be coherent, consistent and without contradiction, according to a set of logical rules. However, the knowledge and objects produced will always emerge within a system that either validates or invalidates them according to the intellectual, social, cultural and political context that prevails at any given moment. In this second perspective, knowledge is always contingent, and it can be neither neutral nor transcendent.

Across the various texts that constitute fictions of technoscience, both of these positions are evident. On the one hand fictions of technoscience may privilege objectivity, however paradoxically, but on the other they locate objective knowledge as contingent, the very antithesis of what objectivity is meant to be. These contingencies are

apparent when texts demonstrate economic and political power as
exerting an influence over the ways in which knowledge can come
into being. Such a double positioning is the case in *Lorenzo's Oil*.
The medical knowledge which accumulates does not exist simply as
knowledge; it can only come to be recognised as such after a number
of political and economic obstacles have been passed. Within the
narrative of *Lorenzo's Oil* ALD, a new and rare disease, is unable to
attract high levels of federal funding because it is so rare: 'ours is
what we call an orphan disease, it's too small to be noticed, too small
to be funded'. Instead, research funding is dependent on the efforts
of the parents who raise cash and give donations, those very same
people who are the non-experts. The absence of funding not only
limits the research, and the associated accumulation of knowledge,
but also restricts communication between the different parts of the
scientific community. When the Odones raise money for a small
symposium from outside the usual medical-research funding bodies,
the benefits of communication become obvious – a potential therapy
emerges in the form of oil. The contingency of this successful
process is immediately reiterated by the claim that no company will
gear up to make the oil because there is not enough potential
payback in the marketplace. Knowledge and its outcomes are here
clearly dependent on economics – funding to do the research in the
first place, and subsequently funding to make use of the research, to
commodify it. Ultimately, it is only because the Odones themselves
have sufficient economic substance that they are able to find a therapy which can help their son.

   Lorenzo's Oil, then, explores the operations of political and economic power on a knowledge that might emerge to provide a cure
for illnesses. It gives an account of the relationships between medicine as an institution based around doctors, nurses, hospitals or clinics, and suggests that medicine as an institution is linked with
corporate concerns about potential profits from those emergent
knowledges. A number of other films also explore the influence of
funding on the materialisation of knowledge. Such questions are
raised in films as varied as *The Relic* (1997, US), where two scientists
compete for patronage from a benefactor; *Junior* (1994, US), in
which a scientist is evicted from his university-based laboratories
because his research is not commercially viable; and *The Saint*
(1997, US), where a scientist is threatened because she wants her discovery of a cheap source of energy to be given freely to the world.

In the remains of this chapter, I will discuss two particular fictions of technoscience, *The Lawnmower Man* and *Jurassic Park*. Like the films mentioned briefly above, both of these films construct the processes by which the accumulation of knowledge takes place as non-neutral. Instead, its accumulation is presented as occurring in an intersection with systems which only validate knowledge because of the potential commercial market for its products. In *The Lawnmower Man* the intersection is with the military, and in *Jurassic Park* the intersection is with the entertainment industry.

Central to the story of *The Lawnmower Man* is the conflict between the research concerns of an individual scientist and his funding body, in this case a military linked corporation. The film opens with a written commentary on the major technology of the film, virtual reality: 'By the turn of the millennium a technology known as VIRTUAL REALITY will be in widespread use. It will allow you to enter computer generated artificial worlds as unlimited as the imagination itself. Its creators see millions of positive uses – while others see it as a new form of mind control'. The final sentence of this passage sets the scene for a confrontation at the heart of *The Lawnmower Man*, the confrontation between good versus bad uses of technology and science. Aware that such an opposition is not novel to this film, found as it is in many SF and horror films, *The Lawnmower Man* makes this generic history apparent by recalling the *Frankenstein* story in numerous ways. Whilst the protagonists live in suburban California, the new technology is developed in an isolated laboratory on a hill, and although there are no gothic crenellations, it does have a team of paramilitary guards and impregnable high walls. Continuing in the *Frankenstein* mode, Dr Larry Angelo, the brilliant and obsessed scientist of the film, claims of his research that: 'The potentials for human advancement are endless, virtual reality is the key to the evolution of the human mind'. Unlike Dr Frankenstein (Victor in the novel, and Henry in the James Whale films), who animates dead bodies, Angelo animates by enhancing the intelligence initially of primates, and then a human, Jobe. In each of the stories, the scientist feels he is contributing to humankind in a profound and life-enhancing way.[21]

Although continuing the long tradition of the misguided scientist theme, *The Lawnmower Man* is set in a more contemporary scenario. Angelo is not a self-funded individual; instead, he is supported by a military-oriented corporation. It is this corporation, referred to as 'the Shop', rather than Angelo that is presented as immoral; their motivation to fund research depicted as governed by their need for ever more sophisticated fighting machines which they can sell on to buyers. Whilst the film is clearly critical of an alignment between militarism and research, Angelo's place within this scenario is more ambivalent – his relationship to the Shop is based on both resistance and dependence. In making Angelo's relationship to the Shop ambivalent, *The Lawnmower Man* starts out by not making a simple opposition between a mad scientist and society, a monster and society, or for that matter, a scientist and a monster. Instead, the operations of power that structure the emergence of knowledge become visible in the confrontations between an institution and a scientist that are mutually dependent on one another.[22]

The Lawnmower Man begins by straightforwardly foregrounding Angelo's position as one of resistance to the militarism of his sponsors. The credit and opening sequences, filmed in a blue-hued darkness, feature the laboratory as a series of enclosed spaces – lengths of windowless corridors end in security doors and the experimental subjects, chimps, live in cages. Angelo, arguing with Timms, the Shop's go-between, is seen through the point of view of Roscoe, a caged chimp. Through this perspective Angelo, framed by bars, is trapped by Timms and the Shop's demands on him. Angelo's experiments, which are not necessarily limited to a military application, are designed to enhance intelligence through the use of both 'neurotropic drugs' and sensory stimulation through virtual simulations; however, they have been co-opted for use in training the chimps to use a special infrared battle helmet. The visual entrapment of Angelo continues into the first post-credit scenes of the film. In the aftermath of the death of Angelo's best primate subject, Roscoe, in an attempted breakout from the research institute, a breakout which is linked to a side-effect of the aggression factors included in the battlefield simulation protocol, Angelo comes into conflict with Timms. During this confrontation, Angelo refuses to carry on working with the Shop, claiming that they are preventing the development of his research to its full potential as a learning aid. When he indicates that he will get funding from elsewhere, he is reminded by Timms that he has signed 'an iron clad disclosure deal', which makes it impossible to use his knowledge in any other context. As Angelo rails against the obstacles to his research project, moving from an open-plan area and up some steps into the enclosed space of the narrow viewing balcony, the camera tracks his movements. As it does so, it moves behind columns, literally putting obstacles in the way of a clear view of Angelo, reiterating the idea of obstacles being put in Angelo's way. In the final shot of this sequence, Angelo is framed inside the small viewing balcony, an effect that echoes his entrapment by the Shop.

In making explicit the sequestration of Angelo's knowledge for military uses, these scenes explore questions about the ownership of knowledge. As the narrative of *Lorenzo's Oil* made connections between money and access to knowledge, so too does *The Lawnmower Man*. Angelo's research, and the scientific knowledge he has accumulated through it, does not belong to him; it is owned by the funders of his research. Not only does the Shop have the right to allow or limit access to the knowledge created by Angelo activities; they can also control what could become possible through managing the provision of money for facilities. Here, the funders own and regulate the knowledge, not the individual who creates and develops that knowledge. In this way, *The Lawnmower Man* presents a perspective in which the production of knowledge is not simply based on creativity, but equally on the seemingly more mundane decisions about how it can be put to 'good' use. The figure at the centre of the production of knowledge, in this instance still an individual, is caught up in the decision making, sometimes in productive ways, though often, as is the case for Angelo, in ways which are not considered productive by the individual.

As read above, *The Lawnmower Man* presents a relatively straightforward critique of the technoscientific process of a military-corporate institution, a process which both exploits the creative work of scientists, and entraps them. However, Angelo is not simply an innocent figure caught up in the machinations of a powerful organisation. In the opening segments of the film, Angelo appears actively resistant to the use of his research for military purposes; however, as the narrative progresses he becomes more complicit with the Shop through his reliance on their research equipment. Furthermore, his ethical position comes into question when he unilaterally embarks on a human study. After Roscoe's escape attempt Angelo is given enforced leave. In this period, when he is depressed and obsessed with the research he is unable to carry out, Angelo decides to act on his own and entices Jobe, a young man with learning difficulties, to be his first human subject by offering to let him play his video games. This means of seducing Jobe into being a part of the experiment operates on the audience as well. *The Lawn-mower Man* was one of the first films to attempt to show virtual reality, and much of the special-effects work of the text depicts the fictionalised virtual reality.[23] Prior to the moment when Angelo asks Jobe to play his games, *The Lawnmower Man* made relatively little use of its graphic effects. There are glimpses of the battle simulations played by Roscoe, as well as Angelo's floating and falling sequences. But it is only at the point when Jobe and Peter (a boy who lives next to Angelo and is one of Jobe's friends) play a game together, that the exhilaration of experiencing this new reality is displayed within the text. In part, this exhilaration is mediated through the reactions of the characters. When Peter and Jobe play the game, the spectacle of the cyberscenes themselves gives a sense of the speed and action experienced by players inside a game, but this effect is heightened by hearing the shrieks of the two players. Later in *The Lawnmower Man* the cyberscene graphics continue to combine speed with action. As Angelo loads learning patterns for Jobe, the information is seen spiralling inwards, whilst a 3-D image of Jobe's brain actively responds to the stimuli. However, the most spectacular scenes are the ones involving the fluid transitions of the cyberbodies of Marnie and Jobe (the former is a woman whose lover Jobe has become). The double articulation of seduction is most explicit here; the images depict bodies in sexual play, using a series of transformations in body shapes which display the computer-generated graphics to their greatest effects. Significantly, it is at the height of this seductive sequence, at the moment when a viewer might be most impressed with the graphic sequences, that the images begin to turn more menacing. From this moment in *The Lawnmower Man*, though the special effects are still impressive, the story being told through them is no longer playful; instead it is one of destruction. When Jobe's cyberbody, re-forming into an uncontrollably ejaculating primal thing, attacks Marnie's cyberbody, it causes her to lose her sanity in the real world. The technology here shifts from being seductive, into having the potential to become a hostile environment. As Angelo's wife says to him early in the film: 'It may be the future to you, but to me, it's the same old shit'.

This shift in the construction of technology from seductive to potentially hostile is mediated primarily through Jobe, and Angelo's role in precipitating the events that lead to this shift suggests, as I mentioned above, that he is not an innocent figure within the narrative. Angelo initially wins Jobe over to his cause by getting him to play a virtual-reality game against Peter. With the game over, when Jobe expresses his humiliation over his bad game-playing, Angelo offers his own expertise to make Jobe more intelligent. In a nicely ironic scene, Angelo, sitting side by side with Jobe on his sofa so they can talk as equals, gains Jobe's consent. He persuades Jobe that if he is more intelligent people will not be able to take advantage of him – all the while taking advantage of him. The experiments to enhance Jobe's intelligence begin in Angelo's cellar; the low lighting and heavy shadows of the room echo the look of the facility in which his primate research was carried out. This visual link back to the VSI Institute outlines how compromised Angelo's resistance actually is. No longer the outraged scientist, whose work of great potential is subverted by the specific requirements of a military-corporate complex, he is playing at being god, pushing Jobe further and further, without really considering the effects of the experiments on the latter's life. Angelo's integrity is finally jettisoned when, finding his own facilities insufficient, he goes back to the Institute despite what he already knows about how it operates. This progression of events suggests that individual scientists in *The Lawnmower Man* cannot function either on their own, or on their own terms. In this fiction of technoscience, the nature of contemporary research, dependent on expensive equipment and facilities, inevitably results in the incorporation of the researcher into a system that they cannot fully control. And, indeed, once Angelo is back in the VSI laboratories he is again subject to the machinations of the Shop. In taking Jobe into the laboratory, Angelo has compromised both himself and Jobe's safety – Timms subverts Angelo's experiments by swapping the drugs Angelo had been using on Jobe.

The effect of subverting the experiment is to alter Jobe's personality radically. Although the experiments had already begun to have unexpected side-effects such as telepathy, Jobe had remained unaggressive, unless he was provoked. Once given the drugs substituted by Timms, he no longer simply becomes more intelligent, but develops into an aggressive and vengeful figure. In a discussion of Jobe's aggressive masculinity, Claudia Springer puts forward the view that increasing his intelligence turns him into a 'hypermasculine hunk'.[24] Jobe's subsequent violence, Springer argues, is an attempt to protect this masculinity when it is threatened by the boundary loss of both real and virtual heterosexual sex; furthermore, she indicates that this suggests the film's ambivalent attitude towards virtual-reality technologies. This argument rests on a comparison between Jobe and fascistic soldiers, whose masculinity must be kept hard, both physically and emotionally, and must be protected from the menace of feminine fluidity.[25] The connection between fluidity and femininity here relies on the notion that at orgasm, a man gives himself over to the moment in such a way that he is no longer whole, that the boundary of his subjectivity is broken in the 'little death'. Within the construction being used by Springer, women act as both reminders of this potential loss for heterosexual men, as well as the figure who engages the man in this threatening act of sex. Accordingly, Jobe's aggression towards Marnie is motivated by his need to protect his newly found masculinity from the fusion of sexual encounter with a woman in both the real and virtual worlds.

An alternative reading of *The Lawnmower Man* is that Jobe's violent activities, in an echo of the Creature in *Frankenstein*, are a reaction to a more general experience of living within the human world. Jobe's personal history, as depicted within the film, includes being physically beaten by the repressed priest, as well as being punched and taunted by another character because he is 'dumb'. Jobe's murder of Peter's abusive father is motivated by his desire to protect Peter, a motivation that is maintained through to the ending of the film. Jobe's violence against all the characters that he attacks can be read as a commentary on the violence of the world that he inhabits, and his desire to be a god-figure is a megalomaniacal desire to rid the world of its 'sins'. Nonetheless, there does seem to be a distinction between Jobe's apparent reason for attacking Marnie and his aggression towards the other characters. In the other cases, each character threatens either Jobe or someone he cares about. In contrast, Marnie stands in for what Jobe perceives as some kind of perverse sexuality. When Jobe becomes telepathic he is shocked about the things that go in the heads of the people he meets. And, as women have so frequently done in the history of cinema, Marnie acts as the representative of this within the text. As such, she is punished more for what she represents to Jobe than for anything she herself has done. The different acts of violence that Jobe carries out, however, cannot be easily linked to an ambivalence towards the virtual-reality technologies in themselves. These technologies have certainly enhanced his learning in ways that have been unpredictable, but the savagery with which Jobe's violence erupts is linked to the subversion of Angelo's protocols, rather than the protocols themselves. When Timms subverts Angelo's experiments by swapping the serum, replacing the human version for a primate one containing aggression factors, the film visualises Jobe's mind 'being blown', and his extreme violence follows from this event. But, even though Jobe's violence can be made sense of in this way, his actions are not condoned. Within *The Lawnmower Man*, Jobe is not a hero. As such, the version of violent masculinity performed through Jobe is presented as a problem, not a solution. And by implication, the activities of the Shop which caused the transformation of Jobe into a violent aggressor, are also problematised.

The interference with Angelo's experiments not only alters Jobe's personality, it also changes the prospects for the resolution of *The Lawnmower Man*. Up until Jobe's transubstantiation into a 'Cyber-Christ', the narrative conflict has been between the Shop and Angelo. In this conflict, Angelo is a scientist who resents the Shop, yet needs it if he is to carry on with his research. As such, he is not a neutral figure subject to the operations of a power greater than himself; instead, he is in an ambiguous relationship with that power. With Jobe's violence unleashed, the central conflict of the film becomes three-cornered, and his activities are the ones that cause the collapse of the control of the Shop, and the destruction of Angelo's work. With Jobe as the narrative agent who promotes this resolution, the ambiguity of the relationship between Angelo and the Shop remains unresolved. *The Lawnmower Man* problematises, then, the aggressive actions of a monstrous character, a character created in the power play between an individual scientist and the institution for which he works. However, in so doing it displaces the question of a scientist who is both resistant to and complicit with the operations of power in contemporary science.

The subversion of Dr Angelo's experiment in *The Lawnmower Man* exposes an uneasiness over who has the right to control the means by which scientific knowledge is acquired: the scientist or their paymaster(s)? There is a similar conflict in *Jurassic Park*, though here the anxiety revolves around who has the authority to make use of scientific knowledge. The central theme of the narrative in *Jurassic Park* is that an entrepreneur's privately funded scientists have been able to clone dinosaurs, and these creatures are to be used as the central attraction in a theme park. The concern of *Jurassic Park* is not with science in itself, but with a science that operates outside of a domain authorised by the legitimised institutional practices of science. The explicit criticisms of *Jurassic Park* are aimed at John Hammond, the entrepreneur who has co-opted the skills of scientists, taken individuals out of a scientific domain and relocated them in a corporate one where the processes of legitimisation are defined by potential profit, rather than by the generation of potential knowledge.

The science at the centre of *Jurassic Park* is the ability to clone dinosaurs from fragments of DNA found in prehistoric mosquitoes preserved fossilised in amber. The recreation of the dinosaurs represents, within the science of the film, the pinnacle of achievement. It also represents an extraordinary degree of human control over nature – extinct animals are brought back to life. However, these very creatures, once they have escaped, come to represent the illusory nature of the control that Western science exerts over nature. But even prior to the release of chaos signified in the escape of the dinosaurs, a series of events serves to emphasise the unpredictability of both life and nature. These events are a combination of technological and natural occurrences, and they include the shutdown of the park's highly sophisticated electronic fencing system; corporate espionage; a storm that hits the island; and finally, the spontaneous swapping of the dinosaurs' sexes. These individually minor occurrences are soon superseded by their outcome, the escape of the dinosaurs, but nonetheless they do reinforce the emphasis in *Jurassic Park* on the impossibility of full predictability.

It is this questioning of the predictability of events in the world, whether they are natural or technological, which functions as the route through which the central critical commentary of *Jurassic Park* emerges. Prior to the dinosaur breakout, the question of control is posed through the three scientists – Ellie Sattler, Allan Grant and Ian Malcolm – invited to validate Jurassic Park as a safe entertainment venue, and it is through their points of view that the audience receives their first view of the dinosaurs. After arriving on the island where the theme park is about to go into operation, the three witness their first real-life creature. The suspense of this moment of revelation of the main spectacle of *Jurassic Park* is drawn out and mediated by the jaw-dropping reactions of the characters as each in turn is framed gaping. When the dinosaur is finally revealed, its body fills the screen, and low angles are used to give the impression of a creature of enormous size, an effect furthered by the use of trees and human figures to supply scale. As well as providing the spectacle of the outcome of the science practised within the fiction of *Jurassic Park*, the special effects used to create the film's images are themselves a spectacular element. The CGI graphics and the animatronics used to produce the dinosaur images surpass anything previously seen within filmmaking. As in *The Lawnmower Man*, in *Jurassic Park* the special-effects technologies used in the narrative do not simply operate to create images, but are also examples of the capabilities of the technologies contemporary to the making of the films. In both of these films, there is a double articulation of the effects of technology.

Within the story of *Jurassic Park* the awe of the visiting scientists rapidly gives way to unease as they consider the impact of the Creatures on an environment which is alien to them. During a scene in which they watch with fascination as a baby dinosaur hatches, Ian Malcolm discloses his misgivings. After Henry Woo, the chief scientist, has explained how reproduction by the dinosaurs is prevented through cloning only females, Malcolm protests that 'life, uh, finds a way'. Initially Malcolm's protest is greeted with disdain, but in the scenes that follow, the two other experts, Ellie Sattler and Alan Grant, also begin to express their misgivings. For these experts, two scientists and a chaotician, the problem is not simply that Hammond has done something that is flawed and dangerous in its execution – the dinosaurs cannot be controlled; as Malcolm had said, they will find a way. The problem is also that Hammond and his work functions outside of a legitimating domain. Because of his wealth, and the potential income from the research product, Hammond has been able to take the best scientists and put them to work in a specially built laboratory, isolated on the Island like the dinosaurs it produces. The domain that is opposed to Hammond's corporate one is indicated in a long speech by Ian Malcolm:

> 'I'll tell you the problem with the scientific power that you're using here. It didn't require any discipline to attain it. You know, you read what others had done, and you took the next step. You didn't earn the knowledge for yourselves so you don't take any responsibility ... for it [brushes aside interruption]. You stood on the shoulders of geniuses, ah, to accomplish something as fast as you could, and before you even knew what you had, you patented it, and packaged it, and slapped it on a plastic lunch box and now you're selling it [hits fist on table top], selling it ... well ...'
>
> [Hammond replies: 'I don't think you're giving us our due credit, our scientists have done things which no-one has ever done before ...']

'Yeah ... yeah, but your scientists were so preoccupied with whether or not they could, that they didn't stop to think if they should.'

Malcolm's speech implies that there is a way of practising science that requires not only expertise and money, but also an understanding of both the history and the potential of the knowledge involved. Malcolm, Sattler and Grant between them, as representatives of the legitimate academic disciplines of mathematics, palaeobotany and palaeontology, have the knowledge to which Malcolm refers. And Malcolm validates them, not Hammond and his scientists, as having the expertise and authority to judge what is right. Financial power is not enough.

This view is reiterated within *Jurassic Park* when Sattler and Grant, as well as being critics of an improper use of science, become the means through which a degree of order is re-established after the Park has become chaotic. Sattler helps save Ian Malcolm and resets the power switch that reinstitutes the technological capability of the Island, whilst Grant saves Hammond's grandchildren. And, though unable to reassert full control over the marauding and now reproductively active dinosaurs, Sattler and Grant make escape possible. Although, through the actions of Sattler and Grant, science is positioned as a saving presence in *Jurassic Park*, it is not presented as a monolithic entity: the place of Ian Malcolm in the narrative complicates the positions of the scientists as a coherent group. He may be aligned with Sattler and Grant through his status as a scientist, but Malcolm has little narrative function in the latter half of the film. Injured by the Tyrannosaurus Rex during his attempt to divert the creature from the children, Malcolm spends the latter part of the plot either being carried around on a stretcher, or safely placed in a bunker, out of the action. Such a narrative position is appropriate for the type of science for which Malcolm stands. Chaos theory, as presented through this character, is about trying to predict non-linear events, and is not about responding to events.[26] Malcolm was correct in his predictions, but is unable to do anything about them. In contrast, Ellie Sattler and Alan Grant represent a different order of science. As a palaeobotanist and palaeontologist respectively, they represent an order of science that acts to uncover and reconstruct the past. It is their function within the narrative to attempt a reconstruction of a notional scientific authority over the disarray created by the *enfant terrible* conjunction of Henry Woo and John Hammond. That they cannot fully achieve it, and have to leave the island to the dinosaurs, may be seen as something of a failure, but it also reiterates the warnings that they gave earlier in the narrative. That is, it is impossible to control everything even, or especially, through science and technology.

In this reading of *Jurassic Park*, the operations of the institution of science are opposed those of the corporate domain. Like *Lorenzo's Oil*, *Medicine Man* and *The Lawnmower Man*, *Jurassic Park* can be seen as a critique of the ways in which economic power is mobilised to restrict the ways in which scientific knowledge and technologies can emerge. However, *Jurassic Park* differs from the other three films – its solution apparently lies in the proposal that the scientific domain is moral and ethical enough to be above the motivations of profit, that it has the capacity to sort out potential conflicts of interest. Slyly, perhaps, *Jurassic Park* undercuts this seemingly simplistic point of view. Ellie Sattler and Alan Grant only visit the Island because Hammond has promised them money for their research project.

I have argued in this chapter that the institutions of science depicted in these fictions of technoscience are determined by social, political and economic constraints; and furthermore, that the individuals who operate within and through this institutional system are also subject to those same restrictions. As such the individual, the scientist, is no longer the only site of the production of knowledge. The institution is also part of that production. In *Lorenzo's Oil*, *Medicine Man* and *The Lawnmower Man*, the processes of the institutions of medical research, the corporate interests of pharmaceutical companies and the corporate-military nexus inflect the processes of the production of knowledge – what emerges is always contingent on the processes of the institutions within which it operates. *Jurassic Park*, *The Lawnmower Man*, *Lorenzo's Oil* and *Medicine Man* do not, then, depict scientific knowledge as a 'pure' thing, based solely on the creative expertise of an individual or group of scientists. Instead it is more of a technoscience, located within a network dependent on social, cultural, economic and political conditions. As a technoscience, this knowledge does not exist simply because it is knowledge; it exists because the market or social forces in operation allow it to do so. Given this degree of contingency, *Jurassic Park*, *The Lawnmower Man*, *Lorenzo's Oil* and *Medicine Man* could be read as texts that articulate the collapse of the grand narrative of science as a means to say something definitive about what we call the natural world. At the same time, however, they can also be read as texts in which one grand narrative is replaced by another – the legitimating practices of capitalism.

Notes

1 See, for instance, Peter Biskind, *Seeing is Believing: How Hollywood Taught Us to Stop Worrying and Love the Fifties* (London: Pluto Press, 1984); Scott Bukatman, *Terminal Identity: The Virtual Subject in Postmodern Science Fiction* (Durham, NC: Duke University Press, 1993); Annette Kuhn (ed.), *Alien Zone: Cultural Theory and Contemporary Science Fiction Cinema* (London: Verso, 1990); Annette Kuhn, *Alien Zone 2* (London: Verso, 1999); Patrick Lucanio, *Them or Us: Archetypal Interpretations of Fifties Alien Invasion Films* (Bloomington: Indiana University Press, 1987); Claudia Springer, *Electronic Eros: Bodies and Desire in the Postindustrial Age* (Austin: University of Texas, 1996); and J.P. Telotte, *Replications: A Robotic History of Science Fiction Film* (Urbana and Chicago: University of Illinois Press, 1995).

2 Andrew Tudor, *Monsters and Mad Scientists: A Cultural History of the Horror Movie* (Oxford: Blackwell, 1989) p. 147.

3 J.P. Telotte, *A Distant Technology: Science Fiction Film and the Machine Age* (Hanover, NH: Wesleyan University Press, 1999) p. 109.

4 A useful historical overview of depictions of the medical profession can be found in Michael Shortland's pamphlet *Medicine and Film: A Checklist, Survey and Research Resource* (Oxford: Wellcome Unit for the History of Medicine, Research Publications Number IX, 1989).

5 The casting of the lead roles in these films was significant. Paul Muni as Louis Pasteur, Edward G. Robinson as Dr Ehrlich and Spencer Tracy as Thomas Edison added their star status to the heroic scientist role. The joint casting of Greer Garson and Walter Pidgeon in *Madame Curie* is not incidental. They had already played together in *Mrs Miniver* (1942, US). The tag line for *Madame Curie* was 'Mr and Mrs Miniver together again', suggesting that the film was marketed so that the resonances of the earlier film would carry over into the tragic romance of the Curies.

6 Several writers have placed such SF texts within the context of the Cold War. For example, Biskind, *Seeing is Believing*; Lucanio, *Them or Us*; and David Seed, *American Science Fiction and the Cold War* (Edinburgh: Edinburgh University Press, 1999).

7 Although it is not an especially strong element of 1950s texts, *The Creature from the Black Lagoon* (1954, US), *Monkey Business* (1952, US) and *People Will Talk* (1951, US) all have scenarios that involve the problems of getting funding for research. Such questions again reveal the locatedness of science.

8 In April 2000 *Fail Safe* was remade as a television drama directed by Stephen Frears, and was aired in the US to critical acclaim.

9 Tudor, *Monsters and Mad Scientists* p. 156.

10 Stanley Jeyaraja Tambiah, *Magic, Science, Religion, and the Scope of Rationality* (Cambridge: Cambridge University Press, 1990) p. 115.

11 Examples of such critical work include Evelyn Fox Keller, *Reflections on Gender and Science* (New Haven: Yale University Press, 1985); Bruno Latour, *Science in Action: How to Follow Scientists and Engineers through Society* (Milton Keynes: Open University Press, 1987); Mary Jacobus, Evelyn Fox Keller and Sally Shuttleworth (eds.), *Body/Politics* (London and New York: Routledge, 1990); Janine Marchessault and Kim Shawchuk (eds.), *Wild Science: Reading Feminism, Medicine and the Media* (London and New York: Routledge, 2000).

12 W.H. Newton-Smith, *The Rationality of Science* (London: Routledge and Kegan-Paul, 1981) p. 1.

13 Children who have ALD all have higher than normal levels of a particular set of fatty acids in their blood. The experimental protocol is designed to reduce these levels by reducing the dietary sources of the fats. Within the narrative of *Lorenzo's Oil*, the results indicate that the effect of the diet is to increase rather than reduce the fatty acid levels.

14 Like many films that tell biographical stories, *Lorenzo's Oil* ends with statements about the on-going status of the people who featured in the story. This reminder of the factual basis of the events is further underlined in *Lorenzo's Oil* by short video sequences and photographs of real-life boys whose survival has been made more possible by the treatment. This transition, from the melodramatic story-world of *Lorenzo's Oil*, to the events that inspired it, heightens the impact of an already emotive film.

15 *Species* (1995, US), through its use of an ensemble cast to represent different ways of knowing in the role more conventionally played by a single hero figure, does allow objective and subjective knowledges explicitly to function together. The subjective knowledge of the empath, Dan Smithson, operates in conjunction with the more traditional scientific knowledge of Laura Baker, a molecular biologist. At the same time, however, the separation of the two positions into different characters reveals the deepseatedness of the opposition.

16 The collection of essays *The 'Racial' Economy of Science*, which aims to critically re-evaluate the sciences, especially those whose origins were outside of the Western paradigm, has a section on the construction of objectivity. Sandra Harding's work on the philosophy of science has questioned the gender neutrality of objectivity, as has Donna Haraway. Sandra Harding, *Whose Science? Whose Knowledge? Thinking from Women's Lives* (Milton Keynes: Open University Press, 1991); Sandra Harding (ed.), *The 'Racial' Economy of Science: Toward a Democratic*

Future (Bloomington and Indianapolis: Indiana University Press, 1993); Donna J. Haraway, *Simians, Cyborgs and Women: The Reinvention of Nature* (London: Free Association Books, 1991). See also the collection *Feminism and Science*, which includes several essays that address this construction of objectivity. Evelyn Fox Keller and Helen E. Longino (eds.), *Feminism and Science* (Oxford: Oxford University Press, 1996).

17 It is at this point that the double meaning of the film's title becomes apparent. The title 'Medicine Man' does not simply refer to Campbell, it also refers to the tribal Medicine Man, the figure who knows about the cure.

18 A clue about the ants is inserted relatively early on into the narrative of *Medicine Man*. Prior to a discussion about why this particular community is free of disease, Crane asks Campbell what he is giving to the children to eat; he replies, 'sugar coated ants'.

19 Although this breakthrough is somewhat ambiguously presented in a dream sequence, it would be mistaken to think it just comes to Augusto like a vision. The dream is more a crystallisation of the things he is already thinking about.

20 Donna Haraway has made this argument in 'Situated Knowledges', in Haraway, *Simians, Cyborgs and Women* pp. 183–201; but it is also implicit in those studies which seek to reveal the ways in which scientific research practices have become embedded in particular social practices, especially those of race and gender. See, for instance, Thomas Laqueur's *Making Sex: Body and Gender from the Greeks to Freud* (Cambridge, Mass.: Harvard University Press, 1990); Vernon A. Rosario (ed.), *Science and Homosexualities* (London and New York: Routledge, 1997); Londa Schiebinger's *The Mind Has No Sex? Women in the Origins of Modern Science* (Cambridge, Mass.: Harvard University Press, 1989); and Jennifer Terry and Jacqueline Urla (eds.), *Deviant Bodies: Critical Perspectives on Difference in Science and Popular Culture* (Bloomington and Indianapolis: Indiana University Press, 1995).

21 In the recently released director's cut of *The Lawnmower Man*, the opening sequence plays more strongly on its Frankensteinien antecedents. In the originally released version the primate subject, Roscoe, dies in his attempt to break out of the institution. In the director's cut, Roscoe instead escapes to the shack where Jobe, the lawnmower man, lives. Here, the technologically enhanced simian bonds with Jobe, who, not knowing better like the blind man in Mary Shelley's *Frankenstein: Prometheus Unbound*, mistakes Roscoe in his I-R helmet for his favourite comic hero, CyboMan. It is only after this event that Roscoe is located and killed by the paramilitary guards.

22 In the sequel, *Lawnmower Man 2: Beyond Cyberspace* (1996, US), the military link is absent. The narrative revolves around the machinations of a megalomaniac figure, Jobe, who wishes to control access to all the

information in the world, or all the information that is networked. The story is a simpler one than *The Lawnmower Man* in that it has a more obvious 'good guy versus bad guy' scenario.

23 Walt Disney Productions, the makers of *Tron* (1982, US), attempted to create the equivalent of a virtual reality ten years before *The Lawnmower Man*. The computer-generated graphics in *Tron* were innovative for the period, but because of the time taken to generate them, it proved difficult to sustain their use across the narrative. The filmmakers had to resort instead to more conventional animation sequences to complement the computer-generated sequences such as the motorbike chase. At the time *The Lawnmower Man* was made, the computer technologies were more advanced, making it easier to create even more sophisticated graphics than had been used in earlier films.

24 Springer, *Electronic Eros* pp. 91–94.

25 Springer is here drawing on the work of Klaus Theweleit on soldiers in the Freikorps. According to Springer, the 'fascistic soldier fears a loss of control so intensely that he avoids sex and despises women, onto to whom he projects sexual temptation and what he perceives as the dangers of bodily fluidity'. Springer, *Electronic Eros* p. 94.

26 In the sequel to *Jurassic Park*, *The Lost World* (1997, US), the character of Ian Malcolm returns in a much more assertive role. The narrative of *The Lost World* is, however, quite different to that of *Jurassic Park*, the ethics of making the dinosaurs is no longer at issue, and there is little in the sequel which relates to the debates about science evident in the first film.

2

Resistance is futile?

In *Enemy of the State* (1998, US) Robert (Bobby) Dean, an affluent African-American labour lawyer, is getting on with having a successful life. Suddenly, he gets caught up in the surveillance strategies of a rogue section of the National Security Agency (NSA), surveillance strategies that include the use of the most sophisticated of technologies. It is the startling effectiveness of these technologies that forms one of the main spectacles of the film, and their supremacy is shown through a particular sequence of images, one that is repeated several times within the text, a device that reiterates the power of the technology. The sequence always begins with a call on a cell-phone, a call that provides a set of co-ordinates; these are then passed through a computer-controlled relay to a satellite even as the co-ordinates are heard in the dialogue. Almost as soon as the number sequence ends, the satellite is seen tracking into its new position. There follows a montage of images which demonstrate the satellite focusing in – roofs of houses and their different colours are clearly delineated, figures and cars are visible even though this satellite is about 155 miles above the ground. The first time the satellite is seen in action within the narrative, it is being used to hunt down a figure running across the rooftops. In this instance, the satellite images are intercut with a second series of more conventional cinematic images – the figure being chased and his pursuers running across roofs, jumping off walls and leaping across fire escapes – as well as swooping helicopter shots from the airborne members of the chase team. Rapidly edited together, and scored with music and a dialogue from the technologically assisted network of voices telling the pursuers where to go, these sequences give the impression of an omniscient system. Each time the pursuers seem to have lost their man, he is found again running either through buildings or down alleyways. The breathless relentlessness of this chase is captured in the constant camera movement of whips, pans and tilts, until finally, the man dies in a collision with a fire engine.

Dean becomes the target of this same surveillance technology after a chance meeting with the man who is being chased, Daniel Zavitz. Zavitz, an old university friend of Dean's, puts into the latter's possession information that the NSA agents want to get hold off, which reveals their complicity in the murder of a prominent politician. The dead politician had been taking a stand against a government bill, the 'Telecommunications, Security and Privacy Act', a bill that would make it easier for the authorities to carry out intrusive surveillance practices. The position of *Enemy of the State* on such strategies is clear from the outset, as it fictionalises the effects that such executive powers could have on people's lives. In an environment in which surveillance technologies are already everywhere, it only takes a few switches for an individual to come under scrutiny – ATMs, blimps, and police-officer cameras, as well as footage from in-store security CCTV, make public spaces fully accessible to a surveillance team. Even traffic-tunnel surveillance technology can be turned to the pursuers' needs. These moments in *Enemy of the State* give the impression that nowhere is safe. A single car and a single figure can be tracked across complex road systems, rooftops, through tunnels, buildings and subways. The near complete accessibility of the public space to surveillance is also carried over to domestic spaces, so that there remains no such thing as private space. Visual and audio devices can be put everywhere: inside smoke detectors, telephone handsets, Christmas-tree baubles, behind ventilation grills and into buttons. Tracking devices are no longer limited to cars, but can be put inside everyday personal items: watches, pens, shoe soles, clothes, mobile phones and pagers.

Like *The Conversation* (1974, US) before it, and which it explicitly references, *Enemy of the State* tells a story about how an organisation can intrude into the privacy of an individual's life through the use of technologies.[1] The rogue NSA controller has the power to mount a smear campaign through the media, break into banking records, personal histories and telephone bills. Everything which is computerised or electronic makes an individual potentially subject to increasing levels of surveillance. The essence of *Enemy of the State* is the attempt to take control of information, and to turn it into a resource for power, financial or political. This is not dissimilar to the theme examined in Chapter 1, where scientific knowledge was a contested site of control. This chapter, however, rather than focusing on the constructions of institutions of power, considers the effects of those institutions upon the individuals who come under their juris-diction. If the previous chapter examined the ways in which human contingencies cannot be transcended in the practices of techno-science, this one adds another dimension to that intersection – the ways in which human relations can themselves be caught up, and determined by the practices as well as the products of technoscience. The films discussed, *12 Monkeys* (1995, US), *D.A.R.Y.L.* (1985, UK/US), *Junior* (1994, US) and *sex, lies and videotape* (1989, US), articulate a series of complex intersections between science and tech-nology and the human figures who are a part of those practices and processes. Each of the texts gives this intersection a different emphasis; at times the relationship is a difficult one, alienating and disempowering, at others it is more productive and constructive. The purpose of this discussion is not to suggest that any one of these posi-tions is the more dominant, only to indicate that fictions of techno-science explore a range of different possibilities. In exploring the different possibilities in these intersections between humans and technoscience, it also becomes clear that what is central to these texts are definitions of humanness.

Technoscience and its effects

There is nothing new in stating that fictions of technoscience, espe-cially those of the SF or horror genres, depict the effects of science and technology on individuals' lives or that they explore what is understood as humanness. It might even be true to say that the most powerful of these texts have been the ones in which the human race, or more accurately, the Hollywood version of the human race, has to overcome an enemy which is threatening to alter human exis-tence, specifically to dehumanise it. Often, it is the hopes and moti-vations of the central protagonist, the individual who enables the re-emergence of the human figure in the resolution of the film, which become the conditions of humanness celebrated by the text. In *Enemy of the State* for instance, Dean fights back in order to re-establish contact with his family, and in *The Net* (1995, US) Angela Bennett wants to regain control over her life. Between them, *Enemy of the State* and *The Net* invoke the family and individuality as parts of the human condition worth saving, but underlying them is also the desire for the possibility of making choices. In narratives which feature a threat directed towards the whole human race, such as *The Terminator* (1984, US) and *Terminator 2: Judgement Day* (1991, US), as well as *The Matrix* (1999, US), it is freedom from potential or actual enslavement which is at stake. The value systems of the heroes of each of the narratives stand in for the freedom which is about to be lost. Sarah and John Connor, and to some extent Miles Dyson, in *Terminator 2*, stand for ideals of family, and a future not already predetermined. Since the idea of freedom links these various films, it seems to function as a key term in the definitions of humanness. However, freedom here should not be taken as an absolute term, as it emerges in the detail of each of the texts, and as such is contingent on the political operations of the each of those narratives, even if it seems to be presented otherwise.

Critical responses to such films, or more particularly the SF genre, have included two positions: the view that SF is about coming to terms with progress; and the idea that it is chiefly concerned with gaining an understanding of the changing definitions of humanness. Vivian Sobchack suggests that: 'SF film gives concrete narrative shape and visible form to our changing historical imagination of social progress and disaster, and to the ambiguities of being human in a world where advanced technology has altered both the contours and meaning of personal and social existence.'[2] Scott Bukatman argues that contemporary SF, including film, literature, comics and video games, has a particular concern with the shifting emphasis in the ways in which humankind is constructed. In *Terminal Identity* Bukatman makes the claim that since the 1980s SF has explored a slippage in the definition of what it means to be human.[3] For Bukatman, in early SF texts 'being human' – where human is taken to include not only a bodily presence (usually white) but also moral and ethical dimensions – is the subject position that needs to be reasserted in the resolution of the narrative. Accordingly, in contemporary SF the narrative aim is not to view humanness as an undisturbed construct; instead, it articulates the interfaces between technology and human subjects. The relationship between the 'technologies of the Information Age' and humans goes beyond dualities, and the direct interface is the site of a new subjectivity, a hybrid entity that establishes a transformative, and potentially positive, relationship between humans and technologies. Bukatman's emphasis in *Terminal Identity* is on films that depict the changed human body, where changing human subjectivity is actualised in the hybridised or dissolving body. It is not only in such films, however, that the slippage in the definitions of 'human' occurs. Bukatman's argument relies on his position that in pre-1980s SF, the transcendent human subject was one that asserted an unproblematic version of humanness over a problematic technology. There is an assumption here that the human and the technological are separate categories, two distinct sides of an opposition. Consequently, it is only in the loss of definition of the human body that the slippage in subjectivity becomes apparent. An alternative view, and one that I put forward here, is that the human subject has always been prone to slippage, slippage in the sense that the term human gains its meaning through a contingent relationship with other terms that surround it, one of which is technology. As such, humanness and technology are not separate categories, one of which can be transcended by the other. Instead they are always linked, and gain their meaning from an intersection with each other. For instance, and going back to my earlier point that freedom is a key issue in fictions of technoscience made since the 1980s, the terms of freedom emerge in an environment that is contingent on the operations of technoscience. The notion of complete freedom has no meaning here, as it is an ideal that takes on a particular shape in the pragmatic negotiation between what it is possible to achieve and what remains hoped for.

The purpose of this chapter is to explore how the conditions of being human are defined through a series of constructions that emerge in the operations of technoscience. The particular operations I focus on are those which place human individuals as the objects of a particular discourse. *12 Monkeys*, *D.A.R.Y.L.*, *Junior* and *sex, lies and videotape* represent and construct objects of technoscience, and by 'objects' I mean, for the purposes of these texts, human beings (or equivalents) which are operated upon by the processes and practices of science and technology. These include humans who are disempowered by the operations of technoscience, those who emerge with some freedom through a refusal to agree with the practices of those operations, as well as those who fully co-operate with the system. These different instances are meant as an illustration of how fictions of technoscience depict the range of possibilities through which the processes and practices of technoscience constitute the conditions of being human.

Seeing is believing?

The opening shot of 12 Monkeys is the eyes of a young boy. The picture fades to white and then into a series of bleached-out images of a slow-motion shooting, and then of a man's bloodied hand reaching up into the blonde hair of the woman leaning over him. These are the objects of the boy's gaze. In a jump cut, time shifts to a futuristic world, a world where humans live underground, and the characters the viewer sees are inside cages, convicts who are volunteered for duties. In a conversation between the convicts, James Cole and José, about whether or not anyone ever comes back from these duties, Cole says that the ones that do are kept locked away because they are 'messed up in the head, brains don't work.' José responds: 'Hey, you don't know they're all messed up, nobody's seem 'em. Maybe they're not messed up, that's a rumour.' Across these two sets of images the central themes of 12 Monkeys – memory, madness and looking/seeing – have already been introduced. The plot of 12 Monkeys takes place across several time periods; much of it occurs in 1996, with additional events in 1990 and 2035 and a brief sequence in the trenches of the First World War. In the jump cut between the young boy's view of events and the waking adult, the action of the film is potentially placed in two of these time zones in a single instance. The double temporal location is made possible through the device of a dream-memory; the original event took place in 1996, whilst the dream occurs in 2035. This splitting, this falling between places, is a central concern of 12 Monkeys, as it negotiates the different themes of madness, looking, technoscience, time travel and identity.

For the moment, I want to address the theme of looking, or observing. José's response to Cole's comments on the returning volunteers reveals a key concern of the film: that is, the relationship between what you see and what you know. This concern is also addressed through the young boy who is seen looking in the opening and closing moments of the film. The revelation of the boy's identity is withheld until end of the narrative, and so it is only then that an audience unfamiliar with La Jetée (1962, Fr.) will have the opportunity to situate the information they are given throughout the narrative of 12 Monkeys, and so understand the doubled temporality of the opening sequence. This struggle to situate, to create a link between what is seen and what is known, runs throughout the narrative of 12 Monkeys, but the focus of this reading is on the technoscientific

discourse of the text, and the ways it impinges on the connection
between what is seen and what is known.

Being able to see or observe something is a key strategy through
which objects are incorporated into a system of knowledge. In *The
Order of Things*, Michel Foucault comments that the visual has been
the primary means by which the object of science is brought into
focus, and that there is much less emphasis on tactile and auditory
ways of perceiving the object.[4] This is perhaps becoming less true of
auditory perception since technologies of sound recording and mea-
surement are increasing in sophistication. But even there, quantification of sound often involves a visualisation of it in some way. The
scenes in *Contact* where the alien signal is first heard are a good fic-
tive example of such a process. As the soundtrack plays the pulsing
noise of the signal, different visual images of the sound patterns are
shown. Whilst Foucault was primarily remarking on historical
developments in the sciences, more recent critical work supports his
position. Contemporary science and medicine make use of available
imaging technologies. Videos linked up to various types of scanning
devices, such as magnetic resonance imaging and spectroscopy,
ultrasound and CAT scans, make pictures of the body, or parts of the
body. But simply being able to visualise something is only part of the
question. The consequent power of science and medicine to define
and redefine the body has become an important concern amongst
critics of science: 'Science and technology have so rearranged the
boundary conditions for the reproduction of human identity that
the choice is no longer between the natural body and the culturally
constructed body, but between different fields of bodily (re)con-
struction bearing different social and cultural implications.'[5] Whilst
this begs the question of whether there ever was such a choice
between the natural and cultural body, it is useful to point out that
the human body has come to be understood in different ways
through its multiple intersections with technologies, intersections
which bring with them sets of power relations.

12 Monkeys can be read as a text which plays with making objects
visible, or more precisely, visual, and how that object is subsequently
placed within sets of competing power dynamics. From the opening
shot of the eyes of a young boy looking, *12 Monkeys* displays a fascination with looking/seeing. The authorities of the film, a group of
scientists from 2035, choose James Cole for their task because he is
good at observing things; indeed, by the end of the film it becomes

clear that the looking boy, who frames the narrative, is the young Cole. The task set for Cole by the 2035 scientists is a quest that begins in 2035, but which requires Cole to time-travel back to 1996 to obtain a sample of the pure virus that, within the story-world of the film, has decimated the human population, causing it to move underground. The time-travelling device is motivated by the explanation that since its release the virus has mutated, and in order to create a vaccine the scientists need a pure sample. Cole's quest, in the first instance, is to discover, to *see* who released the virus so that a pure sample can be obtained. In this sense, Cole is a part of the process by which something is made visible for the 2035 scientists. Such a description of Cole's scientific mission makes it seem rather benign, neutral perhaps, as it suggests that Cole will simply observe and take note. However, the operations of power in this task are made quite clear in the scenes in which Cole is coerced into taking up the scientists' quest. Cole, one of the criminal underclass of the 2035 world, is strapped, immobilised and then elevated on a chair. The camera, high above him, moves down with a slight twisting motion as though to reorient itself towards Cole, the object of the lens. The scientists arrayed behind a table, seemingly far away in a deep-focused shot, observe him in close-up through their technological eye, as if he had been clamped on the platform of a microscope. This technological eye, a suspended mobile sphere, moves around Cole, focusing in closer and then moving back out again to get another viewpoint; its surface is covered with numerous screens on which are images of the individual scientists.[6] The movements of the sphere are echoed by the camera motion, constantly framing and reframing, moving in and out of close-up and distance shots. In this sequence, Cole is clearly the object of the looking processes of the 2035 scientists, and he is caught and coerced through the eye of their lens. As one of the scientists, in speaking about their request, says to Cole: 'For a man in your position, an opportunity. Not to volunteer would be a big mistake.'

By way of a complex series of shifts within the narrative, Cole does not remain as the object of the 2035 scientists' gaze; although he does initially becomes an extension of it – a human observing machine. When sent back to look for the source of the virus, Cole at first seems to represent a type of science that seeks only to observe, to gather information. Like non-invasive techniques, his presence is not meant to affect anything. But, of course, it does: the knowledge he collects affects the perception of the past, as all non-invasive techniques affect the perception of the thing observed. For whilst Cole does not prevent the release of the virus (and the subsequent death of 5 billion people), he gains knowledge that affects the nature of the quest, he uncovers who really released the deadly virus. A second and important point about the processes of science also emerges from Cole's information-gathering exercise. When he brings back the information he found in 1990, the scientists are only concerned with those parts of it that add to their already existing conceptual, verifiable and delineated framework. But, more importantly, they dismiss information that does not seem important to them. When Cole is taken back to 2035 after his misadventures in 1990, he is again elevated and examined by the technological eye. Cole's initial descriptions of being drugged and incarcerated provoke the combined displeasure of the six scientists arrayed across the width of the screen. However, when Cole recognises the image of Jeffrey Goines, their displeasure is set aside since this information adds weight to the 2035 scientists' hypothesis that a group calling themselves the Army of the 12 Monkeys had released the virus. The scientists here turn the information given by Cole from something he has observed into to something which can be known because it fits in with the already accumulated knowledge. They have the power to fit it into a pre-existing framework, making it into a fact.[7] Although this alignment of Cole's information with pre-existing events, of believing what is apparently seen, turns out to be misleading, it demonstrates the processes of the 2035 scientists at work. They validate as knowledge only those pieces of information that they recognise as belonging within their framework. One effect of this is to construct a premise that is incorrect, and which will have to be reconfigured. The second effect is to provoke a crisis in Cole that causes him to call into question everything that he knows. As this crisis escalates, he attempts to break free of his position within the objective processes of the scientists.

At issue here is not only how Cole's information is made to fit into an alignment with a predetermined set of ideas, but also what happens to the information that is in excess of that set of ideas as it accumulates, and spills over from its intended use. Early on in the film, when Cole returns from his unintended trip to 1990, an example of the imprecision of time-travel technology, the only information of interest to the scientists is that which fits their framework. This, then, is not a neutral process of observation, but is one that serves only to answer a particular question. In itself, seeking to answer a particular question is not necessarily a difficulty, but it may become so if that question becomes enforced as the single means through which something can be known, forcing what is observed to become knowledge in narrowly prescribed ways. One outcome of this pre-scriptive approach can be that as the information exceeds the framing of the question, it begins to turn back on the processes by which a question is put in place. At this point, the information is more than simply in excess of the required outcome, its very lack of fit provides a way of exposing and questioning the frameworks in place. In *12 Monkeys*, those parts of Cole's newly acquired knowl-edge which are not of interest to the scientists begin to inform Cole about himself. They enable him to become aware of his position within a discourse over which he has no control, a discourse that seeks to control him and keep him in his observing place. Once he has become aware of other possibilities, the dilemma for Cole in *12 Monkeys* is how to relocate himself within a series of discourses that limit what he can know and what he can be.

Through Cole's struggles to understand, to make sense of what he knows, *12 Monkeys* explores the ways in which different discourses operate to organise how meanings are made of the world. Within the film there are several discourses in play – technoscience, insan-ity, memory, time-travel and romance. As these come into conflict with one another, the individual who is placed or located through those discourses is thrown into crisis. For instance, within the technoscience discourse the search for the virus only has meaning for the scientists in 2035; when Cole is mistakenly sent to 1990 he is unable to communicate sensibly within the worldview of that period. Cole's actions, his incoherent talk of an apocalyptic virus and subsequent drug-induced frustrated violence, ensure that those in the 1990s think he is insane. When brought before a board of psychiatrists in 1990, Cole is again the object of inquiry. In a scene that visually echoes his previous encounter with the 2035 scientists, he is seated in front of yet another row of investigating individuals. But from the perspective of these 1990 psychiatrists, Cole is just one more mentally divergent person, as his ramblings and confusion present a scenario that fits into the categories defined by the late twentieth-century discourses of psychiatry. In the 1990s, the moti-vation of Cole's quest literally cannot be known, and so it has no meaning. Without a shared context for knowledge, Cole is

disempowered, and he is caught between two points of view that
remain incommensurable.

Unbound and rebound

Before continuing with *12 Monkeys* I want to discuss the ways in
which the idea of being caught between different points of view also
informs the narrative of *D.A.R.Y.L.* This film, which is very different
in style and plot to *12 Monkeys*, is aimed at a child audience.
D.A.R.Y.L. features as a central character a cyborg that looks like a
young white boy of 10 or 11.[8] Daryl, as the cyborg is known, was
'conceived in a test-tube', and is a combination of organic human
parts and inorganic technology; with the exception of his computer
'brain', the boy's body has been engineered as human, complete with
the ability to age, and to grow like any other child. His 'brain' is a
remote microcomputer in communication with a data storage system
that contains all the programming and information about Daryl, in
other words his memory. The conflict between two different positions
develops in *D.A.R.Y.L.* because Daryl becomes indistinguishable from
the human beings which surround him. The dilemma is that Daryl
ceases to be an object defined and explainable with reference only to
its programming, as he learns in ways which cannot be attributed to
his programming. In developing feeling and preferences, Daryl comes
to be perceived as human, and in doing so the cyborg shifts from
being an 'it' to being a 'he'. The struggle in *D.A.R.Y.L.* is primarily
over the right of the people who have funded the research project, the
military, to deny Daryl's rights to exist as a thinking subject. As in *The
Lawnmower Man*, the practices of the scientists occur within the juris-
diction of a military-government committee. This latter grouping has
control over the parameters of the discourse within which Daryl is
allowed to exist. Through the narrative of *D.A.R.Y.L.*, not only does
Daryl move beyond his programming, he also moves beyond the
defining discourse of the technoscience put in place by this military-
science-government intersection, and in so doing exceeds the object
position he was supposed to inhabit.

Whilst *D.A.R.Y.L.* is primarily about Daryl's resistance to this
object position, the first section of the film simply presents him as a
young boy. There is an element of suspense in these sequences, a suspense which resides in the deferral of the information that Daryl is
a cyborg. Initially he seems to have lost his memory, a device used to

allow the audience to identify with him as an ordinary boy. There
are, however, also hints otherwise. The first image of *D.A.R.Y.L.* is
of a helicopter suddenly appearing from beneath the edge of a
precipice, the noise of its rotors breaking into the silence of the
soundtrack. As the sequence continues, it becomes clear this is a
chase; two males, an adult and a child, are being pursued, and the
adult sacrifices himself so that the young boy can survive. After this
the narrative shifts, setting aside the chase. Instead, Daryl is placed
as a young human boy, or at least a young human boy according to
the terms dictated by the representation of a mid-1980s white
middle-class small-town US culture. This placement is evident in
Daryl's transition from a socially inexperienced individual to a 'typ-
ical' young boy, a transition which is presaged by his change in dress.
When first found in the woods by an elderly couple he is formally
dressed in trousers, a shirt and a blazer. His transformation begins
with a change into clothes that are clearly too big for him – presumably because the elderly couple has provided them. Once
around other children, he gets another change of clothes, this time
a set that fits him more closely. In these, he ceases to stand out as different. His incorporation into the narrative as a young boy becomes
more complete once he is placed with foster parents; here he begins
to interact with other children of a similar age, goes to school and
learns to play baseball.

In spite of this incorporation, there remain moments that suggest
that Daryl is not an ordinary boy. Although his lack of knowledge
about his past is explained as the result of trauma-induced amnesia,
that cannot explain all his behaviour. His ability to learn rapidly, his
breadth of knowledge, his aptitude with computers are all marked,
but are never given an adequate explanation. It is only once he is
revealed as a cyborg that such things can make sense to the viewers,
and subsequently the other characters of the film. Daryl's seemingly
extraordinary abilities are things he is programmed to perform, his
speed in learning words and figures, in using a computer with superior skill, and having a perfect capacity to hit a moving target, or to
put bat to baseball, are all part of the process. But this second placing of Daryl within a cyborg framework marks the turning point in
the film. For those very things which made him seem extraordinary
to other humans become quite normal, whilst the things which made
him seem more normal become extraordinary. As a distinction is
made between the things he is programmed to do, and those things

that he has learnt beyond his programming – a capacity for friendship, a relationship with a carer, the possession of likes and dislikes and most importantly feelings – Daryl begins to come into conflict with the technoscientific discourse of the narrative.

As in *12 Monkeys*, Daryl is here initially located by his placement within one system of knowledge, that of military-technoscience, but that system becomes too restrictive and denies him alternative ways of living in the world. When seen in this way, *D.A.R.Y.L.* is about how Daryl, and the people who care for him, enable him to resist the technoscientific discourse of the narrative. Since this restrictive element of the narrative is only introduced after the long set-up in which Daryl is placed within a caring community, such a juxtapositioning makes military-technoscience seem very cold and disempowering. Once the scientists who created him finally trace Daryl, they masquerade as his parents and take him back to their research facility. In a marked contrast with the preceding familial and community scenes, in those leading up to the revelation that Daryl is a cyborg there is a strong sense of isolation. During the car journey Daryl is located in the back of the car, whilst the two adults are placed in the foreground, discussing him as though he is not there. This conversation begins the revelation of Daryl's true identity, a revelation that is carried over into the subsequent scenes in a research institute. After a brief establishing shot of the outside of a fortress-like facility, Daryl is seen alone in a high-ceilinged, starkly lit white room, lying on an obliquely angled bed covered with a white sheet. To a machinic score, the horseshoe-shaped arm of a scanner moves out from the wall and over Daryl's body. It is only at this moment that the camera position shifts, and as it does so the scientists become visible in a window overlooking the room. Through another cut, it is established that they are controlling the machine. And, as the scanner moves back over Daryl's body, this time from the point of view of the scientists within the control room, the editing shifts the image from that of the boy's covered body, the object of the clinical technology of the room, to a digitised image of a cross-section of his chest, complete with beating heart. Already disempowered by his isolation, Daryl's appearance is here renegotiated for the viewer through the use of technologised images, and he is finally revealed as a cyborg when his computer brain is imaged as a constructed object. Here the illusion of an organic brain is fully shattered by the display of Daryl's brain as a sophisticated electronic network in an animated sequence that recalls the computer network of the earlier *Tron* (1982, US). The microcomputer is visualised as a series of interconnecting circuits that are zoomed in on, creating an image of increasing complexity and detail. The final scenes of the revelation sequence, which involve the scientists communicating with Daryl through a computer terminal rather than by speech, also provide an explanation of the acronym D.A.R.Y.L. – Data Analysing Robot Youth Life-form.

Although this sequence literally dehumanises Daryl, its function is to illustrate that whilst he is part machine, he has become indistinguishable from a human. In the scenes that follow this body scan, Daryl's newly learnt human emotions of fear, pleasure and pain are depicted. The crucial device used to prove that Daryl is not simply an extremely sophisticated machine, one whose programming enables him to learn to make decisions that appear to be human, is that of an expression of preference based on pleasure. Although the example used, a preference for chocolate flavoured as opposed to vanilla or strawberry flavoured ice-cream, may seem trivial, it does nonetheless raise the question of how such pleasures can or cannot be defined. Daryl has been programmed to be able to make choices, but he has exceeded his programming in being able to make a subjective choice about which taste he prefers. This ability to have a preference for a particular ice-cream flavour illustrates an opposition between two types of knowledge: first, knowledge that can be predicted and/or explained on the basis of what is known, in this case, knowledge that is acquired through the programming of a computer brain; second, knowledge that is based on experiences which cannot be adequately explained within the paradigms in operation within any given cultural, social and historical moment – that is, the basis for a preference based on pleasure. As Daryl says when asked why he preferred chocolate ice-cream: 'I just did.' It is this acquisition by Daryl of unprogrammed subjective knowledge that causes him to come into conflict with the military funders of the project. They are not interested in his capacity to learn like a human child, most especially they are not interested in the emotions that Daryl has not only come to understand but to display during his stay with his foster family. From their perspective, emotions would limit the efficiency of the cyborg as a fighting machine. As one of the generals says: 'Baseball, ice-cream preferences, friendships? That's all right for America, but hardly what we need at the Department of

Defence.' And from the moment the generals demand the termination of the project, and therefore of Daryl, the film's position on this
denial of emotion is clear – Daryl must be saved because he cannot
be distinguished from a human being, and therefore no one has the
right to terminate him. This desire to save Daryl invokes a duality
that underlies the narrative of the film, the distinction between
human and non-human, but does so in order to destabilise the distinction. A number of films made in the 1980s, including *Blade
Runner* (1982, US), *Short Circuit* (1986, US) and *Android* (1982,
US), do not construct human and non-human through simple biological categories. Instead, the construction revolves around the
ability to be human, in the sense of being a compassionate thinking
being. Clearly, such a proposition mobilises a series of complex
debates around thinking, morality, and ethics. For the purposes of
these films, however, the question can be narrowed down. If a
machine can make the same sort of objective and subjective choices
as human beings, then as a sentient being it is not distinguishable
from humans, and so deserves the same rights. *D.A.R.Y.L.* explicitly
takes up such a plea. When asked by an army general why she thinks
that Daryl is human, Dr Lamb (one of Daryl's inventors) answers: 'A
machine becomes human when you can't tell the difference.'[9]

In the resolution of *D.A.R.Y.L.* the human-machine hybrid is
saved from the military, which only seeks to destroy him because by
surpassing his programming parameters, he has ceased to serve their
purpose. The narrative of *D.A.R.Y.L.*, then, resists the disempowerment of an individual being because they do not fit into a predetermined object position, a position that is put into place by the
operations of a particular institutional framework. Instead, it gives
Daryl an alternative place, a place that is organised around a different set of rules: in this instance, within a family unit. In so doing,
Daryl and his creators finally resist the technoscientific discourse
of the narrative, a resistance performed in the replacement of one
discourse with another. Whilst this resolution can be seen as the
empowerment of Daryl as an individual, a breaking free from a
restricting framework, there remains, however, a problem. The
narrative of *D.A.R.Y.L.* can only engage with Daryl's sameness, by
which I mean those elements that make him seem human. There is
no account of his difference, and so no real answer to the question
posed by Daryl: 'Doctor, what am I?' As the resolution of the narrative involves Daryl being reunited with his foster parents and

friends, his hybrid status is displaced, and his 'what am I' question remains not only unanswered, but also unanswerable within the parameters of representation within the film. This question of the difference of technological beings is something that I return to in the final chapter.

Within *D.A.R.Y.L.*, the problem of being defined through a limiting discourse is resolved through a refusal of that discourse, by the taking up of a different position, one that offers better possibilities of being. However, such an alternative is not always available, as it may not be possible to find a way out of the limiting discourse. Instead, the field of containment of that discourse may be too great. Such a position is evident in *12 Monkeys*. In the narrative of this film, the object of containment, Cole, becomes the site of struggle, a struggle in which Cole attempts to resist the discourse of the 2035 scientists by finding another location to live out his existence. Ultimately, this is a struggle that Cole loses as he becomes enmeshed within the technoscientific discourse of the 2035 scientists. In *12 Monkeys* the dominant order of the narrative put into place by the 2035 scientists is the quest for the pure virus which Cole must carry out, finally at the cost of his life. The other narrative possibilities – romance or madness – compete with and are ultimately contained by this narrative strand. A sense of containment pervades the narrative of *12 Monkeys* in other ways, but especially through the repetitive visual restraint of Cole's body. In addition to the several scenes in which he is arraigned in front of the scientists, when the adult Cole is first encountered he is detained within a caged cell, and then shackled when moved around the underground complex which is home to humans in 2035. This restrictiveness is variously echoed by the enclosed body suits used to travel either to the surface or across time; by his incarceration in an insane asylum in 1990; and in the use of drugs to subdue him in both 1990 and 2035. Outside of these enclosed and enclosing spaces, the constant chase and/or surveillance scenario ensures that even when he is moving, Cole is never in a free space.[10]

These visual instances of containment are echoed in the struggles that the characters undergo in order to locate themselves in relation to the different sets of discourses in play within *12 Monkeys*. This struggle is most evident in two characters, Cole and Kathryn Railly. The latter is a psychiatrist whom Cole encounters in 1990, and subsequently in 1996. As I have already suggested, Cole is part of a quest that, at the beginning of the film, is not personal to him; it is something into which he has been coerced. However, once the technoscientific quest is underway, Cole begins to realise a quest of his own, one that could be framed as a humanist quest for a whole self that is intertwined with his desire for a relationship with Railly. It is Cole's alternative quest which puts Railly into a crisis. Initially secure in her position as a psychiatrist with a 1990s worldview, Cole's presence causes her to question her own perceptions of the world, and like Cole she is presented with two conflicting positions. At the beginning of *12 Monkeys*, Railly is a successful psychiatrist under whose care Cole is put when he is incarcerated in 1990. As such, she is an active agent within one of the perspectives which disempowers Cole, a perspective which positions him as a deluded psychotic, one whose account of a post-apocalyptic world exists only inside his head. In these scenes, Railly is always in control: talking to Cole when he is in shackles, arrayed behind a table with other psychiatrists, or with a guard to help if anything goes wrong. When Cole is returned to 1996 and subsequently kidnaps Railly, he quite literally dislocates her from her normal place in the world. As the quest of the 2035 scientists has taken over his life, Cole acts as a conduit, relaying the power of the scientists of 2035 into the 1990s.[11] This dislocation of Railly is most explicit when she is abducted by Cole and forced to drive him 100 miles to Philadelphia, and then on to the Goines residence. Trapped inside her car with only Cole for a companion, her life as a psychiatrist in Baltimore is left behind, and the effects of Cole's interventions have ramifications that ensure that she can never inhabit it in the same way again.

It is not until Railly returns to her home, after Cole has once again disappeared back to the future, that the extent of this dislocation is established. Again the narrative of *12 Monkeys* uses the strategy of placing information into frameworks. In this instance, Railly begins to find material evidence that Cole's world exists outside, as well as inside his head, and her initial suspicions coalesce into a more substantial doubt as she finds that Cole's protestations have a basis in her version of reality as well as his. Earlier he has claimed to know the outcome of an on-going news story, and this is corroborated when the boy's real whereabouts is discovered and reported by the media. Furthermore, the forensic ballistic report on the bullet that Railly had removed from Cole's thigh indicates that it was fired before 1920, suggesting that his stories of time-travel are not a figment of his imagination. The ballistic report also triggers Railly's recollection of why Cole is familiar to her, and, as she searches the orderly alignment of notes and images on her wall, she finds the photograph that makes her world order finally collapse. Again, *12 Monkeys* is mobilising the idea that something becomes a fact once it can be verified, even though it may be contrary to assumed knowledge of the world. The fact here is a photograph of Cole taken in the trenches of the First World War, *visual* evidence which takes Railly beyond the loss of faith she professes to a colleague, and precipitates her into a crisis that cannot be resolved within the view of the world that is standard to the 1990/1996 time frame of *12 Monkeys*. After her discovery of the photograph Railly is left with two options. She can utilise her psychiatric knowledge by resorting to the view that she is going insane, becoming divergent and constructing an alternative world because she cannot handle a trauma in her life. Alternatively, she can acquiesce to Cole's worldview, and the apocalyptic near future in which the human race is to be decimated by the virus. In the end, Railly has to accept that it is the latter reality that she is about to experience. This reality, however, is one over which she has no control, or even any place. Since Railly is finally irrelevant to the technoscientific quest, her story simply stops with Cole's death.

Cole's character is also trapped between the requirements of the conflicting narrative discourses. Although he has agency within the narrative in a way that Railly does not, he too is finally unable to take control of his place in the world; he is ultimately defined through the quest controlled by the 2035 scientists. The set of discourses that operates in conjunction with the quest is predicated, as I discussed above, upon observation and facts, and certain answers are excluded by virtue of their lack of fit into this particular framework. For Cole, the quest requires him only to seek out the source of the pure virus, and he has no other purpose. Contrary to the quest is the romance theme through which Cole seeks to 'make himself whole'. By this means he wants to determine which of the conflicting stories in operation is correct. Is he mentally divergent as Railly tells him in 1996, or is he a potential saviour according to the rules of 2035? Opting for a madness that he thinks can be cured, Cole also opts for Railly, not simply as his doctor but also finally as his lover.[12] Paradoxically, however, even this line of thinking may not necessarily be his own. It is provided for him by the voice of a character within the narrative whose status in reality, in any of the realities of *12 Monkeys*, remains opaque.

Through Cole and Railly's experience of themselves as caught between the narrative themes of the technoscientific quest and their potential romance, *12 Monkeys* presents a perspective in which human identity is acquired through the location of an individual within a particular discursive regime. Subjectivity is not autonomous, not predicated on the basis of a self-generated 'I' position; rather, it is based on an alignment with different discourses. A lack of fit with, or a resistance to, the available ways of being can determine the absence of a secure identity. In *12 Monkeys* the worldview which dominates the other possibilities is finally that of the 2035 scientists, and within the narrative Cole's identity is inextricably linked to his alignment with that discourse. His tragedy is that he cannot elude the technoscientific process. Its power is too great and it recaptures him, contains him, each time he attempts to escape. Finally, in the ending of the film, it is evident even to Cole that he can only exist according to the rules of that discourse, and he goes to his death fully aware that he is merely following a futile order. Furthermore, the event of the adult Cole's death occurs before the eyes of a young boy who is the young Cole, so his death occurs before his own eyes. In a kind of double erasure, he dies in front of his younger self who does not and indeed cannot yet know who it is who has died. Cole cannot know himself until he learns the discourse that he will not become aware of until he is older, and in knowing that discourse, he will die.

Within the narrative of *12 Monkeys* both Railly and Cole are obliterated through a repressive act mobilised at the request of the scientists. Cole dies because he is forced to carry out an order that he knows will lead to his death, and Railly because her story simply ends when Cole dies. Read in this way, *12 Monkeys* can be seen as a powerful critique of technoscience. The disempowerment of Cole, and also Railly, when they refuse the 2035 paradigm, suggests a criticism of a system of knowledge that restricts an individual to a singular position – Cole is fully determined by his relationship to the technoscientific quest. This restriction to a singular position further represents the assimilation of that individual, a full incorporation of them into the demands of the framework. Technoscience, in *12 Monkeys*, is not about the empowerment of an individual by a journey towards knowledge, it is instead about the quest for knowledge that will improve the human condition, but the individual is only useful in so far as they contribute to that knowledge. Outside of the quest they have no meaning, and furthermore, the quest will continue once they have gone – after Cole is dead his place is taken by someone else, Jones, the woman astrophysicist from 2035. The paradox of such a quest, as *12 Monkeys* seems well aware, is that the sacrifice required to gain this knowledge dissolves what is often understood to be central to the human condition – the possibility of freedom of choice, no matter how limited that choice may ultimately be.

Keeping in line

Both *D.A.R.Y.L.* and *12 Monkeys* play on the idea of an individual struggling to locate themselves in relation to sets of discourses, though they do so with very different outcomes. Whilst in *D.A.R.Y.L.*, Daryl is able to relocate himself successfully, in *12 Monkeys*, James Cole is killed, finally annulled by the operations of technoscience. A related and frequent criticism of contemporary medical science and technologies is that they construct the body in parts instead of as a whole.[13] That is, instead of the body being seen as a whole organism, it is broken down into constituent parts that are used metonymically to reconfigure a perspective on the whole body. This kind of reconfiguring is also evident in a number of contemporary fictions of technoscience. Images of banks of monitors and instruments linked up to human bodies are common in films and television series which revolve around medical matters. In film texts such as *Extreme Measures* (1996, US), *Outbreak* (1995, US), and the television series *ER* (Channel 4), the human being is not only dependent upon the machines, but at times ceases to exist as a human individual. Instead, they are incorporated into another discourse, that of science and technology. Lisa Cartwright's book *Screening the Body*, though primarily about the use of film technology as a tool of science, rather than as a means of telling fictional stories, is a useful account of how technology redefines being human. Cartwright describes how physiologists, at the end of the nineteenth and beginning of the twentieth century, used the technology of moving film to study movement. By reducing the projection speed of the image, they were able to analyse the movements of a human subject – the body was visualised by slowing it down enough to make it measurable and quantifiable. The frame by frame capture of images, which is taken for granted in filmmaking, became a frame by frame capture of the human body. Movement was simplified and reduced to steps, which were in turn categorised into normal and abnormal. These movements became one of the defining parameters of 'normal' human behaviour, and the technology of moving images enabled a particular construction of the human body that could not be seen without its mediation. Whether technological interventions such as these are perceived as a disempowerment or a more benign refiguration of the human, the effect of technoscience on the bodies in question is an important concern.

Junior is a text that makes use of such questions, but does so in a way that is uncritical of technologised intrusions taking control of a body. Apparently a comedy about a pregnant man, an event made possible through innovative research, the narrative revolves around the ability to control the body, in particular the pregnant body. The central character, Alex, is a male research scientist whose topic of interest is pregnancy. His research concern is a drug, Expectane, which is being developed to reduce the chance of miscarriage. In the plot, after being turned down by the Federal Drug Administration to carry out research on human subjects, he is persuaded by his research partner, Larry, to test the drug on himself and join the 'pantheon' of scientists. Together they fertilise a human ovum, stolen from an egg bank, with Alex's sperm and then insert it into his abdominal cavity. The potential to see these activities as a kind of 'monster science' is undercut through the relocation of their activities from a laboratory scenario to a more domestic space. Whilst the 'impregnation' occurs in a fertility clinic, Alex is subsequently moved to Larry's spare room, an excessively floral room whose decor is attributed to the taste of Larry's ex-wife, Angela; the various machines placed in this room seem lost in the eye-numbing awfulness of the *mise-en-scène*. Playing for comic effect similarly displaces the ethical questions surrounding Larry's theft of the ovum. Whilst in the middle of stealing it from a technologically sophisticated freezer, Larry encounters Diana Reddin, an eccentric English scientist. The interplay between the two becomes the focus of attention, instead of Larry's plundering activities.

Although this experiment to prove that Expectane can prevent miscarriage is only meant to continue for the first three months of the pregnancy, Alex decides he wants to go to term. Through this device, *Junior* focuses on images of pregnancy, yet, in contrast to *D.A.R.Y.L.* and *12 Monkeys*, the narrative remains unconcerned with the ways in which it depicts the body as an object of technoscience discourse. Instead, *Junior* more overtly operates as an exploration of masculinity. Alex is initially characterised as a friendless scientist, his absence of personality extending to his dark suits, dark ties and white polyester shirts. As he experiences pregnancy, Alex also begins to experience a more emotional existence. He starts to form relationships with the people around him, changes his style of dress to softer colours, eventually being enveloped in baby pink, and develops his sensuality through touch and food. This play on masculinity functions not only through the device of male pregnancy, but also through the star persona of the actor who plays Alex, Arnold Schwarzenegger. *Junior* can be seen as a part of the progression of Schwarzenegger's star persona from the public-domain hero to the private-domain hero, a progression which has recently ceased to continue with his re-emergence as a public-domain hero in *Eraser* (1996, US), *Batman and Robin* (1997, US) and *End of Days* (1999, US). Nonetheless, seen in relation to *Twins* (1988, US), *Kindergarten Cop* (1990, US), *Terminator 2* (1991, US), *Last Action Hero* (1993, US) and *Jingle All the Way* (1996, US), Schwarzenegger's early 1990s persona progressed from the public-domain hero, an individual isolated from a family but invested in keeping communities intact, to the private-domain hero where the family unit is itself the focus of attention. In *Junior*, as in *True Lies* (1994, US), Schwarzenegger's character operates between the two domains; Alex shifts from the public domain of researching scientist to the private domain of pregnant 'mother', first in Larry's house and finally in a care centre for wealthy pregnant women. Whilst contemporary views of pregnancy do not necessarily equate with nineteenth- and early twentieth-century notions of confinement, there remain few representations of pregnant women who have an existence not completely defined by having a pregnant body. *Fargo* (1996, US) is one of the few films in which pregnancy does not fully determine a woman's character – Marge Gunderson is the investigating chief of police who incidentally happens to be pregnant. *Junior*, however, follows a more traditional view of pregnancy, the difference being that it is a man who is pregnant. As Alex is relocated into a domestic space, his life becomes completely dominated by his experience of being pregnant – he cries over videos of young people marrying, reads maternity magazines, cooks, eats and feels isolated. Although the medical complications of being a pregnant male are the implied reason behind the relocation, by representing the space as something where *only* these events occur, *Junior* moves toward a representation of pregnancy in which the pregnant person is wholly dominated by the activities and

needs of their body. Given that *Junior* is a comedy, it might be argued
that it is a parody of such representations of pregnancy and thus
that the film mounts a critique of them. And indeed there are a
few gestures towards the problems of being isolated, both literally
and metaphorically, but there is little attempt to provide an alternative to them. Such gestures tend, instead, to operate as an opening
for a narrative space for another set of gags – Larry staying late at the
office enables a meal to take place between Alex and the also pregnant Angela, a meal which revolves around jokes about pregnancy
and eating habits.[14]

Although this meeting of Larry and Angela appears to be simply an
interaction between two pregnant people, a sharing of the experience, it also operates in another way. It brings back the figure of the
pregnant woman, a figure who has been almost absent in *Junior*, but
who is really the object of the technoscientific discourse which
informs the text. This technoscientific discourse, which revolves
around the relationship between medical science and technology and
contemporary pregnancy, is taken for granted within the narrative of
Junior. When Alex moves into his house, Larry installs a variety of
monitors, and in 'The Fertility Clinic' the use of technology is a
common practice.[15] There is little to suggest that this technology is
present to do anything else but make pregnancy safer. And whilst it
does indeed seem to function in this way, the problem with such an
uncritical position is that it does not engender any questioning of the
access to and control of the technology, or who controls knowledge
about pregnancy. The clinics in *Junior* are only available to wealthy
people, and pregnancy is incorporated into a market economy. The
figure of Noah Baines, the university administrator whose desire to
capitalise on a market of pregnant women is raised as a problem
within *Junior*, might be said to represent a critical perspective on the
incorporation of pregnancy into a market economy. However, since
Larry's own exploitation of the same potential market is celebrated
in a lucrative deal with a drug company, this critical perspective is
limited to the individual who is presented as the 'bad guy' of the film,
rather than as a commentary on the overall process.

Such an uncritical position extends to the account given by *Junior*
of the drug Expectane. This account reveals a desire to take control
of the body, especially the pregnant body, and make it the object of
the processes of technoscience, and is slipped into the story of *Junior*
right at the beginning. After the opening sequence of Alex's 'babies

in the library' nightmare, the film cuts to Alex at work, a research
scientist whose object of study is female pregnancy. In a space
packed with technological images, Alex strides along at the head of
a group of young students, clearly a man in control. And, from his
monologue, it becomes apparent that his central concern is with the
control of the pregnant body:

> 'The miscarriage prone female reproductive system is merely an exten-
> sion of the body's natural and necessary instincts to reject foreign
> matter, the body mistakenly identifies the embryo as an unwanted for-
> eign substance and creates antibodies to reject it. From this equation
> comes the idea for the drug Expectane which acts to neutralise the
> interfering antibodies and promote successful embryo attachment'.

The aim, then, is to stop this natural, though somehow errant,
response of the body to miscarry a developing foetus. And the focus
of *Junior* is on the potential market for such a drug, the struggle for
control of the drug, and the associated knowledge of the female body,
a struggle that occurs between university and corporate domains.[16]

Whilst almost all of *Junior* is explicitly concerned with a pregnant
man, the narrative is finally about the control of the maternal body,
even though that body is constantly displaced. In this version of a
discourse of technoscience, the maternal body is a site of control, it
is a captured object, but the construction of the narrative around the
male pregnant body makes that object almost invisible. Going further than a fragmentation which occurs when a part of the body
comes to stand in for the whole, in *Junior* as the foetus is fictionally
transferred into a male body, the female body all but disappears.
This sleight of hand repositions the real object of the technoscience
so that it is left without a critical space within the narrative.

Role reversals

Technoscientific control of the body is a common theme in fictions of
technoscience, and this control has been exerted over both male and
female bodies. One of the most well-known fictions of technoscience,
Metropolis (1927, Ger.), brings the two together, as it features a
woman's body being used by a scientist to create a robot in order to
exert control over the male workers. Since then there have been
numerous examples of such stories, especially within the SF genre.
Other well-known films include *Colossus: The Forbin Project* (1969,

US), *2001: A Space Odyssey* (1968, US), *Westworld* (1973, US), *The Stepford Wives* (1975, US), *Demon Seed* (1977, US), *Terminator* (1984, US), *RoboCop* (1987, US) and *Terminator 2: Judgement Day* (1991, US). Whilst all of these films have narratives in which the human body is captured by technology, some of them have also been about resisting that capture. In some cases this resistance has taken the form of humans taking control of the technologies themselves. Instead of resisting the technologies by moving beyond the controlling discourse as in *D.A.R.Y.L.*, in these films the technology remains in place, but is put to a different set of uses. The transition from *Terminator* to *Terminator 2* demonstrates this particular dialogue with technology, as the deadly Terminator of the first film is reprogrammed by the humans for the sequel. This reversal in the use of technology from oppressive to liberatory is also evident in *Enemy of the State*. Dean is able to regain his place in the world through Brill's expertise with the very same technologies that had initially been used to displace him.

sex, lies and videotape similarly uses the narrative device of a technological role reversal. Initially, the narrative seems to have little to do with technologies, as it revolves around the emotional and sexual problems of the two central protagonists, Ann and Graham. Ann finds no pleasure in her sexual life with her husband, and cannot express her needs more generally. Graham, because of guilt over his emotional failures, claims not to be able to get an erection in anyone else's presence, so, as he says, for all practical purposes he is impotent. Unlike Ann, however, he does have a way of gaining pleasure. Graham persuades women to let him video them telling him about their sexual lives and fantasies, and masturbating if that is what they wish to do; in re-watching these recordings, Graham seems to find some pleasure for himself. *sex, lies and videotape* is clearly open to an analysis through the psychoanalytic frameworks of voyeurism and exhibitionism; however, my interest in the text is the way in which the video technology is used both to mediate and to explore sexual and emotional pleasures within the film.

Graham's exploration of the erotic fantasies and exploits of the women he interviews initially appears to fit the pattern of technology as a device of alienation. His dependency on technology for his pleasure causes him to be alienated from both himself and other human individuals that surround him. Graham needs the machinery of video recorders, video playback and television screens to feel comfortable with sexual intimacy. An important difference, however, is that Graham is not alienated *because* of the technology; instead, the technology enables him simultaneously to take pleasure and remain at a safe distance. By using technology as a mediating device, he avoids a confrontation with the reality of his emotional and sexual difficulties, as his intimate relationships with women only occur with their image on the tape. In the sequences where Graham videos Cynthia (Ann's sister), he remains at a distance, placing the camera, and prompting as he asks questions. This habit of asking questions, of taking the conversation in directions of interest to him, carries over into his non-video-mediated relationships. When he first meets Ann, he asks her questions, trying to find out about her life. Unlike the video sequences managed by Graham, these scenes are shot with a constantly moving camera. During the dinner scenes between Ann, Graham and John (Ann's husband and friend of Graham), the camera moves around the table, framing and reframing the three speaking characters. As the emphasis of the conversation shifts around, so the camera moves around the table. The mobility of the camera work in this sequence contrasts with the static framing of Graham's interviewees. In the former, he does not have control over the direction of the conversation, and he may even be the object of the questioning. In the latter, he exerts control, not simply over the mediating technology, but also over the conversation through leading questions and prompts. There is a sense, however, in which Graham's control can be considered to be partial. He may hold the camera and frame the women, but they are in the position of doing what they want, prolonging or shortening the interview as they wish, and are under no obligation to continue. And, in the interview that Graham tapes of Cynthia, she asks him what he wants her to do, to which he replies that she can do whatever she wants. Despite this, it is finally Graham who decides where to place the camera and what questions to ask. And, once the women have gone, he can use the videos as he chooses. For Graham, this level of control establishes an order in his life. It allows him to keep his relationships neatly labelled and lined up in rows in a wooden cassette holder.

Ann is in a similar position to Graham, as she too attempts to keep control over herself, but does so by denying herself any form of sexual pleasure, or even thinking about sex. Prior to her discovery of her husband's affair with her sister, she is characterised as 'hung-up', unable or unwilling to fathom other people's fascination with

sex. The sublimation of her desires into worrying about starving
children, garbage and housework is something of a cliché, but it
does provide the narrative device that enables her to find that other
cliché, the other woman's earring in the marital bedroom. This con-
firmation of her suspicions that her husband is having sex with her
sister provokes Ann finally to do something, to begin to take control
of her life in a different way. Rather than repressing her desires, or
being passive, she chooses to act on them. In so doing she takes up
a place of agency within the narrative, acting rather than reacting.
Ann's first action is to go and see Graham, whom she has not seen
since her horrified discovery of his video collection, to ask him to
make a video of her. This event within the narrative causes Ann not
only to begin speaking about herself, but also to subvert Graham's
control over the video technology, to reverse his dynamic with the
technology as she turns the camera on him. This sequence of the narrative appears in a chronologically disrupted way within the film.
The beginning and the end are shown as they happen within the
story-time, but the rest is mediated through the eyes of John, Ann's
husband, after he has rushed over to confront Graham about video-
ing Ann. The audience's view of the video is here intercut with
John's reactions as he sits in Graham's sitting room, in front of an
image of Ann as she answers Graham's questions about sex.
Throughout, the incessant and distorted electronic note of the score
increases in loudness, and as Ann begins to speak about thinking
about sex with another man, the camera tracks in slowly on the blue-
hued video image of her face. As she is about to reveal her thoughts,
everything changes in the cut to Ann and Graham speaking to one
another without the mediation of his video technology. The score
recedes into the background, the image becomes colour, unframed
by the television screen that John had been looking at, and presumably still is looking at. With this cut a new relationship is established
between Ann and Graham, and also with the video technology. Ann
begins to exert control as she turns Graham's questions back on him.
Throughout the conversation in which Ann shifts from the person
responding to questions, to a person asking questions, to an inquisi-
tor, demanding of Graham that he explain himself, there is also a
series of distinct visual repositionings of the two characters. These
vary from frontal shots, to profiles, and then profiles from the opposite direction. The most dramatic of these shifts are preceded by
shots of Graham's video camera, a reminder that the technology is

still there. Indeed, when Ann asks Graham whether he wants to remain the person he has become, she finally picks the camera up, and taking his place she begins to direct the use of the technology as he backs into a corner. In this sequence, Ann has not only taken up agency for herself, she has also redefined the relationship that has been established between Graham, the women he tapes and the technology he uses. Through Ann's actions, the video technology ceases to be the means by which Graham maintains his distance. Graham is no longer the subject in control, and the women, represented by Ann, are no longer the object of his technologised gaze; they are, instead, the other way around. Once these subject and object relations have been reversed, the technology has little place in the narrative. In the resolution, the technology of *sex, lies and videotape* is neither the thing to control with or the thing to be controlled by, and the relationship between Ann and Graham becomes more direct. Although placed to one side in the resolution, technology in *sex, lies and videotape* has been pivotal in the redefinition of Ann and Graham's relationship.

12 Monkeys, D.A.R.Y.L., Junior and *sex, lies and videotape* can be read as texts that explore the different ways through which the practices and processes of science and technology attempt to constitute their object, in particular how they operate to construct humanness. With the exception of *Junior*, the positioning of such objects is contested. The struggles in *12 Monkeys, D.A.R.Y.L.* and *sex, lies and videotape* revolve around the extent to which technoscience disempowers or erases those constructions of humanness that are not validated within a particular discourse. In *12 Monkeys*, the technoscientific position prevails, with the result that nothing can exist outside of it. Cole, the protagonist of the film, dies because of the operations of power controlled and validated by the discourse of the 2035 scientists; he is finally not allowed to have any freedom of choice in how he wants to be. In *D.A.R.Y.L.* the restrictive framework of the military-technoscience complex is overcome, but only by escaping it and finding an alternative location within which to exist. A different resolution is found in *sex, lies and videotape*. The technology that mediates and delimits the relationship of the protagonist is initially reversed. And though technology is displaced, literally thrown out, taking control of the technology is an empowering act.

The different technoscientific discourses that emerge in *12 Monkeys, D.A.R.Y.L., Junior* and *sex, lies and videotape* suggest that the relationships between humans and technoscience are complex and multifaceted. Across the different texts the humanness which is validated, even if the figure validated is not biologically human, emerges in the struggle with the operations of science. The version of humanness which emerges through these particular texts (which should not be confused with a universal view of humanness, whatever that may actually be) is one founded on freedom of choice, love and emotions. All of these things, however, are not self-contained categories. Choice and emotions come to have meaning because they are juxtaposed with their opposites, containment and rationality. Although there is little in the way of dissolution of the physical body, there is a dissolution of the boundaries of humanness – whilst certain terms do remain constant, they do not have any absolute meaning. They instead take their meanings from their place within competing discourses of the texts, and as such they are contingent categories.

Notes

1 As well as casting Gene Hackman as the loner surveillance geek, the famous opening of *The Conversation* is reprised midway through *Enemy of the State*, as Dean's conversation with a woman is monitored using similar devices and all the same tactics.
2 Vivian Sobchack, 'Science Fiction', in Wes D. Gehring (ed.), *Handbook of American Film Genres* (New York: Greenwood Press, 1988) pp. 229–247; p. 231.
3 Scott Bukatman, *Terminal Identity: The Virtual Subject in Postmodern Science Fiction* (Durham, NC: Duke University Press, 1993).
4 Michel Foucault, *The Order of Things: An Archaeology of the Human Sciences* (London: Tavistock, 1970) pp. 132-138.
5 Susan Squier, 'Reproducing the Posthuman Body: Fetus, Surrogate Mother, Pregnant Man', in Judith Halberstam and Ira Livingston, *Post Human Bodies* (Bloomington and Indianapolis: Indiana University Press, 1995) pp. 113–132; p. 119.
6 In *12 Monkeys* the 2035 scientists are not distinguished from one another. In the end-credits, they are delineated by disciplines botanist, geologist, zoologist, astrophysicist, microbiologist, engineer but who is which remains unclear. As such, the film is about generic science, rather than a particular science.
7 This notion of a fact relies on the view that a factual statement is one that can be 'confirmed or disconfirmed by a scientific method, while "value judgement" cannot be'. Using the scientific method rather loosely as a

system of knowledge, Cole's knowledge is confirmed by what is already known. Of course, it should be added that this notion of fact should not be taken to mean something called 'truth'. Hilary Putnam, *The Many Faces of Realism* (LaSalle, Ill.: Open Court Publishing Company, 1987), p. 72.

8 Although the R in *D.A.R.Y.L.* stands for 'robot', since it is used in conjunction with 'life-form', it is not inappropriate to use the more recently conventional term cyborg to describe an individual such as Daryl.

9 The characterisation of Dr Ellen Lamb appears to be a gender role-reversal. It is her male colleague, Dr Stewart, who initially pushes the idea that Daryl is little different from a human child. Lamb is initially resistant to this position, but is finally convinced. Indeed, in the resolution of the film, it is she who reactivates Daryl, enabling him to return to his foster family.

10 Other references to containment within the film include the story of the boy trapped down the well, and the kidnapping of Dr Goines and his relocation to the inside of a zoo cage.

11 *Vertigo* (1958, US) is an intertext for *12 Monkeys* – Cole and Railly see it together in a cinema towards the end of the narrative, and *12 Monkeys* can be seen as a play upon the question posed by the *Vertigo* character, Gavin Elster: 'Do you believe that someone dead, someone out of the past, can take possession of a living being?' The difference in *12 Monkeys* is that it is someone out of the past and future that takes possession of a living being.

12 By combining the notion of the whole self with that of the institution of a male–female relationship, *12 Monkeys* appears to be alluding to the story told in Plato's *Symposium*. In this story the gods, through the splitting of the hermaphrodite into two distinct parts, created separate sexes. In order to be whole again they have to find their opposite halves. In this scenario, the heterosexual couple is required for wholeness.

13 This has also been a frequent feminist criticism of images of women's bodies. Broken down into parts, the sections of the body generate the meanings for the whole. An example of the bringing together of these two arguments, the feminist criticisms of media images of the female body and the compartmentalisation by technological and medical interventions, can be seen in Monica Casper's 'Fetal Cyborgs and Technomoms on the Reproductive Frontier: Which Way to the Carnival?' in Chris Hables Gray (ed.), *The Cyborg Handbook* (London and New York: Routledge, 1995), pp. 183–202. In this article Casper discusses an example of how the body of a pregnant woman is reconceptualised through medical and technological interventions to keep the foetus alive once the mother has already died.

14 A similar side-stepping of an issue is evident in the scene where Angela sees Larry touching Alex. Unable to see what Larry is touching, only

hearing him and Alex both cooing over the baby kicking in his belly, Angela assumes that the exchange is in some way sexual. The scene is played to deny not only the possibility of sexual pleasure in the touch, and thus a potential gay relationship, but also the possibility that pleasure in touching can occur between men, no matter what its nature. That *Junior* includes this scene is indicative of a need to reassure the audience that Alex, the pregnant and 'feminised' male, remains heterosexual. The need for this reassurance is perhaps more revealing than the scene itself.

15 The fertility clinic run by Larry seems only to be involved with women's fertility. The film does raise the question of male infertility through Larry's inability to fathe a child with Angela. That the resolution of *Junior* enables a reconciliation between Larry and Angela just after she has given birth to a child fathered by another man might be viewed as one of the film's more progressive moments.

16 *Junior* is one of the few fictions of technoscience that does raise the issue of funding in the university sector of research; the majority of texts remain concerned with the corporate sector.

3

The gremlin effect

Apollo 13 (1995, US) is a fictionalised account of the *Apollo 13* mission that almost ended in tragedy because of a small malfunction in the space rocket. The film version of these events centres on the response of various characters to the adversity of a broken-down space vehicle with three men inside thousands of miles from Earth, spiralling and rocking, almost out of control. Although the outcome of this event is known, and a part of space-exploration history, the tension of *Apollo 13* is maintained through a narrative marked by a sequence of events. Each of these events seems worse than the last – oxygen loss, power shutdown, the threat of carbon dioxide poisoning – and each of them must be managed, otherwise the men in the craft will die. The central characters, Jim Lovell, Fred Haise and Jack Swigert, plus grounded astronaut Ken Madingly and flight director Gene Kranz, all provide the focal point of this tension as they each have to work through moments of high crisis. Often this working through involves pulling the teams together, Kranz forcing his Houston Control team to come up with new strategies to get the craft back to Earth, to 'work the problem'; Lovell ensuring that the three in the craft keep their nerve, and work with each other to get through the latest dilemma, whether it is building a carbon dioxide filter, steering a manual engine burn, or dividing out the remains of their food. Clearly *Apollo 13* revolves around teamwork, with the interactions between the human figures central to the narrative. But at the same time as this very human and American story of skill and ingenuity against adversity is taking place, there is also a second one occurring, one less prominent within the focus of the narrative, but central nonetheless. That is the story of the changing interactions between the humans and the technologies which surround them. For this story about a struggle to survive involves the relationships between the humans and technology, as much as it does the relationships between the humans.

In the beginning of *Apollo 13* the technologies of space travel seem taken for granted. Space travel to the moon is considered routine, and the technology is simply a part of the process, managed according to established routines. In the sequences in the flight simulator, even the surprise of the glitch is worked through, outmanoeuvred by the skill of the pilot in control. As well as something that has to be operated, technology is both part of the background *mise-en-scène*, and part of the spectacle. As *mise-en-scène*, apart from in the domestic spaces, it seems always present as machines form a part of the background of key moments – when Madingly is told he will not be flying, in the dressing of the astronauts in their suits, in the pre-launch checks at Houston. During the launch, the technology also constitutes the spectacle of the narrative. Beginning with images of the engines steaming, and the stantions of the gantry falling away against the soundtrack of the deep rumble of the rockets beginning to ignite, to the flames of the ignited engine and the moment when the huge machine begins to move upwards, gaining speed as it blasts higher into the atmosphere to the cheers of the crowd, the technology of space-travel is spectacular. However, as the narrative develops the images of the technology become different, both in the sense that its operational capabilities alter after the accident of the explosion, and also in how it is transformed in the perceptions of the people who inhabit it.

Originally the spacecraft is a vehicle, a fully controlled environment within which the astronauts could undertake their journey to the surface of the moon, but in the course of the mission it becomes instead a life-boat. As this shift is made, parts of the machine are required to function in ways which were not originally intended. In a discussion about whether or not the engine on the lunar module could be used to fire in space, Kranz says to the Houston team: 'I don't care about what anything was designed to do, I care about what it *can* do'. This statement encapsulates the central dynamic between the humans and the technologies of *Apollo 13*. Technology is no longer perceived in terms of what it usually does, but in terms of what it can be made to do. Square filters are repackaged to fit into round holes using a whole series of unrelated bits and pieces; the crew have to do a manual burn with the Earth as their guidance system instead of a computer; Madingly reverses the flow of power between the command module and the lunar module in order to get the remaining amps needed to bring the navigational computer back on-line for re-entry. In this series of shifting relations, the technology ceases to be a static object which performs in pre-determined ways, and instead becomes something which can be redefined through the activities of the humans who operate in conjunction with it. The relationship is transformed from one of control and expectation, to one of uncertainties and instabilities: it is open to renegotiation.

In taking up the perspective that the relationship between technologies and humans is open to renegotiation, this chapter explores a different set of possibilities to those seen in the earlier chapters. There, my readings of the films illustrated the different perspectives which different films generated on the processes of technoscience. In *Lorenzo's Oil*, *Medicine Man*, *Lawnmower Man* and *Jurassic Park* technoscience was viewed through the focus of knowledge formations and institutions. Through *12 Monkeys*, *D.A.R.Y.L.*, *Junior* and *sex, lies and videotape* the different effects of technoscience on humans were explored. In both chapters, the images of technoscience are presented as being contingent on a variety of influences, but nonetheless there is a tendency for the individual films to take up singular positions on technoscience. This chapter draws on an alternative framework, one in which multiple meanings replace singular ones. A particular version of this shift from singular to multiple meanings is seen in instances where the meanings associated with technological objects are renegotiated and transformed within an individual film. *Gremlins* (1984, US), *Gremlins 2: The New Batch* (1990, US), *Strange Days* (1995, US) and *Fresh Kill* (1995, US) are discussed as texts in which the meanings of technological objects are not necessarily secure, or anchored to a singular dynamic between individuals and technoscience. Rather, the meanings of technological objects are viewed as contingent and unstable, renegotiated by the shifting patterns of connections across the narrative.

Renegotiations

The concept of technoscience that is central to the readings of the films in this study has often been used to discuss the processes by which knowledge and objects are produced through the practices of science and technology. However, it is also relevant to discussions of how technologies and knowledges operate within a social world after they have been produced. When science and technology appear in the world as systems of knowledge and objects, they can become multiple social objects, and as such they are open to a range of uses or interpretations, reinterpretations, or even misinterpretations. Each usage generates a different understanding or meaning for a knowledge or object, and the meanings associated with science and technologies are intrinsic neither to the potential of a particular science to give an explanation of phenomena, nor to the pre-determined utility of a technology. Instead, meanings are generated through the intersections created through the social location of the knowledge or object as well as its functionality. John Law uses the term 'heterogeneous elements' to describe the intersecting compo-nents within any given system. 'System' here means something that is constituted by a diverse set of influences that impose some pressure on the meaning of the technology as it operates within a system.[1] The heterogeneous elements are the diverse influences, which when jux-taposed with each other create stresses within a system which had previously been in balance. Any shift in balance can be seen as a reconfiguration of the intersections between the elements, a recon-figuration that has consequences for the meanings associated techno-logical object. In *Apollo 13*, for example, the heterogeneous elements, which might include the initial fault in the oxygen control system, the ground and vehicle crews, the conditions of being in a space environment, the various damages to the physical integrity of the craft, all operate with each other to impose a new meaning on the technology, changing for instance the lunar module from the vehicle that will provide the chance of an astronaut's lifetime, to a vehicle which acts as a life-boat.

The outcome of the idea of heterogeneous elements is that a tech-nology can be analysed as something which is determined not simply by its apparent functionality, but also according to a complex interre-lationship between social locations *and* functionality. This theory moves away from a linear perspective in which functionality is the sole determinant of social uses, towards a perspective in which the tech-nological and the social space actively interact in an on-going process of renegotiation. Such a view overlaps with the idea of patterns of reconnections evident in some of the writings of Gilles Deleuze and Félix Guattari. In *A Thousand Plateaus*, Deleuze and Guattari discuss the idea of connections through the concept of assemblages. The assemblage is a site of sets of interconnections, interconnections in which different influences (these can include the presence of humans, animals, or raw materials as well as cultural, social and political factors) act with and against each other.[2] At the site of active interconnectivity there are at least two concurrent events in process, the disruption of one set of influences and the establishment of another. As this process of territorialisation occurs, the spread of connections through and around any set of interactions is accompanied by periods of disruption, by a loosening of control over patterns of connections. In these periods of disruption the connections become open to new influences, enabling new intersections to appear, new meanings to be made. Inevitably, the period of disruption is itself short-lived and systems of control come back into place, restablising the order of the system and remaking boundaries. However, there may remain changes in the patterns of connection, changes which surface strongly enough for meanings to alter in a tangible way. Seen in conjunction with heterogeneous elements, the concept of assemblages is pertinent to thinking about technological systems.[3] The technology takes its meaning from the assemblages within which it is located, and the changing territorialisations of these assemblages, or to use Law's terminology, the association and dissociation of intersecting forces which constitute a system, change the meanings of the technologies in a social and cultural context.

The films discussed in this chapter all feature narratives in which the stability of the social functions of technologies, and hence their meanings, are open to renegotiation. The four texts have been chosen to illustrate different potential outcomes from this process. My discussion begins with *Gremlins* and *Gremlins 2*; in both of these films the figure of the Creature destabilises the intersections between the humans and the technologies, but the resultant process of renegotiation is short-lived and contained, as the destabilising element is removed in the resolution of the texts. The next film discussed, *Strange Days*, takes the question of new patterns of connection beyond the parameters of *Gremlins* and *Gremlins 2*. Instead of being isolated in such a way that they can be set aside at the resolution, the intersections of the technology and the humans occur within a series of communities in which relationships of love, friendship, law and order, and economic power all influence the meanings of technological objects. As such the technologies of *Strange Days* are central to and embedded within social processes depicted within the text. *Fresh Kill*, the final text I discuss in this chapter, also has a narrative which is open to an exploration of the shifting patterns of connections between humans and technologies. However, unlike in *Gremlins*, *Gremlins 2* and *Strange Days*, in this video-feature the small changes in the power relations that occur within changing patterns of intersection between the human figures and the technologies remain open to the possibility of further transformations.

Gremlins in the system

Gremlins and *Gremlins 2* both explore a series of intersections between humans and their technological environments, and the ways in which a new alignment of elements can result in the renegotiation of the social meanings of technological objects. In *Gremlins* and *Gremlins 2*, this process of renegotiation becomes possible through the figure of the Creature, a green and scaly embodiment of the gremlin.[4] The Creature operates within the films to disturb the equilibrium between humans and technologies by transgressing and then renegotiating the boundaries initially in place; in so doing, new sets of connections are established. The Creature is a kind of catalyst, a catalyst which disrupts the balance between the different elements that make up the system. Superficially, the Creatures enter into the plots of *Gremlins* and *Gremlins 2* via a similar route – Gizmo, a Mogwai, comes into the possession of Billy, the main protagonist of both films.[5] In *Gremlins*, Gizmo is a Christmas present; in *Gremlins 2*, Billy rescues 'him' from the clutches of the twin scientists. However, the transformative effect of the Creatures varies between the two texts, and the distinction resides in the different kinds of technological environments that *Gremlins* and *Gremlins 2* depict. In *Gremlins* the technological environment is primarily domestic, and features everyday technologies; *Gremlins 2* occurs in a different kind of system, in a heavily technologised workplace environment. Between the two films, the action has moved from a private space to a public space, as the battle shifts from domestic to office gadgets.

The everyday setting of *Gremlins* is established with the first shot of the town – a parodic picture-postcard scene, with the spires and roofs of the houses covered in a fall of snow. However, this is not a prosperous town since the people of Kingston Falls find it hard to pay their rent, and are without employment. The absence of a major employer within the community accentuates the sense of an economic and industrial recession which is the context for the narrative.

Technology is introduced into *Gremlins* primarily through two characters – Murray Futterman and Randall Peltzer. Futterman is a depressed blue-collar worker who constantly complains about the lack of American technologies in the marketplace. Citing his 15-year-old Southern Harvester as an example, he expresses nostalgia for the old days when the US could produce long-lasting technologies, ones that did not constantly break down, as do the 'foreign' goods to which Futterman constantly alludes. Futterman's position, however, seems to go further than simply bemoaning the short lifespan of contemporary everyday technologies such as cars, 'radios that go in the ears', TV sets and stereos. His direct alignment of the lack of American goods with the increasing amounts of foreign goods would seem to make him something of a techno-xenophobe: 'How would you like to open up your car and find it filled with foreign parts?' And although Futterman's attitude is not explicitly condoned within *Gremlins*, as it is displaced by the progression of the narrative, his outbursts do connect the Creatures with things from outside of the US, a connection reiterated by the Mogwai being found by Peltzer in a Chinese community. The second figure who introduces technology is Randall Peltzer, a self-employed inventor who makes small technologies for the home. Perhaps an extension of the figure of the individual inventor, Peltzer is far from the successful figure of that myth. The various devices he invents, which include the Bathroom Buddy, the Peltzer Juicer, an egg breaker, a remote light dimmer and phone control, all fail. Their ability to function is short-lived, as they work well for a couple of weeks and then begin to malfunction. Peltzer, in contrast to Futterman, could be seen as a metaphor for the technological capabilities of the USA of the period. And these technologies are presented as being not quite up to the competition of a world-wide marketplace. Futterman and Peltzer, then, present two distinct views. One suggests that the US has been invaded by foreign devices, and the other sees US technology as both uncompetitive and also prone to failure. In either view, there is unease around technology.

The problem of living with unreliable technologies is explored through the Peltzer family. Living in a house surrounded by malfunctioning inventions, their life is constantly interrupted by breakdowns that they endure because of family loyalty. This antipathetic relationship between humans and technology is nicely illustrated through the workings of the Peltzer Juicer. Beginning a sequence set first thing in the morning, the juicer is shown in close-up, filling the lower corner of the screen, an apparently benign domestic object made suspicious by the discordant note in the score and its unusual framing. Billy, the son of the Peltzer family, walks into the kitchen, behind the machine to get a glass of juice, all the time glancing suspiciously at the juicer from the back of the frame. As he begins to operate the machine, pausing to steel himself against the possible chaotic outcome, Billy visibly relaxes as the juicer initially seems to function, only for the machine to then cover him and the kitchen with orange-pulp. This scene characterises the initial relationship between humans and technology in *Gremlins* as one of a resigned accommodation to something that does not function correctly. However, as the film progresses and the Creatures hatch, the technology becomes something altogether different. The Creatures introduce a new set of forces into the system, ones that are aggressively destructive and chaotic, compelling a reorganisation of the elements which surround the technologies, a reorganisation which sees them being redefined as weapons with which the humans defend themselves. This is especially apparent in the sequence in which Lynn Peltzer defends herself against the gremlins in her kitchen. Here the various kitchen utensils – food mixer, microwave, knives – are used to dismember and pulp the creatures. Whilst this sequence seems also to be making a comment on the ways in which domestic items are easily turned to alternative and often violent uses, it also reveals the continuation of a gendered dimension to the dynamic between humans and technologies presented within *Gremlins*. Lynn Peltzer, the mother of the family, is only able to operate in any active way within the kitchen space. Prior to the emergence of the Creatures she is seen making food of various kinds, but once the Creatures are out and about eating her newly baked gingerbread family, she is only successful when fighting them in the kitchen. Once Lynn moves outside of the kitchen, the Creatures become successful, almost strangling her as they reach out from their hiding place in the Christmas tree. She is only saved by the timely appearance of her son, and subsequently becomes marginal to the plot. A similar positioning is evident in the characterisation of Kate, Billy's girlfriend. Like Lynn she is initially successful, but ultimately causes more problems than solutions. Her success is evident in her recognition that the Creatures harassing her in Dorry's Bar are sensitive to light, and she attacks them with the flash on a Polaroid camera, but when this runs out she too must be saved by Billy. In the final department-store battle, Kate is sent to turn the lights on, but in her lack of knowledge about the switches, turns on the water fountain, almost enabling the Creatures to rise again. The woman characters, then, are not simply marginalised from a successful renegotiation with technology, they also seem to become aligned with the Creatures as a problem within the text. Such a positioning reveals traditional constructions of gender to be a limiting element in the processes of renegotiation, an element that operates at the level of the construction of the characters.

The narrative development of *Gremlins 2* operates in similar way to *Gremlins*, but in contrast to the first film, which first establishes a relationship of resignation surrounding the malfunctioning technology, *Gremlins 2* begins by establishing an interaction that foregrounds alienation. Located in a different setting, New York instead of a frosted Capra-esque Kingston Falls, *Gremlins 2* initially presents technology as standing for an entrepreneurial ethic based on destruction and subordination. The system constituted through the human and technological elements is driven by efficiency and production of profits. The subsequent sense of human subordination within a technologised environment is evident in the *mise-en-scène* of *Gremlins 2*, as much of the action takes place in a 'smart' building in New York City. This building, Clamp Tower, functions with the aid of sophisticated technology that both monitors and controls the environment, building security, and the activities of the employed personnel. The theme of technology as a potentially destructive presence is further emphasised as the plot of *Gremlins 2* opens with the establishment of an opposition between progress and decline. Progress is represented by brash newness, the embodiment of which is Daniel Clamp, a developer who aims to demolish Chinatown and replace it with a simulated Chinatown: 'the Clamp Chinese Centre ... where business gets oriented'. Decline is represented through the character of Mr Wang; originally introduced in *Gremlins* as the guardian of Gizmo, in *Gremlins 2* he is significantly more frail. This frailty is echoed by the dilapidation of his curiosity shop, which, lit only by candles, is dusty and full of old decaying objects. These two images of progress and decline confront each other through a 'visit' by Clamp to Mr Wang's shop. Here the link between progress and technology is established by Clamp's presence being conveyed into the shop via a television monitor and video-player; as such he intrudes into Mr Wang's space as a pre-recorded non-interactive tele-presence. When Mr Wang refuses to accommodate Clamp by accepting his take-over offer, the video and television are left behind, as both disposable items from the culture of progress, and also a symbol of the inevitable displacement of older orders. The voracity of progress is fully effected with the death of Mr Wang, an event that is announced by a CCN (Clamp Cable Network) newscaster multiply present on a bank of television screens. The destructiveness of this progress is made visible as Gizmo, who has only been briefly heard up until this point, escapes from the shop and the screen-filling jaws of the mechanical digger just at the moment they swing across the image to demolish the walls of the old building. In this development of a new Chinatown, Clamp's activities erase a place that used to be inhabited by a living community, and then convert it into a space in which the assumed cultural identity of that community is repackaged into a commodity to be consumed by a different culture.[6] This repackaging occurs not only in terms of cultural identities, but also in terms of degrees of technologisation – the development that will replace this area of Chinatown is planned to mimic the technological supremacy of Clamp's head office and showcase building. However, if it is like Clamp Tower, this development will offer little to the individual. In the latter building, workers are identified by a bar code, and denied the opportunity to customise their workspaces through either plants or artworks which are not authorised. In addition, the surveillance system operating in the building prevents any subversion of the work practices of the Clamp regime; cigarette breaks are stolen at risk of punishment by summary dismissal. Through these various devices, *Gremlins 2* depicts working in the technologically enhanced Clamp building as dehumanising. This is an experience underlined through the figures of Billy and Kate, the characters from *Gremlins* who function within *Gremlin 2* as the representatives of an 'ordinary' humanity – they are the archetypal young couple struggling in an alienating cityscape. This sense of alienation is initially evident by their introduction into the narrative as voices only, their visual individuality lost in a high-angle shot that frames a street crowded with a mass of people hurrying to work. Only the second shot picks them out as individuals, and even then they are jostled by the people surrounding them.

These opening sequences of *Gremlins 2* inscribe several linked oppositions: old versus new, progress versus decline, good versus bad. In so doing a technological imperative is established. The elements of progress and technologies are aligned in a process through which progress occurs at the cost of the individual, the community, and a sense of historical context, and the new system comprehensively obliterates the old. Technology, directed by Daniel Clamp, can only encompass the new; there is no place or space for anything other. The world is held in the jaws of the C of the Clamp Corporate iconic installation, squashed down at the poles and changed in shape. However, as in *Gremlins*, the technological imperative is set up only to be dismantled, for the entry of the Creatures into the narrative disrupts this technological progression towards an alienating newness. The Creatures, the catalyst for the reorganisation of the elements of the system, transform the relationship between humans and technologies in different ways in *Gremlins* and *Gremlins 2*. In both films, as so often happens in cartoons, everyday objects become weapons, and as their function alters, so too does the relationship between the humans and the technology. In *Gremlins*, the department store becomes a source of implements to kill with – sporting equipment, chain saws and buzz-saw blades. Similarly, the photocopier and child's train set become instruments of torture in *Gremlins 2*, the shredding machine a weapon, and the microwave a means to enable the reproduction of the gremlins – the microwave explodes causing the building's fire sprinklers to go off. This latter scene is given further meaning when considered as an intertext to *Gremlins*. It is a reworking of, and possibly an intertextual revenge for, the previously discussed scene in which Lynn Peltzer kills a number of creatures in her kitchen by using various domestic appliances as weapons. In this earlier confrontation, one of the more explosive encounters between Lynn and the Creatures occurred with the microwave. Such transformations suggest that the evolution of a technology need not end when it comes off the production line. Its social meanings are not fully determined by an intended functionality but can continue to alter in unpredictable ways, depending on the reconnections made around it.

Gremlins 2, as well as playing games with functional transitions around individual objects, takes the degree of transformation further. Since the narrative of the film occurs in an obviously technologically controlled and controlling environment, Clamp Tower becomes, metaphorically and literally, a space in which the relations of power embedded in the associations between the technological and human elements become more foregrounded. The building in itself is a kind of system, though one with quite evident limits, which are more or less established through the boundaries of the building. As the organisation of the elements is altered, the power to exert control within the system represented through the building also shifts. The technology of the building is initially used in the pursuit of an alienating employment practice, a practice in which employees are reduced to the status of interchangeable parts of a process, instead of being perceived as individuals who contribute something to that process. These practices of assimilation and de-individualisation are carried over to the homogeneous look of Clamp Tower. The foyer of the building is cold metal and black marble; the spaces in the depth of the shot often seem empty of life. Everything in the office spaces is 'eye-pleasing, colour co-ordinated, authorised'. The implied confinement is made fun of through the entrance and exit doors of the Tower, a 'revolution in revolving doors', as they either stop and trap people, or revolve fast enough to propel their users headlong into the building. In spite of this early indication that all is not quite under control in Clamp Tower, the sense of corporate sameness is further suggested by the costumes of the inhabitants of Clamp Tower. Everyone is dressed in grey, from the chief executive and the office staff to the building tour guides – even the laboratory coats are grey.[7]

The Creatures' eruption throws over this corporate greyness. In terms of the building itself, by the end of *Gremlins 2* much of it in chaos and half-light, the gleaming surfaces covered with graffiti and hand, feet and tooth marks and other less definable prints of the Creatures. This transition does not, however, simply represent a change in the functions of the building. It also represents the trans- formations in the power relations between the heterogeneous elements. Daniel Clamp shifts from his position as a minor deity of progress – the building his plaything, his office a parodic heaven, high above the cloud line with shafts of white light streaming in. By the end of the film he is back down amongst the people; he has seen the error of his technological ways and is ready for his next development scheme: simulations of American small-town communities. More telling is Billy's relationship to the building. Having been chastised for demonstrating traces of individuality, it is his specific knowledge of the gremlins, plus his growing knowledge of the building and how it works, that enables him to lead the destruction of the Creatures. In an echo of the debates about mass culture and rationalisation, Billy refuses his position as a component of the technologised processes of

Clamp Tower. As he does so, his individualism and personal knowledge are foregrounded as they become the means by which he saves
the trapped people, through utilising the centralised communications
systems of the building, the time controls and tele-videos.

The shifting relationships between Clamp, Billy and the Tower are
not, however, simply inversions of a duality, a bad use of technology
versus a good use of technology. After all, the technologies used by
Billy are the remnants of the control and surveillance elements that
had characterised the 'inhuman' centre of the building earlier in the
narrative. Instead, the presence of a third term, the Creatures, complicates the transitions between the uses of the technologies. Technology, rather than being only associated with a dehumanising and
dystopic vision of progress, becomes the means to both capture and
recapture Clamp Tower, with additional and wider implications for
the safety of New York City, and then presumably the world. Clamp
Tower and its various inhabitants, technological, human and gremlin, become elements of a system, within which a conflict is fought
in order initially to destabilise the system, and then subsequently to
reorder it. In a similar way to the photocopier, microwave and
shredder, the functions of the technologies of Clamp Tower are initially renegotiated through the actions of the Creatures, but they are
subsequently renegotiated again through the counteractions of the
human characters. The control of the media technologies is an
example of this. Prefigured briefly in *Gremlins* when Spike, the
leader of the Creatures, appears on all the television sets in the
department store during the final conflict, the media technologies
are utilised by the competing groups in *Gremlins 2*. Initially, they are
under the control of CCN, who broadcast news items and (only)
colour films. As the Creatures take over, the media comes under
their control, and the logo on the screens changes from CCN to the
image of a gremlin. This take-over of the media is also played out
towards the viewer of the narrative. At the moment the head scientist is saying he will never hurt another creature again, the images on
the screen change to make it look as though the film projection or
video-player has malfunctioned.[8] These images soon give way to
more laughing Creatures, signalling the joke of the malfunction.
Briefly, at least on first viewing, the audience is encouraged here to
feel the effect of a technological problem for themselves.

A further dimension of this conflict over the control of the media
is played out through the character of Grandpa Fred. Living out his

dreams of becoming a newscaster, Fred counters the Creatures' control of the cable channel. With the help of Katsuji, a camera-mad visitor to Clamp Tower, Fred takes control of one of the channels and begins broadcasting an alternative version of events to those being told on the outside of the building. Fred and Katsuji's activities are juxtaposed with those of a second set of journalists; the two groups then compete with each other to give media meanings to the Creatures. A similar shifting dynamic is evident in the conflict over the control of the technologies of the building. Just as the Creatures captured the building, and seemed to make it maliciously animate by taking over the environmental controls, the elevators and the telecommunications network, so Billy uses the phone system, the fire system and the centralised time controls to recapture the building. As both groups subvert each other's use of the technologies, as they each make new connections through and with it, the Creatures and Billy reinscribe the system of social relations around that technology. In this process technologies cease to be only alienating things, and become instead a part of the lived space. As Andrew Ross has written:

> But however remote, impersonal, or alienating these processes [technology's precision methods] are, technologies are also fully lived and experienced in our daily actions and practices, and that is why it is important to understand technology not as a mechanical imposition on our lives but as a fully cultural process, soaked through with social meaning that only makes sense in the context of familiar kinds of behaviour.[9]

Following Ross's comments, which echo those of John Law, the activities of the Creatures and Billy provide the context for seeing technologies as part of a cultural process, elements which can be subject to renegotiation, and not simply as something remotely imposed by the operations of a figure such as Clamp. The possibility for renegotiation also entails a transition from the view that humans are passive consumers or objects of technological effects, to one that sees humans as active participants in the processes through which the meanings of technologies are constructed.

The complicating presence of the Creatures is not only relevant to ideas about technoscientific systems. They also complicate the development of the narrative – the gremlins can be seen to act as a tongue-in-cheek demonic realisation of the event that displaces the equilibrium at the beginning of classical Hollywood narratives. In keeping with such a model, the narratives of both *Gremlins* and *Gremlins 2* push towards the re-establishment of the equilibrium, or something close enough to it, through a restoration of normality. This resolution does occur in *Gremlins*, through the eradication of the Creatures in a final showdown between Billy and Spike. *Gremlins 2* has a more complicated resolution. It gestures towards the heterosexual romance, a means of narrative closure common to the classical narrative style – Billy and Kate clear up their misunderstanding, and Daniel Clamp is smitten with Carla, the workaholic chain-smoking red-headed pseudo-vamp. However, this play on closure and the romantic resolution is both subverted and parodied as the film closes with Forster, Clamp's chief of staff, trapped in a room with an apparently female Creature, who wants nothing less than commitment and his body. The final shot is of Forster deciding to engage in this interspecies pairing, just before the words The End appear in a pseudo-romance typeface. As well as parodying the heterosexual romantic closure, this scene also serves to undermine the apparent resolution of *Gremlins 2* through the eradication of the Creatures. For *she* is still very much alive, and in the manner of the paranoid horror film, about to mate.[10]

This potentially open resolution to the narrative also has implications for the renegotiations that have occurred around the technologies of the narrative. I have suggested that it is possible to read the relationship between humans and technologies as one that undergoes a process of transformation. But this poses another question: where do these renegotiations and transformations ultimately lead? It might be expected that these renegotiations represent a departure from the dualities in place at the beginning of the text – progress/decline; new/old; technological/non-technological – and to an extent they are, since they suggest a potential for new patterns of connection between humans and technologies, ones that are not already and always fully determined.[11] However, in *Gremlins 2*, and also *Gremlins*, this has very evident limits. The potential for reconnection is seemingly closed down almost as soon as it begins, and the possibilities for a new organisation of power within the system of elements is placed to one side. The scenes inside the genetic research laboratories – Splice O' Life – encapsulate this clamping down on new possibilities. The work of the scientists who inhabit this laboratory space is focussed on transformation, in this case of mundane things; as such they represent the starting point for the impact of

technoscience on the everyday aspects of human living. Their experiments include creating non-destructible tomatoes suitable for easy
transport, and, in a play on recycling culture, waste scavengers
are turned into sources of electricity by the conversion of the sewer
rat into a new energy source. After the Creatures erupt into Clamp
Tower, the laboratory becomes one of the central sites of chaos
as they ransack it and consume the various experimental potions.
In a spectacular display of the transformative powers of science,
each Creature successfully undergoes an alteration to a gremlin
hybridised variously with a bat, a spider, electricity, vegetables and
brainpower.[12] However, like the monster in many horror films, these
hybrid creatures are unpredictable; they are uncontrollable transformations that destroy the site of their creation, and in a riotous
sequence the laboratory is well and truly trashed.[13] Excepting the
female gremlin, these hybrid Creatures do not survive the activities
of Billy, and so the potential for any sustained transformation is
closed down. In an equivalent way, the opportunities for new patterns of connection and reconnection in the larger-scale system
constituted by the humans and technologies inside Clamp Tower
are apparently dissipated. Although Daniel Clamp has learnt that he
had created a building for things rather than people, he simply
moves on to his next project. 'Billy the Hero' becomes incorporated
into this new plan as he appears ready to design it. In setting aside
the newly reorganised system of Clamp Tower, everything seems
about to continue as normal, and the world clamped in the jaws
of the C begins to turn again. Only the survival of the female hybrid Creature ensures that something remains to keep open the
possibility for future transformations.

Beyond the walls

Gremlins and *Gremlins 2* can be read as films which foreground
technology as a part of a social process, a social process constituted
by the arrangement of elements within the systems of either
Kingston Falls or Clamp Tower. *Gremlins 2*, through the explicit
positioning of Daniel Clamp as the site through which power is
wielded, explores the ways in which power is located within particular sets of connection. In this instance, the sets of connection
cohere around entrepreneurial capitalism. However, there remains
the sense that Clamp fully determines the overall system, rather

than simply being an element within it. In leaving his status unquestioned, the means by which he gains and maintains his power stays
outside of the concerns of the narrative. Because of this absence, the
social processes evident within *Gremlins 2* remain defined within a
relatively limited field of connectivity, and only incorporated into
the restricted system through which the character of Clamp operates. In the remainder of this chapter I move on to discuss two other
texts, *Strange Days* and *Fresh Kill*, both of which have narratives
that are also structured around competing sets of elements. But in
these two cases, the sets of elements stretch out beyond a limited
arena, establishing connections across a variety of different social,
cultural and economic situations. The particular concern of my
commentary on *Strange Days* and *Fresh Kill* is how the technologies
featured in both texts contribute to the networks of connections
established across a range of different situations, instead of more
limited ones depicted in the *Gremlins* films. This reading will argue
that whilst both films present technology as integral to a variety of
social processes, their resolutions suggest very different outcomes.
The resolution of *Strange Days* opts for the appearance of stability,
whilst that of *Fresh Kill* opts for continued openness, an openness
in which the patterns of connection are always subject to the changing conditions which surround them.

Strange Days, released in 1995, is set in the final two days of 1999.
The action of the film takes place in LA, which is depicted as a chaotic
space constantly in transition. The streets are the sites of battles
between the police and groups who want to take control for themselves. The scenes of these activities are often shot from the perspective of a travelling car, an effect which contributes to the continual
sense of movement. The cutting between the inside of the car and the
perpetually changing battles going on outside gives the impression of
elements that are always shifting, impossible to tie down. These
images create more uncertainty than certainty about who is in control
of the unfolding situation. Throughout *Strange Days* it is not only the
power to control the streets that is uncertain, so too is the power
to control the meaning of a particular piece of information, the clip
of the murder of an African-American political activist, Jeriko One.
Central to the elements that assemble around this information is a
technology, the SQUID or super quantum interference device. In this
reading of *Strange Days*, the technology of the SQUID – a device that
can record the full sensory stimulation evoked by any experience of

the wearer – is foregrounded in such a way that the social effects that accumulate around it become apparent. The plot of *Strange Days* is constructed around a series of conflicting territorialisations since the SQUID and the human characters operate as elements which connect together in multiple ways, forming various patterns of connection. Although the term territorialisation overlaps with the idea of systems (as used by Deleuze and Guattari and Law, respectively), for the purposes of this discussion I make a definite distinction between territories and systems. I use territories to stress the notion that the narrative of *Strange Days* operates through a multiplicity of systems, and I make this distinction to indicate a difference between *Strange Days* and the *Gremlins* films discussed above. Each of those films presented a distinct system of intersecting elements, but one that was clearly limited by specific parameters. In *Gremlins* the parameters were established by the town of Kingston Falls, whilst in *Gremlins 2* they were established by Clamp Tower. In *Strange Days* and *Fresh Kill* different systems emerge through the plot of the films, and I use territories to indicate these multiple systems as they interact with other. Accordingly, territorialisations is used to indicate the shifting patterns of human–technology connections that are invested with meaning through the different contexts and power relationships within the individual systems, and especially across the multiplicity of systems.

The various systems of connectivity that operate within *Strange Days* appear through the stories around the different human characters. Starting with Lenny Nero's narrative, the SQUID, originally conceived as a police technology for surveillance and the collection of evidence, is utilised by Lenny as a means of production. The clips he produces, the recordings of people's activities, are his commodities. In this context, the SQUID enables a system based on economic practice with Lenny at its centre, controlling the supply and hustling for the demand. On the side of supply, the individuals who provide the clips are a mixture of genders and races; anyone who looks good enough and needs to make some money can be incorporated into the network. Only people with sufficient money to pay for both the playback technology and a supply of clips constitute the side of demand. Within Lenny's worldview the clips, the packages of sensory experience, are simply part of an exchange system, valued not for what they may or may not mean, but solely for their financial worth.

The economic system put in place by Lenny is, however, only one of several possibilities for the relationship established between the human figures and the SQUID technology. Alternative narrative spaces reveal alternative experiences of technologies, and therefore different systems. Philo, for instance, uses the technology as a means of surveillance, and so for him the meanings of the collected images do matter. Within Philo's paranoiac system, the surveillance of his employees enables him to create for himself the illusion that he is in control of both his life and his business concerns – the club and music scenes. The notion of the SQUID as a means of control is taken to further extremes within *Strange Days*; it is used as an instrument to 'burn out' the neural activities of Philo's and Tick's brains, an action which results in irreversible damage. The figure who uses the SQUID in this way, Max, is also the individual who rapes and murders Iris. Again the SQUID is implicated, not as a means of rape but as a means of control, in this case to control the reactions of the woman who is being raped. The SQUID is used to heighten her terror; force is used to control not only her body, but also her visual and sensory experiences as she is wired to see and feel her own rape and murder mediated through the feelings of the man who is raping and murdering her. If the implications of this sequence are not immediately obvious to the viewer, and they are almost too brutal to think through, they are explained and mediated for the audience through Lenny's reactions to the clip of the rape that he has been sent.[14]

In other less violent ways the SQUID technology also mediates the relationships between people. Tick is another figure who deals in clips, and his links to Lenny are established through this practice. Lenny's relationship with Faith, whether in real time or the one he repeatedly watches on playback, seems to have been based on Lenny watching and recording Faith. These very different systems of connection again suggest that a technology does not accumulate meanings simply on the terms of its functionality; rather, its meaning is contingent on the context within which it is located and used. For Lenny it is part of a process of production or a way of remaining connected to his lost love, for Iris it is the cause of her death, for Max and Philo it is a way of being in control, and for Faith it is a means to heighten her pleasure. Within each of these systems, the SQUID emerges as a different kind of element, not different in substance, but different in meaning.

The sense of contingency is evident within *Strange Days* in other ways. In the economic system put into play by Lenny, images are recycled into different contexts; again nothing has any meaning on its own terms. Although Lenny sells the clips as slices of another person's life, saying to a potential customer, 'this is life, it's a piece of somebody's life, it's pure and uncut, straight from the cerebral cortex', the constructed nature of these clips becomes obvious as Lenny buys the time of different people and gets them to wear the wire and record various actions which are then sold on as 'actual experiences'. The sexual activities, the burglaries may be viewed and felt, pure and uncut in the safety of playback, but a clip is only a simulation, a set-up to be sold and circulated. Everything here is mediated, representations of representations, simulations, performances to the nth degree. And, at the very moment of playback, even the biology of the body, the physiology and biochemistry of sexual acts, fear, death and excitement no longer function in terms of authentic body feelings; they too are incorporated into a system of mediation as they become a part of the information loop. The technology of the SQUID reduces all the recordable senses to objects with an exchange value, displacing them from the experiential into a system of market forces.

Even though these various narrative devices present a new technological sensory experience, the presentation of this experience by *Strange Days* exists in a tension with the limits of contemporary playback technologies of the cinema and the home. Within the story-world of *Strange Days* the SQUID, through superficial surface connections on the head, can record everything that the wearer sees and feels. This includes not only the visual but also the visceral, packaging together the pleasure of the voyeuristic look with the pain of experience.[15] As a demonstration of the visual potential of the device, *Strange Days* opens with a long point-of-view sequence of an armed burglary through a series of images where people are constantly in motion, running through doors and short corridors, through a kitchen and up a staircase. The hand-held on-the-run camera, whip pans and final plummeting drop-off-the-edge shot, give the audience a taste of the visual exhilaration, but cannot make the audience feel pleasure or pain in the way that the SQUID is supposed to do. The representation of pleasure and pain can only be conventional, mediated through the reactions of a character on the screen. This tension continues throughout *Strange Days*. As the narrative depicts the downside of becoming addicted to SQUID playback, and Faith says to Lenny, 'movies are still better than playback ... you know when its over', it also keeps showing playback, giving tantalising glimpses of a new medium of simulation, not to mention stimulation.

Not only is this tension between something new and something old, and the explicit constructedness of images, central to the plot of *Strange Days*; the recycling of images is also an element in the construction of *Strange Days* itself, especially in the use of character and dialogue. The *noir*-ish Lenny is an ex-LAPD vice-cop who operates in the margins of the vice trade, and he also is never in control of the plot. Faith's choice of Philo as a partner is a career move, a prerogative of all the best *femmes fatales*. She also satisfies the convention of a woman to look at, one whose body is exhibited for everyone to see. Max, Lenny's duplicitous best friend, is a psycho bad-guy who thinks he is in control of the plot, even though he has well and truly lost it. The scenarios these characters perform within seem familiar, echoes of too many other films where the streets are dark, the city is LA, and the characters could be using dialogue from old B-movies. Whilst these elements of *Strange Days* provoke a sense of having been here before, seen this before, there is also a push towards something different through the exhilaration of the editing, the use of music and the explorations of light and dark. The rapid editing, combined with a moving camera, is especially evident in the near-dark scenes in which Lenny drives to a meeting. On the streets it is no longer clear who are the lawless. People run in the dark, looting and carrying weapons, chasing and stopping, beating and being beaten in a social world that already seems to have gone beyond breaking point. Counterbalancing these scenes are sequences of long shots in deep focus, where conversations and arguments take place in low-lit spaces, and unknown characters move around in the depth of an alley-way or a long room. A tonal depth is given to these images through a predomination of reds and steely blues, whilst smoky air catches the intermittent beams of white light entering through cracks from the circling helicopters outside.

In employing these different strategies in the construction of the film itself, the makers of *Strange Days* balance banality with difference; familiar images are re-set and pushed towards something different. In a parallel way, through the SQUID technology within the story-world of *Strange Days*, information is created from familiar images but is commodified as something different. And each time it is sold this information accumulates new sets of meanings from its different users and different contexts. However, such re-settings also always carry the potential for an incipient *loss* of meaning. Experiences commodified through the SQUID become incorporated into the realm of simulation and information exchange. Once there, they are no longer located in relation to any originating act, and as they shed meanings they accrue others, becoming territorialised in the process. In such a context, what happens to both the history and the politics of any information?

The question of both politics and history emerges in *Strange Days* through one of the main structuring elements of the narrative, the conflict over a clip which records an event carrying significant political weight – the shooting by two white police officers of Jeriko One, the African-American singer and political activist who had been gaining leadership within his community. Using SQUID technology, the clip is initially recorded by Iris because of the paranoiac need felt by Philo (Jeriko's manager) to know the movements of all his associates. Once it exists, Philo attempts to control the information of Jeriko's death by getting Max to erase all recordings of the event, preventing it from entering the cycle of information. However, Max has his own agenda and he sets in motion a chain of events by raping and murdering Iris. This in turn leads Lenny to think that Faith will also be murdered, and since he is still in love with her, Lenny is desperate to prevent it. So, when Lenny finds the clip of Jeriko's murder it horrifies him, but he primarily sees it as something that has exchange value, for its bargaining power in his game with Philo and ultimately Max. Like Philo and Max, Lenny can only see the clip in terms of the system he seeks to control.

Lornette (Mace) Mason functions within the narrative of *Strange Days* to intercept and interrupt this potential chain of events, and to re-establish the political dimensions of the clip, thus preventing an emptying out of the meanings of the image. Her actions reinforce the trace between the images and the event from which the recording originated. Her presence also invokes another set of connections mobilised through an intersection with the SQUID technology – the spectre of a riot. It is through Mace's threat to leak the clip to the media that the fear of violence, which would erupt if such images were to become public knowledge, is articulated. But this articulation of the fear of the breakdown of law and order in LA is not the same for Mace as it is for Lenny. Mace's relationship to the consequences of Jeriko's death is explicitly constructed within *Strange Days* around her position as an African-American woman, and through her relationship to the African-American communities more generally. Through her, the consequences of Jeriko's death are made to resonate not simply with the activities of Lenny, Max and Philo, but also with the histories of police violence against people of colour, and with histories of racial inequalities within the US.[16]

But these are not the only ways in which Mace's difference is located within *Strange Days*. It is also embedded in the use of the conventions associated with particular genres. The white characters, Max, Lenny, Faith and Philo, have roles with *noir* antecedents, and their interactions with each other are structured into the narrative through stories of the betrayal of friendship and the betrayal of love. The conventions of Mace's role, however, come from the action hero.[17] As an action-hero figure Mace is almost infallible, and it is she who keeps Lenny at the centre of the story. Her actions 'save his sorry ass' as he is betrayed by Max, betrayed by Faith, attacked by rogue police officers and beaten by Philo's hench-persons. Mace is an uncompromised strong woman character, independent, reliable and responsible. Her characterisation is, however, more complex than either of these two points allows. She also has to be seen as an African-American woman, and as a single mother bringing up her son without any help from the boy's father because he is in prison. Since *film noir*, with few exceptions such as *Devil in a Blue Dress* (1995, US), has been predominantly about a white experience of urban culture, the choice to construct Mace's character through a generic tradition which rarely uses *noir* conventions, enables a reading in which the differences of her experiences as an African-American woman are not erased through the simple duality of good versus bad *noir* women, of Mace opposed to Faith.[18]

Like many of the other characters in *Strange Days*, Mace's position in the plot is also contingent on her relationship to the SQUID. Having initially refused to playback any 'porno for wireheads', Mace's inevitable entry into the world of playback has several consequences within the narrative of the film. Whilst issues around a black experience of urban LA resonate through *Strange Days*, much of the narrative remains concerned with the activities of the white people. It shifts from the individual betrayals of white people, and the power that the white establishment controls, towards the threat of chaos caused by the potential of an inner-city riot, whose genesis will lie at the hands of two white policemen. When Mace enters the playback loop, when she watches the murder of Jeriko One as recorded by Iris, through a series of narrative displacements she becomes responsible for preventing the catastrophe of a riot in a city already over-filled with people wanting to celebrate 2K. This passing on of responsibility is made explicit in two different moments. The first occurs when Max asks her if she wants to be held accountable for provoking a riot by leaking the clip of Jeriko's death to the media. Similarly, at the New Millennium party, Mace persuades Lenny that the information on the clip is more important than his self-centred focus on Faith. But having done so, it becomes her job to hand it over to the white establishment, personified in the white chief of police. Mace's narrative function is, then, a double act, a double act that engenders a dislocation of culpability. When Mace is finally aligned with the technology of the SQUID, when she enters the playback loop and acquires knowledge through the SQUID, she problematically becomes the locus of responsibility for whether or not social disorder will occur, regardless of where such responsibilities might really lie. One of the contradictions of *Strange Days* is that this is exactly the message of Jeriko One's music, that the whites are forcing African-Americans to take the blame for something which is not solely within their control: 'and you try to make me think I did this to myself, when the drugs I smoke and the guns I tote both came from *your* shelf'.

Mace's place in this series of displacements is also another incidence of the ways in which patterns of connections can be territorialised in the intersections between humans and technologies. Seen through this perspective, Mace operates differently to the other characters of *Strange Days*. Whilst the activities of Max, Lenny and Philo establish a set of different systems upon which the social meanings of the SQUID technology are contingent, they also remain locked inside the connections of these individual systems. Mace, however, functions as a figure that can forge a new territory of connections across the different systems, breaking down their boundaries. Initially in *Strange Days*, Mace refuses the possible intersections provided through the social and economic circuits of the hustle played out by Lenny, or the paranoia played out by Philo. But, even whilst she does not use it, she can never escape the presence of the technology, as it affects her through the social and economic formations which assemble around it. In finally entering into the playback loop, Mace puts into play yet another potential set of connections, ones which this time include not the personal dramas of Lenny, but a broader context of police corruption and the question of justice. In establishing this alternative set of connections, Mace also alters the social meaning of the SQUID, gives it another set of dimensions. Instead of always being linked to the negative, the information obtained from the SQUID has the potential to be of a broader social use. Mace's relationship to the changing intersections of elements breaks the tendency within *Strange Days* to place the SQUID technology as a deterministic presence, deterministic in the sense that Lenny, Max and Philo all become trapped by and dependent on the operations of the technology, as it functions within their particular system. In contrast, Mace's actions disrupt these individual systems, ensuring that the potential technological determinism of the SQUID is destabilised and open to other territorialisations. In spite of the uncertainty that Mace introduces, however, *Strange Days* does attempt to opt for a kiss and close resolution. In closing on Mace and Lenny's kiss against the backdrop of the Millennial Party, the circuits which have lead to the information about Jeriko's death being given over to the authorities also lead to the romantic closure of the film, displacing, or at least attempting to displace, any uncertainty in what might have been seen, said or done. Of course, the kiss might be read as ironic.

Transformations without endings

In *Strange Days*, the connections created through the relationships between humans and technologies appear to reach toward some form of closure, one enforced through the resolution of the film. As the clip of Jeriko's death is passed onto the police authorities, the shifting territorialisation of the systems appears to restablise, to lock down the potential to keep changing. In the final section of this chapter *Fresh Kill* is introduced as another text viewed through the perspective of systems established through the interconnections between humans and technologies. However, it is different to *Strange Days* in two ways. First, it does not have a simple closure, ensuring that the potential for transformations and negotiations remains active. Second, the use of technologies in *Fresh Kill* is central to the strategies played out by sets of different and frequently oppositional groupings. As such, the technologies can be more easily perceived as an active element in the construction of systems, something which is only implied in the *Gremlin* films or *Strange Days*, where the technologies are already located before they are renegotiated within the narrative of the film. By contrast, in *Fresh*

Kill the processes by which technologies initially become embedded in social practices are always visible.

Fresh Kill is a video-feature, and a very distinctive one at that. Visually striking, with a strong use of deep tones of red, green and blue, its range of references is broad – from melodrama to minimalism; from cybertech to Borges; and from formalistic shots to commercial breakins. The editing crosscuts between an array of different events to create a complex and at times disorienting narrative progression, a progression that is variously passionate, humorous and sometimes cold.[19] As the director and producer, Shu Lea Cheang, describes it:

> There was a certain political agenda we wanted to deal with, in terms of media and environmental racism. That environmental racism was manifested in the transport of industrial toxic waste to Third World countries. Right from the beginning, we made a parallel between the waste and the dumping of garbage t.v. programs into Third World countries. Basically, once that was constructed, it seemed like we kept on making parallels. You have First World/Third World, then you have New York/Staten Island, and even within New York City you have 'Tent City' (a makeshift community of homeless people) as a kind of garbage dump. We set up a bunch of characters with the intention of trying to reverse stereotypes. Right from the beginning we wanted to have this Asian hacker, who was also this really quiet sushi chef, a lesbian couple … There were all these pre-set characters we wanted to put into the landscape. (ellipsis in original)[20]

My interest in *Fresh Kill* arises from the ways in which the narrative elements discussed in the above quotation – pollution, waste and dumping, the control of media technologies, and the characters – are arranged in relation to one another. *Fresh Kill* is a text in which the narrative or narratives are organised around a series of distinct groupings, all of which occupy separate spatial locations. The connections between these groupings are primarily established through the variety of media technologies used by the different characters within the text, rather than through interactions which occur when the characters occupy the same physical space. In *Fresh Kill* the motivation for the making and unmaking of these connections involves a series of political strategies in relation to pollution; such connections are the means by which the opposing groups both come into conflict with one another and resist one another's operations.

These narrative intersections are established across the initially dislocated social spaces of *Fresh Kill* – which include the NagaSaki (a sushi bar), Los Gatos (a village on the Pacific Coast), the home of Jiannbin, and also that of Claire, Shareen and Honey. Each of these spaces, or systems, is distinct, occupying its own section of the narrative, but they also intersect with each other, expanding the narrative spaces in a way that does not rely on any necessary linearity of progression. For instance, Claire (who waits tables at the NagaSaki), Shareen and Honey (Claire's daughter) form a family unit. This family is described in terms of the lesbian relationship between Claire and Shareen, and the domestic relationship between Claire, Shareen and Honey, as well as the location of where they live, and what they do for work and play. It is also described through a series of extensions beyond that discrete location to Mimi (Claire's mother) and Clayton (Shareen's father). These extensions establish another story about extended family relations. Claire, Shareen and Honey's space is also expanded into the theme about pollution. Honey is contaminated by the gifts of Yamakazoo from Jiannbin, who works with Claire as the chef at Naga Saki. The different spaces of the narrative, whether it be the NagaSaki, Tent City, Jiannbin's or Claire and Shareen's home, can be seen as multiple centres of focus within the narrative. Each of these centres of focus is a location from which potential narrative elements emerge, elements which in turn can create a network of connections. The elements, which can be multiple or singular, cohere at different points into a textual organisation created by a network of linkages, instead of a more singular cause-and-effect relationship.[21]

A central theme of *Fresh Kill* is pollution, which is presented as something that occurs throughout the world, and in many different ways. Various instances include: the trash barge taking New York City's waste ('17 tonnes a day') to the Staten Island landfill site known as Fresh Kills; a barge of toxic chemical waste seeking a docking site in Africa; disintegrating H-bombs in the ocean; illegal dumping of radioactive waste in the Pacific fishing waters off the US coast. Less toxically, Shareen's work is based around clearance and redistribution of people's excess furniture and televisions. The problem of pollution, as well as being an event within *Fresh Kill*, is one of the elements that creates a linking device between the different groups of the film – Claire, Shareen and Honey; Jiannbin and Miguel; Mimi; the African Unity Network; GX; and Stuart Sterling. Or to put in another way, the linking device of pollution establishes a territory within which sets of systems interact with each other. As

I have already suggested, each of these groups or systems occupies a distinct narrative location, and in some cases a separate physical space. However, the activities of these groups come together to create a site of action within the narrative. These systems, then, are not simply constituted by the practices of people within a particular location; rather, their existence is constituted and mediated through technologies such as the Internet, radio and television.

In *Fresh Kill* one such site of action operates around the market-place. Although never visible as a particular location within the text, the marketplace is primarily constituted through representative figures from two distinct groupings. Roger Bailey, the director of the transnational company GX, represents the first grouping. The system of GX is depicted within *Fresh Kill* through a series of montage sequences that indicate the extent of its influence. The company is involved in nuclear power production, news production, adver-tisements, telecommunications, cat food and breakfast cereals. These montage sequences also operate as advert breakins into the lives of the television-watching characters within the narrative. As such they are examples of media technologies being mobilised to mediate GX's message to the public within the story-world of *Fresh Kill*. The eco-nomic effectiveness of this media campaign can be gauged through a second group of characters associated with Stuart Sterling, an aptly named stock trader. As dealers and traders on the stock market who talk about nothing but share prices, they act as indices for the success of GX. The intersections of these two systems provide one of the dimensions of the textual organisation of *Fresh Kill*; if GX is suc-cessful in its market operations then Sterling will tell his friends to buy GX shares. Taken together, the GX/Sterling interaction portrays the profit-making orientation of the marketplace.

The intersection between GX/Sterling and media technologies, in particular television, is central to the advertising strategies of GX, and as such they operate as an element in the social practices of the cor-poration. Connections that enable linkages between social practices and technologies are evident in other ways within *Fresh Kill*. Taking as an example the American Communication Corporation (ACC), when this newscasting corporation first appears within *Fresh Kill* it presents a series of stories questioning the problem of pollution. These include a rotting H-bomb off the coast of Okanawa, serious pollution of fishing waters off the coast of California, and a barge of toxic waste seeking a port off the coast of Africa. The interweaving of these newscasts into the story-world of *Fresh Kill* implicitly attaches the different acts of pollution to one another, forming a territory of connections between global pollution and the more local pollution on Staten Island. Each circumstance of pollution is initially isolated, but when they are mobilised by different characters and connected by the media technologies, a larger political space is created. Once ACC is acquired by GX, an event that alters the territorialisation of ACC (causing it to be referred to as American Control Conspiracy), there ensues a new alignment across the spatial organisation of individual systems and their associated groups and technologies. ACC's broadcasts are, through their association with GX, reoriented towards the power field of the economic interests of GX.

However, ACC is not the only source of new information, and a counterpoint to the mainstream newscasting corporation is public access television. Mimi Mayakovsky, Claire's mother, runs the program *Yours Truly Mimi* which solicits calls from the public, and in doing so broadcasts a different set of perspectives, thus providing a competing site of technological interaction. At the outset of the video-feature, the concerns about pollution aired through Mimi's broadcasts are local ones around the Staten Island landfill site. However, they expand to include the question of Los Gatos (the village affected by offshore pollution) once that far-off contamination begins to impinge on the lives of the people in Manhattan and Staten Island. This occurs when either people, or their cats, consume fish poisoned by toxic waste. Between them, ACC News and *Yours Truly Mimi* both use media technologies as part of a social space within which the question of pollution can be negotiated. The contingency of this intersection is made clear when Mimi's programme is taken off-air. Again, the controlling power of GX is exerted in an attempt to orient the media technology towards their perspective, an act of resistance against the activist groups that question their authority.

Another technology through which competing groups operate within *Fresh Kill* is the Internet. Jiannbin Lui possesses a computer system that gives him access to the Internet. A hacker, he displays his skills when he breaks into an on-line shopping site. These skills are later deployed when Jiannbin hacks into GX's system and steals information from their 'Central Data' store. In addition to the interaction between Jiannbin and GX over the Internet, a global connection is established through the deployment of this technology by the African Unity Network (AUN). The AUN introduces yet another system into the territory established around the theme of pollution as it sends activist messages around the global communication networks concerning the dumping of waste in Africa by Western countries. Not only do the AUN make use of the Internet but they also deploy satellite technology when they break into the transmission of newscasts from ACC. This competition over the control of the airwaves is played out in a series of images from Tent City. Tent City is a place where homeless people live, and the place where Shareen brings all the televisions that she collects. These televisions are stacked up, forming a wall of screens on which the competition between transmissions is visible. GX, the AUN and ACC break into each other's broadcasts, and their different words and images compete and collide and collide again. This competition is taken further when Mimi and Claire also break onto the air, after having got into the ACC studios.

From these perspectives, the media technologies in *Fresh Kill* can be seen as elements put into motion by the different and competing groups of the narrative, their interplay of activities assembling as an interplay of resistant systems. By resistances, I do not simply mean a conventionally understood opposition between two groups; rather, resistance is used to mean a series of movements and countermovements made by competing sets of groups. Such movements are a part of the relationships established between social practices and technoscience; never simply progressive or repressive, they are an interplay or negotiation between the two. Resistance, then, is not simply a radical form of action against a dominating force (whether that be economic, military, textual, cultural, political); rather, resistance is a counterpositioning, something which can be radical, but which equally can be reactionary. This definition implies an on-goingness in which movements of resistance are unstable and dynamic, and always in process. From such a perspective, the media technologies are not simply allied to either an oppressive dimension such as GX, or one that seeks to resist such oppression such as the AUN; they are mobilised by *all* groups. To a certain extent, these media technologies function in a similar way to a cyborg. They can be understood as mediating the relationships between individuals/ groups, in the sense that they do not simply operate as a vehicle with which to deliver a message, but become a constituent feature of how that message is conceived and delivered. This notion of cyborg draws on Donna Haraway's influential essay 'A Manifesto for Cyborgs'. Here Haraway states:

[Cyborg imagery] ... means refusing an anti-science metaphysics, a demonology of technology, and so means embracing the skilful task of reconstructing the boundaries of daily life, in partial connection with others, in communication with all of our parts. It is not just that science and technology are possible means of great human satisfaction, as well as a matrix of complex dominations. Cyborg imagery can suggest a way out of the maze of dualisms in which we have explained our bodies and our tools to ourselves.[22]

This reading of *Fresh Kill*, through its attempts to articulate the multidimensional relationship between humans and technologies, moves beyond a simple set of dualisms. In doing so, it touches on an aspect of the cyborg which is sometimes overlooked in the theoretical gestures towards the cyborg as site of political renewal. That is, the cyborg is open to appropriation by anyone who has the means (financial, technological or imaginative), whatever their alignment with radical or conservative positions. Like the technologies of *Fresh Kill*, the cyborg has the potential to be constructive, instructive and/or destructive.

The technologies of telecommunications and the Internet seen in *Fresh Kill* can be understood as elements that give substance to a territory, a territory where the expansionist designs of a transglobal corporation such as GX can be intersected by the systems of oppositional group(s). In themselves these groups do not create the space of negotiation, but do so through the mobilisation of the additional components of technology. In this way a virtual space is created, a space through which the humans and technologies operate together. Technology here is not simply a medium by which a message is delivered; it makes possible the negotiation. Each of these negotiations is, however, limited by its intersection with other systems, which may be economic, political, exploitative or regenerative. Technologically enhanced resistances, when spatialised in this way, reveal their contingencies. Actions cease to be events that gain meanings from a single site (groups or individuals); instead they are only components in a complex and on-going negotiation.

Gremlins, *Gremlins 2*, *Strange Days* and *Fresh Kill* explore the relationships established between humans and technologies. They can be read as texts that refuse simple dualisms between good versus bad, and instead envision patterns of connections and reconnections. In *Gremlins* and *Gremlins 2*, whilst the possibilities for the reorganisation of elements are explored through the emergence of the chaotic figure of the Creature, ultimately these reorganisations remain contained within a discrete system – the Clamp Building or Kingston Falls. *Strange Days* presents the processes of reorganisation in a more complex way. In this text the central technology of the narrative, the SQUID device, is embedded in a series of systems, each of which contributes to it different social meanings. The shifting territorialisations across these systems that are introduced by Mace have the potential to provide a sense of contingency; however, this contingency is displaced in the romantic resolution between Mace and Lenny. In contrast in *Fresh Kill*, where the technologies can be seen to be active elements in the intersections between humans and technologies, the space of negotiation remains a shifting one. The processes of territorialisation evident in this video-feature give an account of the inclusions and exclusions that make up the construction of a space of negotiation, but this is a construction that remains contingent. The anti-pollution grouping may finally damage the expansionist activities of GX, but this damage is not lethal, as its outcome is only a resistant reorganisation of the elements aligned with GX. The on-goingness of such processes can be seen in the operations of Stuart Sterling. He begins the narrative associated with the economic benefits derived from the market strategies of GX, and ends the film associated with the economic benefits derived from the green economy. In *Fresh Kill* a cynical view is taken of this transition. Sterling is presented as exploiting the green economy, as much as he had exploited the stock market. Initially a part of the GX-controlled system of the intersecting elements, he shifts systems, or rather his shift in orientation territorialises another system, one that is constituted by the components of the green economy. Since one of Stuart Sterling's primary functions is defined through his successful financial activities, there is in the end little difference between the green economy and the stock market. As Sterling says: 'The Earth's worth saving, but there's no excuse for not making a profit.' *Fresh Kill*, then, constructs sets of relationships that are always shifting, constantly making and remaking connections across which boundaries of power and control intersect.

This third chapter is a turning point in the progression of my argument about fictions of technoscience. To this point, I have developed a series of positions around images of science and technology which all depend on an idea of contingency. In the final two chapters of *Technoscience in Contemporary Films* I begin to raise questions about the limits of these positions. In particular, I am interested in exploring the extent to which contingency can only capture some of the meanings of technoscience.

Notes

1 John Law, 'Technology and Heterogeneous Engineering: The Case of Portuguese Expansion', in Wiebe E. Bijker, Thomas P. Hughes and Trevor Pinch (eds.), *The Social Construction of Technological Systems: New Directions in the Sociology and History of Technology* (Cambridge, Mass.: The MIT Press, 1987) pp. 111–134.

2 Gilles Deleuze and Félix Guattari, *A Thousand Plateaus: Capitalism and Schizophrenia* (London: The Athlone Press, 1988) pp. 332–337.

3 A similar point about renegotiation, or cycles and circuits, is made by Nick Dyer-Witheford in his discussion of high-technology capitalism. Nick Dyer-Witheford, *Cyber-Marx: Cycles and Circuits of Struggles in High-Technology Capitalism* (Urbana and Chicago: University of Illinois Press, 1999).

4 *Webster's* Dictionary indicates that the use of the word gremlin to mean a malfunction originated in the US airforce during the Second World War. The gremlin was thought to be a goblin-like figure which inhabited machinery. The *Oxford English Dictionary* provides a similar definition of the word gremlin, but attributes its origin to the British Royal Air Force, possibly as early as the First World War.

5 As a slang term for a gadget, Gizmo is another allusion to technologies.

6 In 'Eating the Other', bell hooks discusses the consumption of ethnic and racial identities as a form of commodifcation by a white culture that is seeking difference. bell hooks, *Black Looks: Race and Representation* (London: Turnaround Books, 1992) pp. 21-39.

7 The lack of distinction between the laboratory coats and the rest of the workers in Clamp Tower indicates the embeddedness of the scientific practices of the laboratory within the corporate domain through which it operates.

8 The image used to suggest the malfunction is specific to the medium in play. In the film version, the celluloid appears to melt, and in the video version the hold or tracking seems to shift. If *Gremlins 2* is brought out on DVD, presumably a suitably specific glitch will be inserted.

9 Andrew Ross, *Strange Weather: Culture, Science and Technology in the Age of Limits* (London: Verso, 1991) p. 3.

10 Andrew Tudor uses the term paranoid to describe horror films in which the monster will clearly return in a sequel. Andrew Tudor, 'Unruly Bodies, Unquiet Minds', *Body and Society*, 1:1 (1995) 25–41.

11 As in *Gremlins*, one duality that remains intact within *Gremlins 2*, even if it is ironic, is the gender duality. Whilst Billy runs around inside the

building and Daniel Clamp organises help from the outside, Kate and
Marla remain very much on the side-lines. Marla clearly has her generic
antecedents as she plays up her redheadedness to perfection, whilst also
being a boss. However, once the Creatures take over she either gets
trapped in a spider's web, or simply has to follow Billy's orders. Being
trapped in a spider's web is itself a reversal of the myth of the giant
female spider trapping the unsuspecting would-be hero. Kate is similarly
side-lined as she becomes a parody of her earlier role in *Gremlins* in
which she told the story of her father's death. Whenever she gets the
look that indicates a painful reminiscence she is constantly told, not now.

12 During this sequence, one of the Creatures can be glimpsed reading *The
Double Helix*. This is a narrative of the discovery of the structure of
DNA, and it is still one of the most popularly known versions of that
event. James D. Watson, *The Double Helix: A Personal Account of the
Discovery of DNA* (London: Weidenfeld and Nicolson, 1968).

13 The laboratory scenes invoke a whole series of horror films, not least
through the casting of Christopher Lee as Dr Catheter, a man who collects diseases and *Invasion of the Body Snatchers* style pods. Throughout
both *Gremlins* and *Gremlins 2* there are numerous intertextual references, not only in the use of clips from other films, but in the visual jokes,
such as the alien-style creature pods and the vampire-like gremlin death
scenes, but also snatches of dialogue such as 'the horror, the horror'.

14 The narrative device of hooking up a visualising technology in order to
enable the wearer to see themselves being murdered is also used in *La
Cité des enfants perdue* (1995, Fr) released in the same year as *Strange
Days*.

15 The SQUID technology is similar to the technology presented in *Brainstorm* (1984). The narrative of *Brainstorm* is more concerned than
Strange Days is with the development of the technology in terms of a
clash between the military and the scientists involved in its invention.
Like *Strange Days*, *Brainstorm* spends a substantial amount of narrative
space on the capabilities of the technology, its use as a visual technology
as well as other senses such as taste, hearing and touch.

16 A particularly strong resonance, as others have already pointed out, is
with the Rodney King case.

17 The conventions of action heroes are discussed by Yvonne Tasker in
Spectacular Bodies: Gender, Genre and the Action Cinema (London and
New York: Routledge, 1993).

18 There appears, however, to be a comparison being made between good
and bad action women, through a visual echoing between Vida, Philo's
white woman bodyguad who has dreads, and Mace, who also has dreads.
Vida, who seems little short of psychotic, is contrasted with Mace in the
scenes where the latter saves Lenny from a beating. In this fight sequence,

the movement of both women's dreads features as part of the movement of the images, seemingly captured in slow motion. Here, as is often the case in *Strange Days*, blackness is aligned with the heroic saviour figure, whilst whiteness is aligned with aggressive violence.

19 In an interview about *Fresh Kill* with Lawrence Chua, the director Shu Lea Cheang discusses this aspect of the editing. 'I tell people if they too confused, they should hink about it as someone switching tv channels behind your back. At the same time, people have been finding that it's not passive viewing ... You have to work on it to get that story'. Shu Lea Cheang and Jessica Hagedorn interviewed by Lawrence Chua: http://www.echonyc.com/~freshkill/interview.html.

20 Shu Lea Cheang in interview, *ibid*.

21 Such a perspective on a textual organisation is here influenced by the ideas of Deleuze and Guattari, as already discussed earlier in this chapter. It also owes something to Andrew Gibson's *Towards a Postmodern Theory of Narrative* (Edinburgh: Edinburgh University Press, 1996), a work which also draws on former theorists' writings.

22 Donna Haraway, 'A Manifesto for Cyborgs', in Donna J. Haraway (ed.), *Simians, Cyborgs and Women: The Reinvention of Nature* (London: Free Association Books, 1991) p. 181.

4

It's alive!

Out in the woods, in the middle of the night, Hogarth Hughes finds an Iron Giant. The Iron Giant is an alien creature fallen from outer space, and hungry for metal, roams around Maine eating cars, television aerials and grain silos. It is whilst the Giant is eating the local power relay station that it is discovered by Hogarth, a meeting which leads to a friendship between the two. Hogarth and the Giant are characters in *The Iron Giant* (1999, US), a cartoon feature made for a younger audience.[1] Set in the US in 1957, the friendship between the Giant, an alien technological being, and Hogarth, a young white boy, is placed in the context of a period marked by fears about the effects of technologies, and also of communism. Within the story-world of *The Iron Giant*, 1957 is a time when communities lived with the threat of atomic blasts, duck and cover information films for children, horror movies in which the scientist is attacked by his creation, and also, *Sputnik*. Indeed, the first image of the cartoon is of the *Sputnik*, its star and sickle clearly in view as it circles high above the Earth.

The Iron Giant brings together two key moments, one cinematic and the other historic. The cinematic moment is 1950s SF cinema, a period featuring alien invasion narratives, stories about the side-effects of radiation, and other manifestations of science and technology gone wrong. Various film critics have argued that this period of SF captures something of the cultural transformations of the 1950s – the Cold War, the Atomic Age, Russians in space before the Americans, and McCarthyism, not to mention the increasing social transformations associated with civil rights campaigns and the increasing affluence of the American middle classes following the Second World War.[2] *The Iron Giant* echoes the concern of these earlier films about the threat of invasion from aliens, where alien is often taken as a metaphor for communism, with its opening emphasis on the historic event of *Sputnik*. In this version of 1957, outer space *is* populated by alien beings and Russian sputniks, and there is nothing American out there. The paranoia this evokes is captured by one character, Kent Mansley, a National Security Agent, who is suspicious of anything which is not American. As he says of the Iron Giant, it is 'foreign and all that implies … we don't know what it is or what it can do'. As such, Mansley stands as a figure who is afraid of something different, so afraid that he would rather see it destroyed than attempt to gain some level of understanding. Hogarth is the counterpoint to Mansley; he likes to watch horror films, eat junk food and read comic books. It is Hogarth who befriends the Giant, 'my own giant robot', and attempts to ensure that it will not frighten the community of Rockwell. In the narrative interplay between Mansley and Hogarth, the technology of the Giant is renegotiated from an alien object greeted with paranoid misunderstanding to a friendly being. This negotiation is conveyed within *The Iron Giant* primarily by anthropomorphising the Giant. Although it is a huge metal object, the Giant is invested with a non-aggressive quality through the use of body language, an affect that is most obvious in its small gestures. Combined with its big white eyes and sad hollow voice, these different elements operate to make the Giant seem like a safe object, and an object which Hogarth insists is a he, and not an it. In the resolution of *The Iron Giant*, the Giant also gains a key condition of being human: the ability to make a choice.

In using the narrative device of making the technology seem little different to humans, *The Iron Giant* reconfigures technology through a succession of different terms more usually associated with humanness – choice, souls and heaven, caring for communities and so forth. This reconfiguration renegotiates the elements which cluster around technology as a pre-programmed or alienating object within the world, and places technology within a territory associated with humanness. By taking this approach, technology is made to seem safer, or more manageable; it is not the difference of technology which is at stake, but instead its similarities. Such an emphasis on the use of similarities to reconfigure a technology as an object less threatening to the human world is a central concern of this chapter. Films such as *Android* (1982, US), *Making Mr Right* (1987, US) and *Alien: Resurrection* (1997, US) manage their technological beings by establishing their similarities with conditions associated with humanness. However, the versions of humanness which are used to manage technology are never neutral ones, they are usually ones defined by the choices available within any given text, as well as the cultural context in which that text is both produced and consumed. Within *The Iron Giant*, the choices through which the Giant can achieve self-definition are limited to the heroes of the comic-strip books which are read by Hogarth: he can only choose between Atomo, a violent technological being, and Superman. The choice for the viewer is equally contingent on the representational strategies of the text. The good and bad figures of the text are the Giant and Mansley, and Mansley's demonisation is carried out as a liberalising gesture. He is the figure who encapsulates paranoia about things that are different and foreign, and he is the figure who is ridiculed in the resolution. But in spite of this tactic, the boundaries of difference actually remain quite unclear in *The Iron Giant*. Although the *Sputnik* references suggest that one boundary is to do with communism and the USSR, others are uncertain. Uncertain because we as viewers do not actually know what 'foreign and all that implies' means, and we may not know where foreign might begin in a small fishing community. The second concern of this chapter, then, is the construction of the categories of humanness used to manage the technologies of the text.

Managing technology

Throughout the previous chapters I have argued that the meanings associated with humanness and technologies can be understood as contingent upon one another. Whilst this position is useful, insofar as it reveals the complex network of intersections that link the two terms, there is a danger in coming to the conclusion that all meanings can be captured in such a network. The tendency towards such a capture of meanings can be seen in films in which there is an attempt to manage technology, to try and make technology fully known using a comparison based on its similarities with humanness. This tendency is clearly evident in *The Iron Giant*, as well as in *D.A.R.Y.L.*, a film discussed in Chapter 2. Daryl could be reconfigured from a technology to a little boy on the basis of his similarities with the human community presented within the text; however, *D.A.R.Y.L.* gave no answer to the question posed within the film about Daryl's difference. The apparent erasure of this difference causes a tension in the text, a tension that draws attention to the ways in which many films manage their technological figures by displacing difference in favour of similarity. This chapter looks at films whose strategy is to manage technology through its alignment with terms associated with humanness, a strategy that is especially evident in texts in which the technological figures look the same as the human figures in the film. The visual alignment of the technology with other humans enables a play on the similarities, rather than on the differences. The purpose of this discussion, however, is not simply to point out where similarities are mobilised to establish an intersection between humans and technologies. It is to indicate where such a strategy fails, and where the possibilities for difference are revealed.

One of the key means by which fictions of technoscience establish a similarity between humanness and technologies is through consciousness. In many cyborg, android and robot films, technology is not simply programmed, but is sophisticated enough to be able to begin to think for itself, and to make decisions and choices of its own.[3] *Blade Runner* (1982, US), *Short Circuit* (1986, US), *Screamers* (1995, Can./US), *The Iron Giant*, as well as the films discussed in this chapter – *Android*, *Making Mr Right* and *Alien: Resurrection* – work on the premise that a technology is able to achieve a level of consciousness – that is, an existence that is predicated on the ability to make intelligent decisions. For such texts, the idea that machines, or other synthetically constructed beings, *can* operate consciously and equivalently to humans is not at issue; rather, the question revolves around how intelligent machines *behave* in ways that are equivalent to humans. How, in other words, synthetically constructed beings appear to be indistinguishable from humans. Discussing consciousness more generally, Colin McGinn states:

> [A] conscious being must either be alive or must resemble what is alive, where the resemblance is between the *behaviour* of the things in question. In other words, only of what behaves *like* a living thing can we say that it is conscious. This claim connects consciousness with life, but not with what constitutes life; rather, with what manifests or expresses it. A non-living thing might therefore in principle qualify for the ascription of consciousness, so long as it behaved like a living conscious thing ... It is presumably because of a tacit acceptance of this idea that we are so prone to count the robots of science-fiction films as conscious beings: they do not live, but they act as if they do. (emphases in original)[4]

McGinn's further comment that 'our concept of a conscious state is
the concept of a state with a certain sort of behavioural *expression*'
is useful when thinking about fictions of technoscience.[5] It suggests
that to be 'human' no longer means simply to be biologically human,
but also to behave in ways which are recognised as human. It is
through this displacement that technologies can be argued to be
equivalent to humans.

However, the claim that technologies can behave as though human,
on the grounds that they operate in a way which resembles what is
human, requires a critical attention towards those behaviours which
are used to link and manage humans and technologies within the same
structure of meaning. These behaviours are not necessarily universal,
even if they may be presented as such. To speak of being human, or
human-like, without falling into foundationalist arguments, requires
an acknowledgement of the specific cultural paradigms from which
the notions of being human are drawn. The films I discuss in this
chapter are based around Western, specifically American concerns;
and additionally, they feature predominantly middle-class and white
characters. Each of these texts presents and validates, or invalidates,
certain ranges of behaviour as appropriate to the condition of being
human. But it does not then follow that these texts provide an
absolute definition of humanness; instead, being human and technological is represented through a series of behaviours that exist in
relation to a set of normative values embedded in social relations.

The critical literature that addresses the cultural paradigms used
in images of technology has primarily been concerned with questions of gender, and to a lesser extent with race and sexualities.
Whilst Janet Bergstrom has discussed the stylised android personae
of *Lookers* (1981, US) and *Liquid Sky* (1982, US) as demonstrations
of how unreliable expectations of 'classical sex roles' have become,
it is more common to find the android persona definitively gendered.[6] In making such a point, Mary Ann Doane states: 'there has
also been a curious but fairly insistent history of representations of
technology that work to fortify – sometimes desperately – conventional understandings of feminine'.[7] In *Technologies of the Gendered
Body* Anne Balsamo also considers how a variety of intersections
between bodies and cultural practices – cyborg imagery, bodybuild-
ing, cosmetic surgery, and virtual bodies – are 'ideologically shaped
by the operation of gender interests ... [and] reinforce traditional
gendered patterns of power and authority'.[8] Whilst both Doane and

Balsamo are particularly interested in looking at images in which technologies and women intersect, there is also a parallel concern about the intersections between men's bodies and technology. Steve Best, for example, discusses *RoboCop* (1987, US) as a text that recuperates a traditional version of male masculinity which has come under threat from feminism.[9] Not all of the critical work, however, sees the intersections between humanness and technologies in the cyborg, android or robot bodies as a conservative reinscription of gender categories. Other critics suggest that such films may also investigate new categories of gender, an argument that is made by Thomas Byers in relation to *Terminator 2*.[10]

In her essay 'Envisioning Cyborgs' Jennifer González takes up an alternative position in relation to the hybrids formed in the physical intersection of humans and technologies.[11] She outlines how the term hybrid is usually taken to mean the combination of two pure elements, but suggests that this notion of purity is one that must be problematised. As González states: 'For if any progress is to be made in a politics of human or cyborg existence, heterogeneity must be taken as a given. It is therefore necessary to imagine a world of composite elements without a notion of purity.'[12] By this she means that the term human is not homogeneous, but is constructed through interacting sets of heterogeneous elements. Putting aside the notion of purity provides a useful means to interrogate the neutrality of the term humanness. For González this is especially important in discussions of race:

> Some see cyborgs and cyberspace as a convenient site for the erasure of questions of racial identity – if signs of difference divide us, the logic goes, then the lack of these signs might create a utopian social-scape of equal representation. However, the problem with this kind of e-race-sure is that it assumes differences between individuals or groups to be primarily superficial – literally skin deep. It also assumes that the status quo is an adequate form of representation.[13]

Keeping in view the heterogeneity of the elements through which humanness is composed as a category is, then, essential. And it follows from this position that the elements through which humanness is constructed within any given moment, or in the context of this study, within any given text, can be understood to be selected through a series of processes, and that there is nothing natural in that process. It is contingent on the politics of the text, the casting, the context of the production, and the moment in which it is made. However, rather than seeing texts only as embedded in the cultural and political processes coincident with their production, and therefore as products through which to read unreflective constructions of gender, race or sexualities, it is possible to see some texts through a different strategy of reading. This strategy involves looking at the ways in which the taking on of humanness by a technological being causes an opening up of a critical distance between the performance of humanness and the versions of gender, sexuality, class and race used to designate that humanness. Anne Balsamo suggests that technology can be a seen as a stage for the enactment of gender.[14] But this staging of gender need not be seen as unproblematically accepting such constructions of humanness. Following Judith Butler, who argues that categories of gender, though always performances and therefore constructions, have through constant repetition come to appear natural, humanness is also performance.[15] The idea of performance keeps in place the possibility that all categories of humanness have in some way become embedded within a history of social, cultural and political practices. Furthermore, the validation and invalidation of those categories needs to be understood as contingent on such practices.

In texts where humanness is a state acquired by or attributed to a technological being, the element of performance is especially foregrounded. If a technology can perform as though it were human to the extent that its difference is either not apparent, or is of little consequence, then any notion of an authentic humanness becomes redundant. Instead, what emerges is that particular categories are validated in the recognition of humanness, whilst other categories are explicitly invalidated. The question then becomes: which categories of humanness are in play in these texts, and how are they validated or invalidated? Through this strategy of reading, *Nell*, *Android*, *Making Mr Right* and *Alien: Resurrection* can be seen as more than representations that resonate with transformations in the social world. Instead, they become texts that reveal which categories of humanness are used to manage and make sense of technologies.

Paula, Jerry and Nell too

Android, *Making Mr Right* and *Alien: Resurrection* all feature a technology that is embodied in a form that can be recognised as mimicking that of human beings. In each case, the android or cyborg has been programmed to function as though human; it has the capacity to acquire intelligence, and so to augment its basic programming by learning about being human. My interest in these films is in how they represent technology as human through the conventions of communication, socialisation, sexuality and violence. These constructions of humanness are not only relevant to questions about how images of technology are managed, they are equally relevant to the understanding of the ways that humans themselves learn to be human, or to be acceptable as human. In relation to this point, before moving on to *Android*, *Making Mr Right* and *Alien: Resurrection* I discuss *Nell*. This may seem an odd choice of film to discuss in conjunction with the other chosen texts, each of which features a technological being. However, *Nell* is similar in that it is concerned with humanness as something that is learnt and performed, rather than simply known or innate.

Nell is set in contemporary rural North Carolina; it gives an account of Nell, a white young woman who has been brought up by her mother in a lakeside cabin without any contact with society.[16] She has never been into a village, town or city, heard live or recorded music, seen a television, or read books, though she has been read the Bible. She has no experience of any kind of contemporary technologies.[17] She also is assumed to have no knowledge of social conventions or of sex, and neither does she speak a language immediately recognisable as English. Central to the narrative of *Nell* is the attempt to establish a communicative connection between Nell and the other human figures. Through this communicative connection she is transformed from a 'creature' to a woman who has lived a different life to the majority of people in the USA. This transformation functions in much the same way as the technologies of *Android*, *Making Mr Right* and *Alien: Resurrection*. That is, Nell is the site at which the social and cultural norms validated within the text come into operation, but her own unconventionality makes such norms seem arbitrary rather than natural.

A central opposition in *Nell* is between a contemporary mode of living and the nostalgic evocation of a life built around an apparently simpler set of choices. The film begins with sweeping panoramic shots of dense lush woodland, an idyllic location whose isolated beauty is broken by the insistent whine of a motorbike engine. This kind of juxtapositioning occurs throughout the film, as the themes of isolation, innocence, contemporary life and simplicity are opposed with each other, with Nell operating as the pivot between the two perspectives. When Nell is first encountered, by Jerome (Jerry) Lovell (the local general practitioner who has been called in to verify her mother's death) she is represented as some kind of other. She cannot be communicated with – she does not understand Jerry, and he cannot understand her. In an attempt to establish some form of connection with Nell, Jerry enlists the help of a psychologist, Dr Paula Olsen, who specialises in people with communication difficulties. The introduction of Paula into the narrative provokes a conflict based around the rights of an individual versus social management. Paula represents a form of social management in which the individual is denied agency, whilst Jerry seeks to ensure that Nell's rights as an individual be maintained. This clash of interests between an individual and a group activates a narrative theme in which two competing investigative approaches are mobilised in order to establish a communicative connection with Nell. Jerry and Paula are placed in a very clear opposition through their different methods of investigation. In a reversal of the traditional dualities of rational/emotional and male/female, Paula, the specialist from the city, is placed in the role of the distanced observer. When Jerry first meets her, she is viewing her research subject, a young girl with behavioural problems, from behind a two-way mirror. In these scenes Paula exemplifies the distanced, observing, traditional scientist. She initially continues with this method once she has relocated to Nell's environment, rigging up a video and audio link-up through which she can observe Nell's behaviour at a distance, even whilst Nell is unaware that she is being watched. Paula here is operating not just as an individual, but also as the representative of the medical and scientific institution that validates her particular approach to an object of study. In contrast to Paula, Jerry is introduced as a doctor for whom the rules of an institution would appear to be a last resort. Although he begins watching over Nell whilst she goes about her chores at night, watching like a voyeur hidden in the woods when she is unaware of his presence, much of his research time is spent in her company. Rather than simply sit back and watch using the distance provided by technology, Jerry takes a more interactive approach, trying to gain her confidence and learn her mode of language through an attempt to mimic and use it. In effect, he learns to see, hear and understand again.[18]

Although Jerry's method of learning Nell's language is apparently less dispassionate than Paula's, ultimately both of their approaches are flawed because they are based on the assumptions of the observers, assumptions that obscure their view of Nell. Their closed thinking reveals their tacit presumption that more modern modes of living provide them with the competence to understand Nell. The absence of any real understanding is exposed when Jerry incorrectly assumes that Nell is communicating *with* him after she responds to his animated telling of a story of his childhood, when she is really only talking *to* him. What occurs between them is not a communication, but an exchange of words that are without shared meanings. Similarly, Paula interprets Nell's gestures into the mirror as an example of her having an 'objective self and a subjective self'. These two instances of misrecognition occur from a misunderstanding of one of Nell's utterances – 'Mai' is misinterpreted as 'me'. Part of the strategy of *Nell* at this point is to give viewers enough visual information to know that both Paula's and Jerry's interpretations are wrong, but not enough to know what Nell's words and actions do mean, so keeping the viewer uncertain. Intercut with the scenes of Nell being investigated are images of two girls playing, images of Nell's memories of her long-dead twin. These intercut scenes convey the information that Nell does have a sense of herself, but a sense of self that has not yet been fully included within the narrative. As viewers, we are denied access to a position of full knowledge, just as the methods of Paula and Jerry initially prove to be inadequate in understanding Nell.

Whilst these oppositional approaches are being played out, so are the questions about how human behaviours come to be validated or invalidated. Nell is a young woman who has not been socialised within contemporary human society. Initially, her fear and grief over her mother's death are misinterpreted as animalistic, and she is visually represented as such. Jerry's first glimpse of Nell is as she hides in the roof beams of a dark room, just before she leaps at him kicking and screaming. In the next scenes she mutters and paces barefoot around a room, framed in the doorway like a caged animal. Toby, the police officer, refers to her as 'that creature'. Nell's lack of ability to communicate in a recognisable form of spoken English further problematises her status as a full human being. If she cannot be communicated with verbally, it is difficult to establish a common ground, a base on which to see her similarities with the larger human community of the USA. This absence of any common ground is reiterated within the early stages of the narrative, when there is a lack of an articulation of Nell's point of view. Throughout the early scenes, she remains spoken about and spoken for, but there is also always the sense that these words are wrong, misdirected. This sense of misdirection emerges more clearly in the images. The majority of the early shots of Nell are of her being looked at, with her activities forming a central spectacle in a way that is similar to the spectacles of technological bodies. In beautiful blue-toned night-time shots, she is seen dancing, chopping wood, swimming naked in the lake, or walking across rocks against a backdrop of a deep orange sunset, surrounded by trees that are reflected in the calm water of the lake. These scenes are set up to enchant; the views of the mountains and lakes, the stillness of the water, the softly filter-toned skies, create Nell's space as one of an extraordinary tranquillity. But none of these sequences provides any insight into Nell; instead, they accumulate images *of* her and the place where she lives.

Nell, as an individual, only begins to emerge within the narrative when Jerry and Paula realise that they have been misunderstanding what she has been saying to them. And once the meaning of her words has become clearer, the three can begin to communicate with each other. Once this common ground of communication is established, her patterns of behaviour and her language are placed within a recognisable framework of human behaviour comprising various kinds of emotion and the capacity for communication. Nell's fear of daylight is explained as a 'deliberately implanted phobia', a strategy used by her mother to protect Nell from being seen and so the potential victim of an assault or rape. Within the narrative this strategy is not treated as irrational, but as an outcome of the rape of Violet Kelty which resulted in her becoming pregnant with Nell and Mai. The images of the two children are also explained, revealing the existence of Nell's dead twin, and the source of her odd language as the shared private language of the two sisters. Through these revelations, Nell's transformation from being a creature to a young woman is ensured as her experience of a series of emotions – fear, grief, pleasure – provides her with a set of circumstances that appear to be similar to the stories of other people's lives. The similarity of these experiences, whilst juxtaposed with her still evident differences, makes her seem less difficult to accommodate as a person with rights and feelings. This accommodation of Nell is furthered once

Jerry and Paula can decipher her speech, allowing her words to be translated into English.

The depiction of Nell as recognisably human because she experiences emotions which are familiar within Western perspectives is, however, as much about the acceptable limits of such emotions, as it is about her having them. Within the worldview of *Nell* – a predominantly white, Southern USA inflected humanism – Nell's position as human is implicitly tied into her learning acceptable codes of behaviour. For instance, her expressions of fear and her pleasure in dancing have to be restrained and retrained through social conventions. She is taught not to be afraid of daylight, and about male bodies, though in a way which is not supposed to be sexual. However, after her encounter with Billy Fisher in the bar, in which he exploits her lack of knowledge about sexualised bodies, Nell is taught about sex. Using a manual she learns about men's and women's sexual bodies, apparently so that she can learn when it is inappropriate to show her body. These elements of the film, in which Nell is taught the right behaviours, suggest that many of the behaviours associated with being human are things learnt, rather than things that are done naturally. The idea that behaviours evolve through learning within the family unit, or equivalent, is also evident in that Nell initially learnt from her mother. Hers was not an unknown language, but the combination of a speech degradation learnt from her mother, who had been paralysed on one side of her face from a stroke, with a private twin language that Nell had developed with her dead twin sister. Nell, then, has learnt to communicate in much the same way as other humans; that is, from the observation and copying of the people around her. Similarly, her behaviour has been learnt through the lessons from her mother, which seem to have been predominantly biblical. However, since these people, her mother and twin, did not conform to the social, linguistic and cultural norms of the people who find her, neither does Nell, until she has learnt about their different ways of living. This intersection, between the family and the social, reveals the competing pressures on the ways in which individuals learn to behave as human.

Although many of Nell's actions are explained through the narrative of the film, some remain unexamined to the extent that they reveal the assumptions underlying the constructions of humanness mobilised by the makers of *Nell*. This is especially true of the constructions of her sexuality and gender. Her learning about the physical act of sex seems to operate to inform her about heterosexuality, as well as to warn her of other people's desire to exploit her body. However, there is nothing within the film to suggest Nell's own sexuality, the desires that she might feel, whatever the orientation they may turn out to have. This apparent sexual purity problematically underpins the construction of Nell as the representative of a different mode of living. There are several other ways in which Nell's humanness is embedded within versions of femininity unquestioningly attributed to women. For instance, Nell's empathy for suffering, either in the case of Mary, the troubled wife of the police officer, or Paula and Jerry when they argue with each other, falls into traditional constructions of gender that *Nell* leaves unquestioned. This seems a little strange in a text that has explicitly raised a question about the origin of gender roles – early in *Nell* Paula's head of section, excited about the prospect of bringing Nell into the Institute, speaks about wanting to know where gender roles come from.

These criticisms of the gender constructions notwithstanding, other elements used to attempt to relocate Nell into the mainstream of contemporary social and cultural norms of the American South are put into question. Rather than simply make Nell a figure who is easily assimilated into the conventions of a modern society, *Nell* does begin to address the problem of being different. Just as the film criticises the way in which Nell is placed as an object to be studied by science, it also criticises the practices through which the media appropriate Nell as a spectacle, a spectacle which can be packaged and sold. The violence done by such an appropriation, of taking something out of one space and placing it in another, even with good intentions, is directly articulated through Nell. In an attempt to protect her once the media arrives, Paula and Jerry take her to the Institute in the city. Her journey in the back of Paula's car, a journey which takes her into unfamiliar spaces, is characterised by Nell's fearful reaction to the noise of the helicopter, the chasing news van, and the huge reflective surfaces of the high-rise offices of the business district of Charlotte. Once at the Institute, Nell's loss of place is made more tangible through the use of images of her dead sister. Utilising again the device of making visible what Nell imagines, inside the hospital Nell 'sees' her sister. Unlike the previous sequences in which Mai has been seen as a healthy young girl, in this sequence she is clearly sick. And as the apparition vanishes, it acts as a symbolic repetition of the loss of Mai when Nell is unable to reach her because of the barrier of a window, a barrier that she has not seen because it is outside of her previous experience. The loss of Mai, which precipitates a crisis in Nell, is more fully repeated when, in another location within the city, Nell continues to grieve within a space that is completely alien to her. A diminutive figure amidst the anonymity of the architecture of a modern city, Nell's view of the tall buildings reflected in a shallow pool of rainwater is a poor echo of the view of tall mountains that she used to have. The flat greyness of the cityscape is reiterated in Nell's eyes, which had previously echoed the blue of the skies of her lakeside home. In this context of alienation, Nell's final images of Mai are not memories; instead, they are a reimagining of her death as Mai walks into the water, vanishing beneath the surface, leaving only a trace of herself behind in a ring of flowers on the surface of the water. These images of a final loss and letting go suggest that Nell's entrance into modern life and her acquisition of the 'right' kinds of humanness is not a release from a rural isolation; rather, it is something that occurs at a great cost to herself.

Mr Right in the making

Nell reveals the ways in which humanness is learnt, and also seeks to validate human community. The films *Making Mr Right* and *Android* use the same tactic to manage the technological beings which appear within the narrative. The repetition of this tactic in a different context, technological bodies instead of human bodies, allows it to be seen more clearly for what it is. That is, the behaviours that come to stand for being human are not absolute attributes, but are subject to the norms of convention particular to cultures, places and histories. In the following discussions of *Making Mr Right*, *Android* and *Alien: Resurrection* I discuss how these attributes are used to make sense of technological beings, and how that process can be seen as attempt to make them manageable and safe.

Making Mr Right features Ulysses, an android that has been created in order to undertake a seven-year journey into deep space, something which a human is considered unable to do because of the psychological effects of isolation and containment. This need to maintain relationships with other people is central to the definition of humanness that runs throughout *Making Mr Right*. The plot of the film revolves around three characters: the Ulysses-Android simply called Ulysses, its creator Jeff Peters and its teacher Frankie Stone. Within the story-world of *Making Mr Right*, the Ulysses-Android is to be socialised, but only to the extent that it will seem less disturbing to humans. The intention here is not to enable Ulysses to pass amongst humans unrecognised as a technology; rather, it is simply to make Ulysses acceptable, a technology with human behaviours as well as a human face. Since the creation of Ulysses as an acceptable social being requires it to acquire aspects of human behaviours, which involves teaching it to be sociable through a particular set of conventions associated with maleness, *Making Mr Right* denaturalises conventions surrounding masculinity even as it reconfigures the technological being into a 'he'. What is acceptable as normal, it becomes clear through a variety of comic interludes, has nothing to do with nature, and everything to do with consensus. This immediately poses the question of whose consensus; within *Making Mr Right* that consensus appears to be one provided by a group of white individuals, male and female, who live a relatively wealthy lifestyle.

The playing out of the processes of Ulysses' socialisation within the narrative of *Making Mr Right* serves several functions. It operates as a double critique of the construction of technological objects as coldly rational and alien to humans, and a critique of male masculinities, in particular, those versions of masculinity in which men are unable to express emotions.[19] It also also plays with certain conventions of female femininity, in particular versions of heterosexual femininity.[20] The opening credit sequence parodies the stereotype of women drivers who do their make-up in their cars (and male drivers who similarly use their electric razors). Driving along a freeway, headed toward a grouping of high rises which characterises the business centre of many US cities, Frankie shaves her legs and armpits, as well as doing her mascara and lipstick. Fun is also made of the joke about what women carry around in their handbags when, like an inquisitive child, Ulysses pulls out the contexts of Frankie's handbag. Rather less playful, however, is the construction of Frankie through the stereotype of the nurturing woman. One of the functions of Frankie within the narrative is to teach both Ulysses and Jeff what they need to know to enable them to get along with other people. And although Dr Ramdis's remark, 'I think a woman would be a good influence on him', appears to be treated with some scepticism by Frankie, this is finally what she does.

The critique of rationality and masculinity which emerges in *Making Mr Right* does so through the establishment of a relationship between Ulysses and Frankie, a relationship that results in their becoming a romantic couple. This device of the romantic couple installs yet another version of humanness within the narrative, the ideal of romantic love. In this context, Frankie doubly fulfils a traditional Western gender role, both as a socialising influence who can teach Ulysses the kinds of 'social graces' he will need, and as one half of a heterosexual couple. The particularities of Frankie's socialising influence revolve around creating a technological figure that can participate within a social framework. Her promotional campaign entails making Ulysses seem less like a sophisticated piece of technological hardware, and more like a sociable being that can perform on network television, appear in magazines and attend fundraising events. This sociability is contrasted with the perspective taken by Ulysses' creators, Chemtech, whose focus is restricted to the functionality of the android. Their publicity video emphasises what a Ulysses-Android can do, that is things which are hazardous to humans – handling toxic chemicals, explosives, radioactivity, and so forth. Frankie's presence serves to bring something different to the persona of Ulysses, a capacity that will make him appear less coldly rational; in other words, something more than the functionality that he already possesses.[21] This gendered role is carried over into the *mise-en-scène* of the text. When Frankie first drives out to the Chemtech site, she passes a series of anonymous concrete buildings without another human being in sight. A high-angled, light-drenched panoramic shot provides a view of wide concrete grey roads which are placed around flat opaque domes, which reveal nothing of what is going on inside them. Frankie, in her bright red car, is by contrast a vibrant presence as she drives amongst these buildings. This play on femininity and vibrancy continues into the scenes inside the Chemtech buildings. The inside of the complex is brightly lit, the walls are either cold blue or shiny stainless steel, with heavy security doors that pneumatically open and close. Such is Ulysses' 'birthplace', as Dr Ramdis, the director of the facility, refers to the robotics laboratory. As in the previous scenes in which her red car contrasted with the grey of the buildings and the road, Frankie's bright clothing provides a significant increase in the colour environment of a laboratory characterised through lab equipment, glassware, luminescent liquids and hazard-suited individuals. Throughout

Making Mr Right, Frankie is presented as a direct visual contrast to these austere and impersonal spaces. The bright reds and yellows of her costumes literally bringing colour into the grey institution, in much the same way as she is meant to enhance Ulysses beyond his functionality.

The constructions of gender mobilised within *Making Mr Right* become more explicit with the introduction of Ulysses creator, Dr Jeff Peters. Jeff has invented Ulysses (as a physical copy of himself) with the intention of using him in the place of humans during long-term space exploration. The scenes between Ulysses and Jeff serve to make a distinction between technologies and humans, one in which technologies are rational, and humans, especially women, are subject to the vagaries of their emotions (this is a distinction that will be reversed in the resolution of the film). Since the aim of the Ulysses Project is to overcome the potential psychological difficulties that a human might encounter during years of isolation in spacecraft, it is unsurprising that Jeff perceives anything which is characteristic of emotion to be antithetical to his plans. And although this kind of positioning clearly and deliberately echoes the rational/emotional and male/female dualities, the character of Jeff is not presented as a figure who simplistically privileges the rational. It becomes clear that Jeff is not only concerned with the emotional life of his project; he is also concerned with his own. Characterised as an inventor who can do wonders with machines, he is a version of a benign mad scientist, as he is brilliant but cannot engage with the humans around him. And in spite of his pejorative remarks about emotions, Jeff's inability to engage with other humans is not presented as a privileging of rationality over emotions. Rather, it is engendered by an inability to know how to communicate with other people; as he admits himself: 'I'm not good with people.' Jeff's construction of Ulysses as a copy of himself is, then, not simply physical, as Ulysses is also a copy of Jeff's emotional existence. However, because his programming has enabled Ulysses to learn about human behaviour without fear of intimacy and vulnerability, he remains unafraid in his communications with people. Thus, he is able to learn about behaviours that his more repressed creator is even unable to consider. And in so doing, he becomes constructed as a technology that is less disturbing because it is more able to closely understand human experiences. This distinction between Jeff and Ulysses reiterates the key condition of being human within *Making Mr Right*, that is, the need to communicate and form relationships. Additionally, it also opens up a distance between the performance of masculinity and the processes by which those masculinities come into being. The view that behaviours are the result of convention is made explicit in a conversation between Ulysses and Frankie. After Ulysses has grabbed Frankie's foot to give it a foot rub, she says to him: 'You know Ulysses, you can't go grabbing people's feet like that' Ulysses asks, 'Why not?' 'Because, it's just isn't done.' 'Why?' 'There are rules for social behaviour ...'.

In many ways, then, *Making Mr Right* frames technologies and humans within the same discourse of gender, and refracts both Ulysses and Jeff through a similar set of issues (that both Ulysses and Jeff are played by the same actor, John Malchovich, reiterates their similarities). Through this process it seems to manage the technological difference of Ulysses, reconfiguring him through codes of masculinity that stress his similarities with the human figures of the text. In itself, this tactic is not a new one, and *Blade Runner* is perhaps the most well known contemporary version of this story. But what is more interesting is that in the closure of the film the difference of Ulysses is neither fully resolved nor erased. Ulysses is presented as a technology that has become both rational and emotional; however, he is not simply allowed to pass as human because he has accumulated experiences of emotions to complement his programming. Although Ulysses has come to *seem* as human as the next human, the resolution in which Ulysses and Frankie are united as a romantic couple does not close off the difference of Ulysses. Unlike many films in which the romantic couple is used to displace contradictions within the text, this couple is very clearly a hybrid one in which the switch between a human and a technology does not occur. That Ulysses experiences some technical difficulties when kissing Frankie reiterates his status as an android, a piece of technological hardware that has learnt to combine rationality with emotions. This re-establishment of Ulysses's 'androidness' enables a displacement of the conventional heterosexual romantic closure of the film, a displacement which has tended to be resisted throughout the workings of the text by making Ulysses seem like a human male, right down to his having a penis. Finally, however, Ulysses is not a human male, and Frankie Stone, or Frankenstein, has been able to tame the monster *and* will take it to her bed, an event that makes Ulysses a queer bedfellow. This undercutting of the romantic closure's potential to

fully assimilate the technology of the Ulysses-Android into an acceptable version of heterosexual masculinity is intensified by Jeff Peters
taking Ulysses's place on the space mission. As *Making Mr Right* does
not completely erase the difference between humanness and technology, it also does not erase the existence of different kinds of masculinity. The masculinity embodied in the character of Jeff Peters,
one that is afraid of intimacy and has difficulty in participating in the
most validated version of humanness in *Making Mr Right* – the capacity to communicate and be a part of a community – cannot be simply
changed in a happy ending, so he is sent into outer space.

As the end-credits roll to the Turtles version of 'Happy Together',
it becomes apparent that there are two ways in which humans
and technologies can be happy together. But only one of these is
validated within the text. Through the couple of Frankie and
Ulysses, queer though it may actually be, the human–technology
relationship that establishes communication and inclusiveness is
celebrated through the terms of romance, love, sex, friendship.
The other version of this relationship, the one that is predicated
on distance, but which is equally based on conditions of being
human – of feeling alienated, afraid, suspicious, all of which
involve the hurt and miscommunications of an outsider – is set aside.
However, in closing on the figure of the outsider, this setting aside
serves as a reminder that there is heterogeneity in the constructions of both humans and technologies, and this cannot always be so
easily managed.

Androids in space

Between them, *Nell* and *Making Mr Right* construct a version of
humanness which is based not only in the particular communities
which appear in those texts, but also on the apparently universal
conditions of community, communication and love. The theme of
community is also evident in *Android*, but it is placed in a context of
violence, rather than love and communication. *Android* is set on a
space station where the enigmatic Dr Daniel is attempting to create
the perfect android. Sharing the space of the station is Max 404, an
early model android known simply as Max, who appears to be male.
The routines of Dr Daniel and Max are altered by the arrival of a
group of escaped convicts who take refuge on the space station. Like
Blade Runner, which was released in the same year, *Android* can be

read as a contemplation on what it means to be human. Commenting on both films J.P. Telotte suggests that:

> [W]orks like *Blade Runner* and *Android* articulate a simple yet ever more pressing question: what does it mean to be human in the modern world? And the response they offer is often a relative or comparative one, a response that looks at our own *in*human practices and thus sees the artificial being not so much as a menace but as a potential aid in drawing us back to a sense of humanity.[22]

Telotte here is suggesting that the engineered figures of texts, the replicants and the androids of *Blade Runner* and *Android*, enable a thinking about the modern condition of being human, where the key terms of being human are not blood, flesh and bones, but sets of practices or behaviours. But for Telotte these artificial figures seem to have little to say about the circumstances of being technological, serving instead as an 'aid in drawing us back to a sense of humanity'. Whilst I agree that *Android* (and *Blade Runner*) do look at human practices, both also reveal much about the images of technological beings. These images in *Android*, however, are more ambivalent than those which appear in *Making Mr Right*. In the latter film, Ulysses was the only technological figure, and he was set up to be the 'nice guy' of the text. By contrast, in *Android* there are several technological figures within the text, each of which operates in a different way, providing a more complex construction of technology.

Variously described as low-budget, generic SF, cult and avantgarde, *Android* is a bleakly humorous meditation on human and technological conditions. The story centres on the android Max, and introduces him through his experience of the very human state of loneliness on a space station. In the film's opening scenes, when it is not yet obvious that Max is an android, his isolation is emphasised by his surroundings of computers and monitor screens. Max's communication with the other occupant of the space station, Dr Daniel, only occurs through the mediation of an intercom, further underlining his isolation. The final image of this opening sequence, one that is repeated several times within the film, is a long shot of the darkened room with Max alone in the distance. The depth of the perspective is enhanced by the arrangement of the columns of computer hardware, which echo the monolith shapes of *2001*. In this isolated environment, Max feeds his fascination with humans through a consumption of twentieth-century human artefacts, including films, video games

and teaching tapes. This use of popular culture as a resource by which
a non-human can learn about being human is common to several
films including *The Man Who Fell to Earth* (1976, UK), *D.A.R.Y.L.*
and more latterly *Species* (1995, US). It is a device that again accentuates the denaturalisation of human behaviours. Not only can a
technological being be seen to learn to behave as though human, but
it can do so via the mediation of images of humanness which are
themselves clearly constructions. Max does not learn from experiences accumulated through contact with human figures, as occurred
in *Nell* and *Making Mr Right*; instead, he acquires information from
images of human behaviour in order to simulate human behaviour.
But *Android* goes further than only suggesting that images of humanness can provide a template of behaviours usually associated with
humanness, it also shows constructions of humanness being used to
make sense of the behaviours of characters – Max makes sense of
Daniel's actions by comparing him to the 'evil' inventor Rotwang in
Metropolis. Constructions of humanness, then, are not only devices
from which to mimic human behaviour, they are equally devices
which place behaviours in a context, and so give them meanings.
Again, there is nothing natural in any of this.

     With the arrival on the space station of the escaped convicts,
Maggie, Gunther and Mendez, Max has the opportunity to expand
the influences through which he has learnt to perform human behaviour. Prior to their arrival, he had the routine of his work for
Dr Daniel, and the unchanging repetitions of old films and videos,
as well as the songs to which he has listened. In contrast, the new
figures bring with them elements of unpredictability, something that
is alien to the rationalised and technological worldview that has
been Max's experience. But not only do they bring unpredictability,
they also bring violence, the antithesis of the images of humanness
in which Max has immersed himself. Mendez, the physically largest
male, constantly moves around, visibly seething with discontent and
aggression. Gunther, a slighter figure, represents a more thoughtful,
though equally violent, masculinity.[23] Maggie is also a violent figure,
though coded differently to either Mendez or Gunther. Like Gunther, she is a thinker, but she figures differently as she is also the
centre of the sexual tensions of *Android*. Max, who has never seen
a woman, is fascinated by her; Mendez, as the dominant male,
operates as though he owns her physically, killing and probably
raping her when she refuses him sex. In addition, Daniel wants to

make use of her in his experiments to activate his female android, Cassandra.

Through his intersections with the unpredictable Mendez, Maggie and Gunther, Max becomes more humanised, at least within the parameters set up by the film. Initially, he is a hesitant, seemingly innocent figure, but also one who is beginning to rebel against the authorities that surround him. This rebellion takes on a more tangible form with the arrival of the humans, and in particular Maggie. Not only will her presence on the station enable the activation of Cassandra, but she also seems to activate Max's capacity for sexual desire. Max, programmed to learn and perform complex patterns of behaviour, like Ulysses in *Making Mr Right*, begins to act out an attraction for Maggie. This acting out is intertwined with a second narrative strand, one in which Daniel wants Maggie to enable his activation of Cassandra, an event that Max associates with his termination. The two narrative strands come together in a distorted version of heterosexual humanness in which two males compete with each other for an available woman, with Max perceiving Daniel as a threat to both his desires and himself. As a consequence of this, *Android* can mobilise traits not usually associated with rationality, such as petulance and jealousy, when Max destroys Daniel's prized orchids and begins to associate him with the villain of *Metropolis*.[24] At the same time that Max becomes caught up in his desire for Maggie, he begins to lose his definition as a technological being, and is instead reconfigured with a range of human-like behaviours.

Through the dynamics of his relationships with the other characters of the film, Max is represented as a technology that has acquired the behaviours associated with humanness, such as decision-making, anger, jealousy, self-preservation, sexual desire, petulance and pleasure. But unlike the learnt behaviours in *Nell* and *Making Mr Right*, not all of these are validated within the text; this combination of validated and invalidated aspects of humanness makes Max an ambivalent image of a technological being, and not one that is simply managed. This ambivalence is most evident in Max's capacity to act violently. In many ways *Android* seems to oppose Max's lack of knowledge about violence in the world with the menacing violence of Mendez, a character who performs humanness at its most violent and aggressive. When Daniel forces Max to kill Mendez by removing his moral governor, and then giving him an order to carry out, Max seems to be contaminated by the process. The mobility of

Max's expression as Daniel manipulates his neural chips conveys a violation of the former's innocence. And when the voices he hears in his head, as he walks back from killing Mendez, remind him that 'murder is a serious crime, Max', he pauses as though reflecting on what he has been made to do. In these scenes the horror seems to be that this innocent technological figure has taken up the violence of humanness, allowing us, as Telotte says, to look at our own inhuman practices, practices that make murder into a kind of justice. However, there is something else going on in *Android*, something else which does not have an easy explanation, but which makes Max seem more ambivalent than he appears to be in the Mendez murder sequence. Prior to the removal of his moral governor, Max already has the capacity to kill. When the first police patrol arrives at the station, Max uses his defence mechanism to kill the police officers as easily as if he had been playing space invaders. This link is emphasised by the defence grid screen being the same as the one on which he played the video game; the graphic representation of the real target echoes that of the simulated one. Later, when Max is forced to murder Mendez, Daniel's actions seem like a disempowerment of Max, a forcing of him to do something that is against his 'nature'. However, given the previous events, this is not something that is against Max's nature, but rather an action for which he seems to have no motivations of his own. Max, then, accumulates a complex set of attributes as he operates both as killer and as an endearing android. Given this characterisation, *Android* is not only commenting on the modern human condition, but is also presenting an ambiguous image of its central technology.

This ambiguity carries over to other images of technologies within the text. Throughout *Android* there is a play with mimicry, representation and simulation, one that hints at a concern with not being able to know the visible difference between the authentic and the inauthentic human. On one level, *Android* makes fun of the inability of technology to replicate or mimic organic objects. An example of this tendency is the food replicator. Although now a staple of television SF series such as *Star Trek: Deep Space Nine*, the food replicator, the *Chef de Cuisine*, is a chemical computer intended to combine chemicals to simulate the taste of particular foods, but it never actually works. Similarly, just as Max informs Daniel that there are visitors on the station, the bird in Daniel's garden explodes, revealing itself as a mechanical model. Whilst the inauthentic status of the bird and the products of the replicator are made clear, the boundary between the authentic and inauthentic is not always so clearly demarcated. For example, the simulation of space invaders and the killing of the police patrol are represented using the same visual cues, collapsing the distinction between an actual event and an event reproduced on a computer screen. The same lack of distinction is evident in the androids of the film. Until the closing scenes Daniel, the creator of both Max and Cassandra, is presented as though he were human. His android status is only revealed when he is decapitated. Thus, Max and Cassandra's programming as close approximations of humanness are derived not from the human experience of humanness, but from the android experience of humanness. As such, the origins of these experiences remain unclear. That this distinction is not obvious is evident through the continual misrecognition of android for human. Whilst Max's identity as an android is revealed to all but Maggie, Daniel's identity remains human to all but the other androids. This continual misrecognition ensures that authentic human identity is always in question.

In contrast with Max and Daniel, Cassandra remains a technological being whose role within the narrative is relatively obscure. Although only fully activated towards the end of *Android*, her point of view has already been visible. In the two segments where Daniel examines her, there are views of the ceiling that are clearly meant to be from Cassandra's point of view. Although these can be explained by Max's comment that she is already alive, her ability to see into the future is unexplained. Twice Cassandra's view of the ceiling and light fitting is superimposed with a view of Max doing something he has not yet done, but is seen to do later in the narrative – laying the table for Maggie and Daniel's lunch, and finding the torch under Maggie's body. But whilst the mythological Cassandra could never act on what she saw, this technological version does have agency. Her power is initially evident in her refusal to allow Daniel to touch her breasts, and it is her intervention that allows both her and Max to survive at the end of the narrative. What all this might mean remains uncertain within the film, making it easy to suggest that Cassandra as a female android is, unlike Max, unknowable within the framework of *Android* that emphasises the activities of the male characters in its constructions of humanness. As such she could represent the frightening aspect of technology, the one that is too different to be managed through its similarities with humanness. But if Cassandra is read as a figure that is unknowable, she can only be a witness to the constructions of humanness – a witness that carries all the weight of her different gender, which in turn becomes a site into which other differences settle and merge. Cassandra is the unknowable woman and object of desire, the unknowable technology, and an unknowable other that disturbs and then disrupts the domain organised around Daniel and Max. To think of Cassandra in this way, however, closes down any further meanings that she may carry. Simply seeing her as a mark of difference ensures that she has no meanings beyond that difference. And if she is only different to the other figures in the text, she can contribute nothing to the constructions of humanness that the figures in the text generate.

An alternative to seeing Cassandra only as a mark of difference is to view her as a figure who ensures heterogeneity in the constructions of humanness and technologies. Like *Making Mr Right* and *Nell*, *Android* uses the idea of community as a key term in its construction of humanness. Max does not want to be isolated; he desperately wants to be a part of a community, and that is his motivation for going back to Earth. Cassandra shares this desire, saying 'there are more like us on Earth'. In having this need for community Cassandra, like Max, is a technology that shares in one of the definitions of humanness. But where he simply wants to go to Earth, she wants to join others like them, indicating that there may be more than one kind of community on Earth. Through this contrast, Cassandra ensures that the existence of different kinds of community is not erased in a simple opposition between humans and technologies. Instead, humanness and technologies in *Android* can be seen to be composed of sets of heterogeneous elements, not just pure categories.

Images of the new Eve

The majority of films featuring androids, robots and cyborgs, especially those made since 1980, have tended to gender their technological figure as male. Exceptions include, perhaps most famously, *Metropolis*, but also *The Perfect Woman* (1949, UK), and *The Stepford Wives* (1975). A more contemporary selection of films comprise *Blade Runner*, *Running Delilah* (a.k.a. *Cyborg Agent*; 1994) *Eve of Destruction* (1991), *Weird Science* (1985, US), as well as a number of low-budget cyborg films such as the *Cyborg* series, in particular *Cyborg 2* and *3* (1993 and 1995, US). As with the male technological figures, the female technological figures can be seen as performing particular versions of humanness, but with a different emphasis on the gender construction of the technological being. Few of these figures have, however, been central to critical commentaries on the constructions of humanness. Those that have been discussed, including Maria from *Metropolis*, Rachel from *Blade Runner*, and Eve-8 from *Eve of Destruction* have tended instead to be used only to discuss gender.[25] Perhaps this is because the female technological being is constructed in such a way that it is difficult to see beyond the constructions of gender in play within the text. For instance, through the doubling of the characters of Dr Eve Simmonds and Eve-8 as the creator and the created, *Eve of Destruction* enables a dual representation within which the difference between the cyborg and the human marks the divide between what is acceptable behaviour and what is not. But this division operates solely through what is acceptable behaviour for women. As in many films of this kind, the different behaviours of the cyborg and the human double begin with Eve-8's damage. After being damaged by gun-fire, Eve-8 marks out her difference from Eve by recreating her image with a new set of clothes – a red leather jacket and a short black leather dress. This contrasts sharply with the more restrained clothing she had previously worn, a beige business suit with a white shirt, which echoed the clothing favoured by Eve, who, when not in a lab coat, was seen wearing pale cream jumpers, beige wool trousers, long camel coats – items which connote a certain degree of wealth and propriety. The change in image that Eve-8 undertakes emphatically indicates the change in perspective from a woman who displays an anonymous correctness, to one who has little regard for the middle-class social conventions that Eve operates within. Instead, Eve-8 becomes a malfunctioning and gendered technology, a bad daughter, a threatening mother, and a cyborg who has a nuclear device where a human woman would have a womb. In *Eve of Destruction* the presence of the technological being functions wholly within the narrative to demonstrate constructions of gender which are validated and invalidated around a female figure.

A recent addition to the line of female technological beings, however, presents a different kind of construction. The *Alien* series has always featured an android within its narratives, and in the latest – *Alien: Resurrection* – the android is gendered female. And as with the other android figures in the series, when Call first appears in

Alien: Resurrection, there is nothing to set her apart from the other characters. She is simply another of the figures who stands silhouetted against the lights of the *Betty* as they wait to be transferred onto another spaceship, the *Auriga*. But this alignment with the rest of the crew is quickly dissipated when she becomes the figure whose reactions are most often intercut into the narrative actions in which she is not directly participating. A facial reaction, a snort or a comment is edited into the interchange, often making no difference to the event, but nonetheless inserting Call's responses and locating her in the action. Her presence is further emphasised by her positioning, though only through the dialogue, as an object of desire, especially in the eyes of some of her male colleagues. The role that Call plays within the narrative has, however, nothing to do with sex, and everything to do with preventing the spread of the alien creatures. Call, it turns out, has come on this expedition to kill the newly cloned Ripley, and 'make it all stop'.

Like any figure within a film, Call's characterisation accumulates across the different narrative events that structure the progression of the narrative. Even if her motivations remain uncertain, her similarities with the apparently human characters are evident. As she variously performs as angry, fearful, brave, ruthless, and foolhardy in her quest to kill off the aliens, she is incorporated into the dynamics of the other crew members as they form a group to get back to the *Betty*, appearing to be as human or inhuman as the rest of them. Her role as the naive terrorist also tends to confirm her status within a framework of humanness. As a character later says to her: 'I thought synthetics were supposed to be logical, and shit, you're just a psycho girl'. The scene of Call's first confrontation with Ripley reveals the former's naivety, as she seems to believe that she alone can stop everything, a belief that is mocked by the Ripley of *Alien: Resurrection*, one who is not quite the Ripley of the previous films, but is the hybrid human-alien construct No. 8. Call begins this scene apparently in control, and although diminished in size by the vast dimensions of the vessel, she is free to move through the spaceship and gain entry into Ripley's containment chamber. Call's control over events rapidly dissipates when, knife in hand, she leans over Ripley's prone body, but in the moment of Call's hesitation, Ripley asks: 'Well, you going to kill me, or what?' Call's physical advantage of being above Ripley is similarly reversed, when the latter smoothly repositions herself, face to face with Call, and demonstrates that she is not afraid of Call's knife by forcing it through her own hand. The scene closes with Ripley echoing Call's words, 'I can make it stop', before she dismisses her into the arms of the waiting patrol, a gun against her temple. Call's lack of power is further emphasised when the other crew members of the *Betty* override her assertion that Ripley should be left behind, telling her she has no authority here. Paradoxically, it is at such moments of Call's disempowerment that she also begins to be incorporated into the group. The new alliance between the remaining members of the crews of the *Betty* and the *Auriga* plus Ripley, requires that they work together in order to survive the aliens. It is only their collective knowledge that will get them through. Although Call's visual separateness remains apparent, this distinctness is now used to attach elements of humanness to her, rather than to disrupt the cohesion of the group. She is the only crew member to accompany Ripley into the chamber of horror that holds the failed experiments, and goes to comfort to Ripley after having hit Wren, the chief scientist, on her behalf. Call's reactions to the impregnated survivor also suggest a growing investment in individual humans, rather than the greater task of stopping the aliens at any cost.

Taken together, these scenes establish Call's place within the narrative of *Alien: Resurrection* through a set of characteristics which do nothing to locate her as anything other than human. The construction of humanness with which Call intersects, however, is based around a series of heterogeneous elements, and is not a unified position. Between them the group comprises white and black, male and female, fully able-bodied and partially able-bodied. These different figures perform a different range of characteristics that are given a coherency by the desire to survive the creatures, and Call's behaviours do not finally disrupt this grouping. It is Ripley who sits more uncomfortably within the group of potential survivors, since she keeps disrupting its cohesion by acting unexpectedly. This group organisation is evident in the spatial arrangement of the scenes where they find Purvis, the man impregnated with the alien being. When Ripley tells them that he has one inside him, the framing cuts from Ripley and Purvis to the rest of the group. As they discuss it amongst themselves, shots of Call, with Ripley and Purvis out of focus behind her, are intercut with shots of other members of the group, a dynamic that is punctuated by a shot of Purvis as he repeats his question: 'What's inside me?' When they are finally silenced by their inability to respond to Purvis's increasingly desperate repetition of his question, the camera frames the group, with Call in the foreground as she drops her gaze to the ground, before cutting back to Purvis, and then to Ripley. The spatial arrangement of this sequence underlines the positions within the group. The pirates are roughly aligned, and for the moment with Wren, Call is closer to that group than Ripley, who as the hybrid human-alien is set apart, placed next to Purvis, the man who has an alien inside him. In the next sequence, this spatial organisation is reformulated as everyone has to do the same thing, to swim underwater to get to safety. Even Call, so often singled out in some way, remains anonymous within this grouping.

The revelation of Call as an android, then, follows a series of narrative events, each one of which is a crisis around which the characters of the film form and re-form alliances. At each crisis, as the chances of survival get progressively smaller, Call is gradually further incorporated as one of the elements that constitute the group. Her shooting by Wren seems to end all this, and as she falls into the water her apparent death is marked by Vriess's cry of anger. However, the time for recriminations is cut short when everyone's attention is diverted by the next alien attack. As the plot moves on, Call's death is left behind, as the deaths of the other crew members, Elgyn and Hillard, had to be left behind in the progression of the chase. In contrast to this rapid progression through the plot, Call's moment of resurrection, which itself displaces the aftermath of Christie's death, is one of the few moments of relative inaction in *Alien: Resurrection*, a difference that marks it as a significant event. Just after Christie has fallen into the very same hole as Call, the door alarm begins to sound. The pace of the narrative goes almost into slow motion as a series of cuts shows each character lining themselves and their weapons up for the next event. When the door finally opens vertically, only revealing Call from the feet upwards, the rest of the group are dumbfounded, finally able to move when Call tells them to. It is Ripley, of course, who first realises that Call is an android, and proves this by putting her hand into the wound in Call's side. But Call does not want to be recognised for what she is, an android who has risen from being damaged, not from the dead. She turns her back on the other crew members as they react to her android status, Distephano becoming especially excited when they realise she is a second-generation model, a robot designed by a robot.

As I have already argued, Call's incorporation into the group until her revelation as an android has relied on her accumulation of humanness through her performance of characteristics shared by the other group members. It is only after the revelation, however, that she begins to speak about herself, acquiring a set of emotions that ensure that her accumulation of humanness continues. Once the survivors realise she is the technology which can help in their escape, they persuade Call to patch into the mainframe, an action that Call is initially reluctant to carry out because it destabilises her sense of self: 'I don't want to go in there, it's like my insides are liquid, it's not real'. Although what real may actually mean in this context is uncertain, her resistance seems to resonate with a fear of her loss of individualism, as though to go inside the mainframe computer will make her lose her boundaries for ever, to become incorporated into the technological domain. The absence of any visual clues to Father, the *Auriga's* mainframe computer, which is only heard and never seen, makes this a fear of a technological unknown. However, the unknown of this computer does not carry the same technological determinism as did the computer on the *Nostromo* in *Alien*. That mainframe, Mother, referenced in the use of the associative term of Father, was programmed to ensure the survival of the alien at the cost of the human crew. In contrast, Father seems to have no such intent, and Call has no difficulty in taking it over, her voice becoming the voice of the computer as she takes control, apparently simply by accessing it. Through this device, the computer technology of *Alien: Resurrection* is brought under the control of the technological being whose allegiances fall in line with those of the human characters. There is nothing nasty lurking in the electronic circuits of this text.

It is not only Call's fear of a loss of individualism that ensures her place within the domain of humanness. As Call and Ripley sit in the *Auriga's* chapel, symmetrically framed in front of an image of a cross, Call reveals her 'true' nature: she is programmed to care. Ripley, in calling her the new 'asshole model', makes fun of her predicament, but it is predicament that reveals a comment on the state of humanness; that is, humans do not care enough anymore. Since Call is gendered female it would be easy to see this aspect of her programming as a comment as much on her being female as about her passing as human. This potential collapse of humanness into gender is also evident in the opposition between Wren and Call. Wren was the leader of the scientists who cloned Ripley – the same scientists who as a group who took an orgasmic pleasure in the extraction of the alien from Ripley's chest. In a conversation with Ripley, Wren had virtually shivered with anticipation at all the wonderful products and cures that the alien could bring to humanity once it had been tamed, studied as a specimen and incorporated into the paradigms of the United Systems Military, the organisation which runs the cloning experiments. Wren is here constructed as a scientist of the Frankenstein school, a scientist who cannot see beyond the narrow rationalism of their experiment. Call might seem like a simple opposition to Wren's perspective, as she is the one that does care. However, the kind of care that Call represents takes the form of considering the outcomes of experiments on people and the world. This distinction displaces the traditional gender lock between rationalism and emotionalism: Call considers the outcomes, she does not simply feel them. What Call represents, then, is an amalgamation between rationality and emotions, a version of humanness that is celebrated by her survival as in the resolution of *Alien: Resurrection* she looks out from the *Betty* towards the Earth below. Even this ending, however, is not a simplistic celebration of a unified humanism bringing together rationalism with emotionalism. The final scenes have a different tonal quality. The colour is bleached out as all the survivors are bathed in the new sunrise, a sunrise that follows the cathartic double inferno of the exploding *Auriga* and the burn of the *Betty's* re-entry into the atmosphere of the Earth. But this new day dawning is not followed by certainty. When Call says to Ripley 'What happens now?' and Ripley responds, 'I don't know, I'm a stranger here myself', the outcome remains open to anything.

In *Alien: Resurrection*, *Android* and *Making Mr Right*, the central characters are sites through which technological beings are managed as they acquire humanness. Through this device, the technological beings are renegotiated as objects in the world through their similarities rather than their differences. As in *Nell*, the technologies acquire their status as human through their intersections with behaviours that are validated or invalidated within the narrative progression of the individual texts. These processes of validation and invalidation suggest that what is taken to be human is not the result of naturally given categories which can be attributed universally to all biological humans. Instead, the categories are validated or invalidated according to the cultural, social and political dynamics of both the operations of the text and the context within which it is produced and consumed. The constructions of the technological beings of *Alien: Resurrection*, *Android* and *Making Mr Right* appeal, quite conservatively, to a version of humanness dominated by whiteness, middle-classness and heterosexuality. And through these categories the common themes of communication, caring, rationality balanced by emotions and the need for community emerge. However, even as these films appeal primarily to a set of conservative categories, these categories are not always so simplistically constructed around unified positions. Instead, some of them are heterogeneous ones, constituted by different elements. Whilst the racial profile remains white, the gendered heterogeneity of community is evident with *Making Mr Right*. However, this gendered community is not as straight as it seems, since the romantic couple is a hybrid human–technological one, not a hybrid male–female one. This potential for hybridity also comes through in the resolution of *Android* and *Alien: Resurrection*. Whilst both texts present a straightforward version of humanness based around the need for community and the need to survive, they also give other possibilities. In *Android* Cassandra indicates the possibility of different kinds of community, whilst in *Alien: Resurrection* the surviving figures offer uncertain prospects for the future. But even though *Making Mr Right*, *Android* and *Alien: Resurrection* provide the possibility for heterogeneous communities, these communities remain embedded in different versions of humanness, versions of humanness which manage technologies through their similarities to humanness, rather than their difference from it. In all of this, there still remains the question of technology on its own terms, rather than on human terms.

Notes

1 The screenplay for *The Iron Giant* is based on the Ted Hughes's story, *The Iron Man* (London: Faber, 1989).

2 Examples of these kinds of commentary include: Peter Biskind, *Seeing is Believing: How Hollywood Taught Us to Stop Worrying and Love the Fifties* (London: Pluto Press, 1984), Mark Jancovich, *Rational Fears: American Horror in the 1950s* (Manchester: Manchester University Press, 1996), David Seed, *American Science Fiction and the Cold War* (Edinburgh: Edinburgh University Press, 1999), Andrew Tudor, *Monsters and Mad Scientists: A Cultural History of the Horror Movie* (Oxford: Blackwell, 1989) and Susan Sontag, 'The Imagination of Disaster', *October*, 40 (1965) 42–48.

3 Alison Adams gives an overview of recentadvances in AI in *Artificial Knowing: Gender and the Thinking Machine* (London and New York: Routledge, 1998).

4 Colin McGinn, *The Problem of Consciousness* (Oxford: Blackwell, 1991) pp. 206–207.

5 McGinn, *The Problem of Consciousness* p. 207.

6 Janet Bergstrom, 'Androids and Androgeny', in Constance Penley, Elisabeth Lyon, Lynn Spigeland and Janet Bergstrom, *Close Encounters: Film, Feminism and Science Fiction* (Minneapolis and Oxford: University of Minnesota Press, 1991) pp. 33-60.

7 Mary Ann Doane, 'Technophilia: Technology, Representation, and the Feminine', in Mary Jacobus, Evelyn Fox Keller and Sally Shuttleworth (eds.), *Body/Politics: Women and the Discourses of Science* (London and New York: Routledge, 1990) pp. 163–176; p. 163.

8 Anne Balsamo, *Technologies of the Gendered Body: Reading Cyborg Women* (Durham, NC: Duke University Press, 1996) p. 10.

9 Steve Best, 'RoboCop: The Crisis of Subjectivity', *Canadian Journal of Political and Social Philosophy* 13: 1–2 (1989) pp. 44–55.

10 Thomas B. Byers, 'Terminating the Postmodern: Masculinity and Pomophobia', *Mfs* 41: 1 (Spring 1995) pp. 5–33.

11 Jennifer González, 'Envisioning Cyborg Bodies: Notes from Current Research', in Gill Kirkup, Linda Janes, Kath Woodward and Fiona Hovenden (eds.), *The Gendered Cyborg: A Reader* (London and New York: Routledge in association with The Open University, 2000) pp. 58–73.

12 González, 'Envisioning Cyborg Bodies', p. 67.

13 González, 'Envisioning Cyborg Bodies', p. 71.

14 Balsamo, *Technologies of the Gendered Body* p. 11.

15 Judith Butler, *Gender Trouble: Feminism and the Subversion of Idenity* (London and New York: Routledge, 1990) pp. 1-34.

16 This image of the cabin deep in the wood also resonates with the pastoral tradition of American writing through nineteenth-century authors such as Henry David Thoreau.

17 Nell has, however, experienced older forms of technology. Prominently displayed in her home is a spinning wheel.

18 The point about needing to relearn is key throughout the film. The apparent innocence and simplicity of Nell's life is used to counterpoint the alienating modern existence of the people she meets.

19 Much of the literature on masculinity has focused on forms of male masculinity. Recently, however, studies on constructions of gender have begun to consider modes of female masculinity. See for example Judith Halberstam, *Female Masculinity* (Durham, NC: Duke University Press, 1998).

20 I specify heterosexual femininity here since all of the main women characters have a preference for male lovers. However, this is not meant to

suggest that the versions of femininity in the film are exclusive to heterosexual women.

21 That Ulysses only learns about emotions from the women characters of the film is problematic, since it reinscribes the dualities of men/women and rational/emotional, even as it attempts to break them down. Although operating to validate emotions as a human competency, it aligns only women with emotionality. Within the world of Chemtech there are no women scientists who can inhabit the rationalised programming side, and whilst there may be men with emotions in *Making Mr Right*, they are not the figures from whom Ulysses learns.

22 J.P. Telotte, *Replications: A Robotic History of Science Fiction Film* (Urbana and Chicago: University of Illinois Press, 1995) p. 20.

23 The antipathy between Mendez and Gunther continues throughout *Android* as they constantly argue. Mendez's claim to superiority extends to being the man who will penetrate another man. When Gunther, speaking of *Alice in Wonderland*, mentions the Red Queen, Mendez reacts to this as a suggestion that he is a queen and immediately tells Gunther that he will take him where he is. This would seem to be following the stereotype that 'real' men penetrate, whatever the sex of their partner.

24 The connection between Daniel and Rotwang is made using two sets of video monitors. One is the video link to the garden where Maggie and Daniel are having lunch, and the second is a video replay. Max sits looking between the two images, clearly making associations between the white-haired Rotwang and the blond Daniel. The clip of *Metropolis* used within *Android*, of the robot-Maria being created, obviously resonates with Daniel's intentions to create a female android.

25 See for example Cynthia Fuchs, '"Death Is Irrelevant": Cyborgs, Reproduction and the Future of Male Hysteria', *Genders*, 18 (Winter 1993) pp. 113–133; Ludmilla Jordanova, *Sexual Visions: Images of Gender in Science and Medicine between the Eighteenth and Twentieth Centuries* (New York: Harvester Wheatsheaf, 1989) pp. 111–133; and Claudia Springer, *Electronic Eros: Bodies and Desire in the Postindustrial Age* (Austin: University of Texas, 1996).

5

Technology untamed

What can*not* be said about images of technoscience? A brief look at the two *Terminator* films reveals the gaps that exist in the thinking about images of technoscience. *Terminator* (1984, US) and *Terminator 2: Judgement Day* (1991, US) each have as a central character the figure of the terminator. This terminator, the T-101, is a technological being, a cyborg entity, a machine covered over with an organic skin so that it looks the same as a human being. In *Terminator* the T-101 is not made safe by its alignment with humanness; instead, the technological being poses a threat to the human race. The T-101 is characterised through the physical presence of Arnold Schwarzenegger, and as the narrative progresses, through SFX and make-up. Schwarzenegger's early 1980s physical bulk alone gives the T-101 a dominating presence on the screen, a presence that is enhanced by its initial meetings with the human characters. The baiting of it by the three young men is made to seem puny in contrast to the terminator's brutal strength. Whilst the technological status of the terminator is not revealed until about a third of the way into the text, its difference is obvious not only from its size and strength. The impassiveness of its expression, and its overly deliberate body movements, especially in the turning of its head, give the impression of something different. This physicality is coupled to a programmed intent to kill the soon-to-be mother of the saviour of the human race, Sarah Connor. This intent is visible not only through its actions, but also through its complete lack of responsiveness to its surroundings, its only reactions being to keep on and on, without any change of expression in either its face or its body language. As Kyle Reese says to Sarah Connor when he explains that the T-101 is a machine: 'It can't be bargained with, it can't be reasoned with. It doesn't feel pity, remorse or fear, and it absolutely will not stop, ever, until you are dead'. As the impossibility of revoking the T-101's programming becomes clear, as it gets up again and again and again, the cover of the cyborg is gradually stripped away, revealing its technological construction. And although this technological construction echoes human skeletal structures, its metallic constitution makes the structure strange, disturbing. The combination of this strangeness with its relentless pursuit of Sarah Connor places the T-101 outside of constructions of humanness. This is a machine that cannot be communicated with, it has no common ground with the humans of the text, and it only stops when it is destroyed.

In the second film, *Terminator 2*, the physicality of the T-101 remains, but it is combined with a different programmed intent. Unlike the terminator of the previous film, this one is sent back in time to ensure the continued existence of the now living saviour of the human race, John Connor. Given this new set of parameters, the foe of the film must also change, and instead of fighting humans, it fights other technologies, in particular the T-1000. The transformation of the T-101 between *Terminator* and *Terminator 2* reveals the different strategies by which the two texts manage their technological beings. Since the T-101 of *Terminator 2* is on the humans' side, it is invested with humanness. This occurs by attributing to it the capacity to learn about caring, a narrative device put in place through its developing relationship with John Connor. As John teaches the T-101 to understand something about the ways in which humans care for each other, so the technological being is renegotiated from the threatening figure of *Terminator* to the less threatening one of *Terminator 2*. This transformation is brought about not only by the T-101 learning why humans cry, but also in its positioning in relation to the other technological being of *Terminator 2*: the T-1000. This latter technological being is altogether different to the T-101. Not only does its human form look different – the slight Robert Patrick versus the still bulky Arnie – its technological condition is different. This terminator is constructed from a fluid and mutable liquid, and is able to change shape through the wonders of 1992 state-of-the-art morphing technologies.

Much of the critical literature which surrounds *Terminator* and *Terminator 2* has tended to focus on the masculinities portrayed by the T-101 across the two films, and the different cultural resonances being played out in 1984 and 1992, the years in which the films were released. However, little has been written about the technological beings as images of technologies, and whilst the terminators can be viewed as differing constructions of masculinity, they can also be seen as different constructions of technology. In *Terminator*, the T-101 represents technology as something different and threatening. It literally attempts to take the place of the human, but in the end is remodelled, overcome and revealed for the imitation that it is. In *Terminator 2* this technology returns, looking the same but with a new user-friendly interface. This friendlier interface makes the revelation of the T-101's metallic skeleton different than that of the earlier text. In *Terminator 2*, the technology's underlying metallic structure seems less disturbing, perhaps even familiar after the first film, its echoing of the human skeleton now a gesture of connection rather than disconnection. Instead of being an image that insists on the difference of the technology, the uncovered T-101 might be seen as a link between the humanness being performed by the machine, and the humanness being performed by the humans. In contrast, there is nothing familiar in the T-1000, and the more its technology is revealed, the more difficult it is to grasp. In spite of its capacity to look superficially human, it is without any traces or echoes of humanness. Underlying its surface features, there is no solidity, it is ever changing, a flow of aggregations which can assume the look of any object, animate or inanimate. And since the T-1000 bears no similarities to constructions of humanness, it cannot be made safe, or managed with any degree of certainty. This uncertainty makes the T-1000 disturbing: it is a technology which is not made to perform like a human; it is technology which is different.

Beyond human games

I have argued throughout this book that the meanings given to humanness and technologies in fictions of technoscience occur in the intersections between the humans and technologies of the texts. These meanings are embedded in the cultural, social and political operations of the given text. However, it does not follow that such intersections can encompass all the possible meanings of either humanness or technologies. Whilst the possibility for multiple versions of humanness emerged in the previous chapter's discussion of *Nell*, *Making Mr Right*, *Android* and *Alien: Resurrection*, these possibilities emerged more as hints, rather than anything more definite, suggesting that the ideological concerns of these films is to encompass not difference but sameness. But difference can rarely be contained, it is always escaping, present in the gaps and unresolved tensions in the texts. This question of escaping difference is relevant not only to humanness, but also to technologies.

Although the possibilities for multiple versions of humanness are evident in the technological beings of *Android*, *Making Mr Right* and *Alien: Resurrection*, they remain primarily as manageable and safe objects. The same can be said of the T-101 of *Terminator* and *Terminator 2*. In re-negotiating the technological beings by placing them within a framework of human behaviours, they can be understood, whether they function in positive or negative ways. The limitation of this position is that technology is fully assimilated into the frameworks of humanness that operate within a given text, and the difference of technology as technology is displaced and tamed. The T-101 of *Terminator* is managed by locating it outside of humanness, whilst in *Terminator 2* it is given a share of humanness. The T-1000 of *Terminator 2* is characterised in a similar way to the first terminator: it is inhuman, a technological horror. In the critical discussions that surround the *Terminator* films, it is the conditions of humanness that primarily concerns the critics. Whilst the purpose of the readings varies, the figures of the terminators are frequently used as explorations either of humanness generally, or more often of different constructions of gender.[1] But, in spite of this tendency, technologies are not simply stages upon which humanness or gender can be performed. Technologies are also technologies, objects in the world that are difficult to comprehend to those of us not familiar with their construction, and difficult to manage through the terms made available through constructions of humanness. The difference of the T-101 in *Terminator* and the T-1000 of *Terminator 2* finally resides in what cannot be said about them, rather than what can be said.

The purpose of this chapter is to look at what texts cannot or do not say about the technology central to their narratives. *Wargames* (1983, US), *Edward Scissorhands* (1990, US) and *RoboCop* (1987, US) each features a technology that has the capacity to learn either to communicate with humans or to behave as though human by becoming part of a human community. But unlike the technological beings of *Android*, *Making Mr Right* and *Alien: Resurrection*, despite this capability the technologies exist, at least in part, beyond the framework of humanness: their difference as a technology remains untamed. Although many fictions of technoscience represent the difference of technology as a problem, this discussion does not aim to reinstate the view that technology is alien and alienating, or, indeed, that humanness and technologies are separate categories with a distinct and essential basis. Instead, I argue that the categories defined as human are unable to capture completely the meanings of technology. I take up this position to suggest that constructions of technology retain a degree of difference, in the sense that how they are understood is open to other possibilities, possibilities beyond those put in place by the limiting constructions of humanness. Whilst the first three films discussed in this chapter, *Wargames*, *Edward Scissorhands* and *RoboCop*, are used to make this point in relation to technological objects, the final film considered, *GATTACA* (1997, US), extends this argument to take in the discourses of technoscience.

Building connections: games and warfare

Wargames opens with the high tension of a nuclear attack. Two men, locked behind an inches-thick steel door, have to follow a set of counterattack procedures. As the pressure of the responsibility for launching nuclear missiles that could kill millions of people mounts, they fail to carry out the launch. This scenario, which turns out only to be a test to assess the responses of military personnel, sets up the rest of the narrative. Since the humans are unreliable in their responses, it is decided that a machine will take their places. Through such a device, *Wargames* is centrally concerned with a dependent relationship between humans and technology; it is a narrative that is informed by fears of a potential disaster caused by an over-reliance on technological systems. In many ways *Wargames* is a technologically updated remake of *Fail-Safe* (1964, US). This latter film, which was remade for US television in 2000, was released shortly after the Cuban missile crisis, and is concerned with the consequences of the introduction of technology into the military chain of command. Within the story of *Fail-Safe*, through a series of malfunctions a nuclear bomber is sent beyond its fail-safe point by the mechanised system, and cannot be recalled. Additionally, all attempts to shoot the bomber down fail, and so the crew drops its bombs on Moscow. In order to prevent Soviet retaliation, the US president decides on the strategy of dropping a nuclear warhead on New York. Closing on this event, *Fail-Safe* suggests that there can never be winners in a nuclear war, and that such a war would be futile. Released twenty years after *Fail-Safe*, *Wargames* again takes up this theme of the futility of nuclear warfare, but instead of using the narrative device of a malfunctioning switching system, relocates the problem of technological control onto an advanced computer system that has the capacity to learn. Through the presence of the AI technology, the need to learn about the futility of nuclear war is shifted from the human figures to the technological figure. And as the technological being of *Wargames* learns about futility, the human figures and the technological figure engage in a rudimentary form of communication. However, the capacity of the technology of *Wargames* to communicate, unlike Max or Ulysses in *Android* and *Making Mr Right*, does not ensure its renegotiation as a safe object.

The complex AI technology that replaces the human figures in *Wargames* operates through a strategy-game program that provides the machine with the capacity to learn from its mistakes. This machine, the NORAD-controlled WOPR (War Operations Plan Response), simulates tactical responses in the event of war, and as one of the film's characters says: it 'spends all its time thinking about World War III. It has already fought World War III – as a game – time and time again'. In a discussion of *Wargames*, Paul Edwards comments that 'Joshua [another name for the WOPR] has neither comprehension of, nor stakes in, reality; its world is the microworld of the game'.[2] Edwards makes this statement in the context of a discussion of the AIs of the 1960s films *Colossus: The Forbin Project* (1969, US) and *2001: A Space Odyssey* (1968, UK/US). He considers the AIs of these two films, Colossus and Hal, to be more inherently threatening than the WOPR, because they develop a distinct and controlling relationship towards humans as they take an interest in the particularities of human ways of living. For Edwards, the animosity of the machines is specifically directed towards the human characters. By contrast, the actions of the WOPR are motivated solely within the logic of the game; for this machine there is nothing outside of the parameters of the game strategies. Whilst I agree with Edwards' description of the different nature of the relationship between humans and Colossus and Hal, this difference does not serve to minimise the threat that the WOPR represents to the human world. Both Colossus and Hal can communicate with the human figures that share their environment, and the humans can understand both of them; they are aware of their relationship to the human world. But the WOPR, because it plays games according to an internal logic based on calculated predictions and outcomes, has no awareness beyond those calculations. It is the very absence of a stake in human reality, and the absence of any means of understanding human reality, that makes the WOPR so much a threat. Since the machine cannot recognise the distinction between a game world and a real world, once the human world comes under the control of the WOPR it becomes part of a game plan, and nuclear devastation simply the end of a game.

The tension of *Wargames* revolves around whether the mismatch between the realities of the human and machine worlds can be overcome, and given the echoes of *Fail-Safe* a happy outcome is by no means certain. Although the resolution of the film is about finally getting the machine to understand, since many of the obstacles to this resolution occur because of the human figures' misunderstanding of the technological system, *Wargames* is as much about human ignorance as it is about machines. The lack of human understanding is played out in two ways within *Wargames*, both through a figure who is new to the technology, and through those who are meant to be familiar with it. The first misunderstanding occurs when the WOPR begins to play a 'game' of global thermonuclear war at the request of a young hacker, David Lightman, a request that David makes because of his assumptions about computer systems. Seeking out the computer system of a new games-making company, David misrecognises and misunderstands the system that he has entered as a new game, a mistake that results in the activation of the game plan that involves a potentially lethal simulation of nuclear warfare. David's lack of understanding of the WOPR technology is reiterated by the actions of the NORAD staff, the group of civilian and military personnel who are in control of the defence systems, and who are therefore meant to be familiar with it. Inside NORAD, where the WOPR is physically located as an ominously humming big black rectangular box, complete with arrays of flashing lights, the military and their civilian advisors are dependent on a range of technologies to represent the outside world. Deep inside a mountain, they rely on highly mediated representations of the world to 'see' what is occurring. Without an easy means of verification, they are unable to tell the difference between what is real and what is simulated, and the two collapse into one another. The control room, where a significant portion of the drama of *Wargames* is set, is a highly technologised environment. Much of the floor space is taken up with rows of terminals operated

by military personnel; the focal point of the room is a series of
screens that take up the whole of a high wall. On these screens are
military strategy maps that can zoom in and out of detailed locations,
as well as providing a global perspective. These maps and computer
terminals contain and control the flow of information about military
movements, and they are the means through which the people inside
the mountain perceive the outside world. Excepting the sequence in
which fighter planes are sent to make visual contact with a missile,
the people in the mountain are constantly uncertain about the relationship between what they see on the screens and what is in actual-
ity occurring. And although they become aware of some degree of
contradiction, they fail to recognise that the WOPR has control of
their representational systems, and that it is playing out a strategy
that will have fatal consequences. The reality of the people inside the
mountain is both literally and metaphorically put into question by the
intervention of a technological system.

The overwhelming presence of the technological system is, then,
signified not only through the information that the WOPR constructs on the screens inside the mountain, but also through the
ranks of terminals and looming screens that take up the majority of
the frame. The contingency of this space is most palpable in the
scenes where the NORAD command have to wait and see if the
incoming Soviet weapons are real, or whether they are the WOPR's
constructions. Using a narrative device from *Fail-Safe*, a communication link to a potential target site is kept open as the command
group wait for verification of the strike, whilst the screens behind
them explode with the lights of simulated nuclear explosions. Even
this device displays a dependency on the technological system. A
telephone link is required to maintain contact with the outside
world, as the command team cannot go outside and see with their
own eyes. The sequence in which the nuclear explosions are relayed
by the WOPR, which is strong even on a small screen, must have
been powerful in a darkened auditorium, particularly in 1983.
Bright white lights flash up and spread as huge circles of destruction
across the big screen to signify the extent of the catastrophe. However, unlike *Fail-Safe*, in which the nuclear strike does occur, in
Wargames it does not, revealing the disparity between the outside
world and the representation controlled by the WOPR

The euphoria that follows the realisation that the nuclear attack is
a simulation acts as a release of narrative tension which is mediated

through the celebrations of the human characters on the screen. But this euphoria is rapidly replaced by horror as the humans notice that the game is not yet over. The WOPR is still playing, trying out different possibilities in order to win its game, and as it attempts to do so by launching the US rockets which would precipitate a real Soviet strike, the NORAD command realise that they are completely in the control of a machine intelligence that they do not understand. And, furthermore, a machine intelligence for which their existence, or lack of existence, is of no consequence. That the WOPR does not succeed is due to the intervention of David Lightman, who establishes a communicative link with the WOPR by playing games. It is significant that David has throughout referred to the WOPR as Joshua, the password that let him onto the system in the first instance. The use of this more human name might suggest that David has more knowledge of the system, but what he really knows about is game strategies. He knows that tic-tac-toe is an unwinnable game, and so uses it as a device to teach the WOPR that some games cannot be won, and so it is futile to play them. The WOPR translates this new knowledge to its nuclear war strategies, and decides that this is a game which is futile to play, coming into line with the thinking of the humans, or at least some of the humans.

Through its position that global nuclear warfare would be futile, and that an over-reliance on technology is not necessarily useful, the resolution of *Wargames* remains close to the narrative of *Fail-Safe*. However, *Wargames* also poses another set of questions concerning the relationship between humans and technology. A key device within *Wargames* is the degree to which humans are made vulnerable by their inadequate understanding of the technology that surrounds them. David accidentally puts into motion a game that nearly leads to nuclear war, and the NORAD command simply does not understand the capabilities of the WOPR, and so cannot tell the difference between its constructions and reality. An understanding is only obtained when a common ground is reached, and in the context of *Wargames*, this common ground is games strategy. In enabling the WOPR to learn that total destruction is not a viable option, the technology is recuperated from its threatening flashing lights and black-box position. Writing on this turnaround, Paul Edwards argues:

> Disembodied AI turns to fearful foe, but then turns back again, rehabilitated by the touch of innocents (the teenagers David and Jennifer).

This pattern of cyborg rehabilitation through communion with caring human beings recurred frequently in the 1980s, as computers were transformed from alienating instruments of corporate power to familiar tools of entertainment and communication. With his final line – 'How about a nice game of chess?' – Joshua has completed its transformation into a player and companion in an adolescent world returned to innocence.[3]

Edwards here seems to suggest a full transformation of the technology of the WOPR, which he significantly refers to through its designated human name of Joshua. And whilst it may be recuperated through the witticism of 'How about a nice game of chess?' this is only a partial renegotiation. The WOPR cannot be re-presented through the terms of humanness, as 'a player and companion in an adolescent world', because it has never been managed through those terms. Instead, the WOPR remains a sophisticated piece of technology, and in spite of the attempt to elide its difference in the resolution of *Wargames*, that it can play chess is only one of its capacities: something of the WOPR remains beyond a humanised world-view.

Keeping technology beyond the picket fence

The limits of the assimilation, or the appropriation, of technology are also evident in *Edward Scissorhands*. Although constantly displaced onto a theme of tragic romance – the opening and closing framing devices locate the story as one of impossible love – the film explores a similar theme to that of *Wargames*: the limits of the relationship between technology and humans. Unlike the WOPR, Edward Scissorhands is a technological figure who is introduced into a human community, and, except for his scissorhands, he is almost fully like a human. Within the opening sequence Edward is described as a man, though a man created by an inventor who died leaving 'him incomplete and all alone'. The tensions in Edward's story, which is narrated in retrospect by the woman who loves him, emerge most clearly through the 'will they won't they' of the romance thread. But the tensions exist in relation to the difficulties experienced by Edward as a different sort of being when he is introduced to a human community, a human community that is based around conformity.

The human community central to *Edward Scissorhands* is that of an anonymous small American town. The period is uncertain; it has echoes of the 1950s but also incorporates more contemporary technologies such as answerphones, CD-players and modern cars into the story-world. The look of the town encapsulates a sense of superficial difference that is underpinned by conformity and enclosure. The buildings, predominantly bungalows, are similarly shaped but distinguished from each other by a limited range of pastel colours, a range of colours which is often repeated in the costumes of both the women and men. These buildings are linked into a distinct and enclosed location by an overhead shot that shows the squat bungalows joined by roads, paths, picket fences and patches of grass. Within the narrative, there are only a few occasions when the action moves outside of this space. Edward's home forms a contrast to this suburban conformity. Situated at the end of a street of pastel bungalows, it rises up, untidily angular, grey and menacing. However, unlike the fictional inhabitants of most gothic houses, Edward is not initially invested with a menacing difference. That is something that only emerges once his place within the human community cannot be secured.

Edward is initially discovered, alone in his decaying home, by the well-meaning Peg Boggs. Peg, the local Avon representative, is at first frightened by Edward, his scissorhands being a threatening difference, but she takes the android back to her home once she realises the extent of his isolation. Once in the Boggses' home the process of Edward's assimilation into the human community begins.[4] Peg's actions literally serve to hide his difference, as she gives him some of her husband's old clothes to wear, to cover over his black leather suit. This cover-over also becomes a make-over as she attempts to hide Edward's facial scars with a variety of Avon products, none of which are sufficiently effective. Yet, even as this process of assimilation occurs there are persistent references to Edward's difference – he cannot dress properly because he does not have human hands. This tension between fitting in and being different is nicely played out in the sequence in which Edward eats his first meal in the Boggses' household. Kevin, the young son of the family, constantly makes gestures towards Edward as an exotic outsider: 'Can I bring him to show and tell on Monday?' In a parody of good manners, Peg keeps telling her son not to be rude, whilst her husband attempts to engage Edward in a conversation about the view from his home on the hill. All the while Edward is unable to eat because he cannot handle a knife and fork, but no one will acknowledge this by helping him. The visual emphasis on Edward's difficulty in eating peas, a point-of-view shot of a single pea precariously balanced on his finger blades, discloses the impossibility of Edward's incorporation into humanness, something that becomes more explicit throughout the rest of the film.

The community into which Edward is introduced, and from which he will be excluded, is an exaggeration of white suburban life. With the exception of Peg, who has her work as a sales rep, the women stay at home whilst the men go to work, taking their cars with them. Throughout the day, these women create a community that is based variously around what they try to hide from each other and what they share with each other. This community of hide-and-exchange materialises in a network of communication over garden fences, via the telephone, out on the street, and even through the route of Peg's door-to-door selling. The operations of this network ensure that nothing is missed, that all information will ultimately be shared, and finally, that resistance is futile. This sharing, however, is far from benign, as it verges on a process of annexation, an annexation that materialises in the degree of copying that occurs. When Edward's cutting skills become apparent, the word spreads with the result that every home has a topiary figure in its garden; and every woman and her dog a new hair or fur cut. There is even an attempt to take Edward's novel influence beyond the local community. Exploiting his appearance in the media Joyce, one of the Boggses'neighbours, has plans to commodify his skills by setting up a beauty parlour at the local shopping mall. Throughout the human community, Edward's difference is displayed only in order for it to be consumed. Edward's entrance into this group can be seen as the plight of an innocent, an innocent who is almost entrapped within the seething resentments and boredom that characterise the community. And, through the portrayal of Edward as a naive figure who attempts to accommodate the possessive gaze of the other characters, *Edward Scissorhands* very obviously portrays the difficulties of being different. There is, however, some displacement of the nature of this difference – that is, Edward's technological construction. Edward is not simply an innocent human figure who has grown up outside a particular community; he is a technological being.

The impossibility of Edward's relocation into the community that initially strives to assimilate him becomes explicit at the moment when the possibility of a lovers' relationship between a human and a technology opens up. The crisis is precipitated when Edward takes part in a crime because of his attraction to Kim Boggs, the daughter of the household and the narrator of the story. Through this event, Kim realises her own attraction towards Edward. No longer seeing him as a weird being brought into her household, she begins to respond to his attention towards her. The anxiety around a human–technology relationship is expressed through the jealous reactions of Jim, Kim's boyfriend. After Kim has told Jim she no longer wants to see him, he responds: 'I'm going to lose you to that? He isn't even human'. This is the first moment within *Edward Scissorhands* where any of the human characters have acknowledged Edward's difference, and it occurs only once Edward's position has already become less secure within the community. Jim's actions further ensure that the community comes to see Edward as a threat. And as they begin to see him as a threat, the group that had sought to assimilate Edward's difference instead becomes a mass that wishes to see him destroyed. The transition from consumers to eradicators is clear when Joyce, the fatal *femme* of the piece, aids the turn against Edward. Depicted throughout the film as a sexually assertive woman, Joyce attempts, but fails, to seduce Edward, and she eventually takes revenge by claiming he attacked her. The figure of Joyce exemplifies the problematic constructions around women in *Edward Scissorhands* and the displacement of the technological condition of Edward. Because the construction of the community primarily revolves around women, it appears as though Edward's fall from grace is ultimately the fault of women. And even though the crowd that marches on Edward's home, demanding that he be brought to account, is of mixed gender, it is Joyce and her friends who lead the way. Even prior to this moment of mass hatred, Edward's life with the Boggses is altered because women have acted on their desires. Not only is he alienated from the community because of Jim's jealousy, the impossibility of his ever belonging to that community is also revealed. In the sequence where Kim asks Edward to hold her, eventually placing herself within the circle of his arms, Edward has his final flashback. In this flashback, Edward's inventor is about to give him his hands, but just at that moment he falls dead to the floor. The combination of these chronologically distinct moments brings together the two impossibilities of Edward's life. He can never be fully human, be a part of a human community, and because of this, he can never have a relationship with Kim. In the final images of the film, as the elderly Kim finishes her story for the little girl, the problem of Edward as a technological being is apparently displaced onto a problem of impossible love.

Despite these displacements, Edward's difference does remain, and is marked by his appearance. His scissorhands and his gothic appearance are both out of keeping with the human figures that surround him.[5] Yet in spite of this, the fact that Edward is a technology is rarely remarked upon. Apart from Jim's outburst, the only moments when this is made clear is during the flashback sequences. And these flashback sequences in which his origins are revealed are only available to the audience, not to the human figures who appear within the text. The first of these occurs when Edward is helping Peg in the kitchen. The rotating mechanism of the tin opener acts a visual link to a previous event. The flashback, which is not a memory since it depicts an event prior to Edward's construction, shows the moment of Edward's conception. The inventor, a seemingly benign old man, whilst watching his biscuit-baking technology system in operation, decides to create Edward, a thought conveyed as he holds a heart-shaped biscuit up against the metallic chest of an automaton. This automaton, like Edward, has scissors for hands. A second flashback uses the device of pages turning in a book to indicate the progression of Edward's construction as he is transformed from the tin can-like figure into a fully human-like figure. However, the limits of this transformation are apparent in Edward's unfinished state. He is clearly not the embodiment of the 'well presented' young man in a suit, the image that was depicted on the final page of his inventor's plans, and his scissorhands remain as a mark of his evolution from his origins as a slicing machine.

The presence of these flashback sequences, with their emphasis on the making of Edward as a technological being, enables a reading of *Edward Scissorhands* as a film concerned not simply with difference or impossible love, but with the relationship between humanness and technology, a relationship that is distinct from those discussed through the technological figures of *Android*, *Making Mr Right* and *Alien: Resurrection*. These figures are incorporated into humanness through their acquisition of human behaviours, and as they do so, they become a part of a community. To the extent that their social construction is appropriate to a particular community of humans, their difference is erased, and in this moment of erasure they are managed and made safe. In comparison, for all its use of the melodramatic tragic romance, *Edward Scissorhands* does not allow a simple collapse of technology into humanness. Edward is a technology, and as such 'he' is different. And it is this difference which causes him to be excluded from the human community.

Hybrid beings

The technological beings of *Wargames* and *Edward Scissorhands* are both materially distinct from humans. That is, they are constructed from non-biologically human parts. Questions about technologies are also relevant to the figure of the cyborg, or cybernetic organism, which is understood to be a hybrid being, a figure constructed from both organic and inorganic components.[6] Within fictions of technoscience, the cyborg is often a hybrid derived from human organic material as well as inorganic material. *RoboCop, Universal Soldier* (1992, US) and *Running Delilah* (a.k.a. *Cyborg Agent*) (1994, US) all feature humans that are reconstructed after a trauma which would have been fatal without technological intervention.[7] *RoboCop* features a hybrid entity that is constructed from a policeman, Alex Murphy, and sophisticated technology. The only portions of Murphy that remain are his face, usually hidden behind a helmet, and his spinal cord and brain, a point that remains opaque throughout *RoboCop*, and is revealed only in the sequel *RoboCop 2*. What appears to be at stake in these films is a redefinition of humanness, a redefinition which is inevitable as the boundaries of the human body are blurred as technologies encroach and become an inseparable part of the functioning hybrid being. My particular concern here is the extent to which the hybrid figure of the cyborg exposes ideas about technologies as much as it does humanness.

The redefinition of humanness within *RoboCop* occurs in the dystopian version of the American city of Detroit, a place that is marked by violent conflict between organised drug gangs and the police. Controlling, and generating, this conflict is Omni Computer Products (OCP). Within *RoboCop* there are two sets of relationship between humans and technological beings, and the technologised figures of RoboCop and ED209 (Enforcement Droid 209), both of which are products of OCP, provide a focal point for these differing relationships. The first kind of relationship is a relatively conventional one, involving a good technological-cop versus a bad technological-cop. The ED209 is a fully technologised being, but one that malfunctions in ways that suggest that it is dangerous to humans. The physical construction of the ED209 further encourages such a perspective. It is a large metallic biped machine, with angular and machinic movements accompanied by hydraulic sounds, whose awkward bulk dominates the space it occupies. The machine is often shot at a low angle, making it tower above the human figures that surround it. The threatening power that the ED209 embodies is evident during a demonstration of its capabilities, a demonstration that goes wrong when the machine goes out of control and kills its human target. Subsequently, the machine is allied with the corrupt figure of the film, Dick Jones, an alignment through which the machine gains more negative status when Jones uses it in an attempt to destroy the other technology of the film, RoboCop. RoboCop is a visible contrast to the ED209; it is a much slighter machine, and its approximation to a human shape makes it appear visually less menacing. Whilst it is larger than humans, and much more deadly than a human, its threat is not indiscriminate since its violent actions are only directed against figures characterised as thieves, terrorists and rapists. Through the different characterisations of the technological beings, the battles between ED209 and RoboCop become a contest in which the all-menacing technology is vanquished by the technology that is programmed to 'serve and protect'.

The second kind of relationship between humans and technologies occurs *within* the cyborg figure of RoboCop, and it goes beyond the good-versus-bad duality evident in the conflict between the ED209 and RoboCop. After his murder, Alex Murphy is transformed into RoboCop by the rematerialisation of his biological body into a hybrid mechanised–organic body. The theme of transformation not only operates through the human body in *RoboCop*; it also operates through the alteration of the cityscape. *RoboCop* is set in Detroit City where the old city is to be demolished, and a new and better version, Delta City, is to be constructed in its place. Murphy's murder in the disintegrating hulk of a derelict steel mill and his subsequent reanimation as a cyborg inside a high-tech laboratory is a similar kind of transition. The old Murphy is almost entirely demolished, and the remains are re-configured into a bright new titanium-covered object. This transition is displayed in the scenes that link Murphy's murder and his subsequent reanimation. The death of the fully human Murphy is shown in a sequence of cuts from a close-up of Murphy's face showing his unresponsive pupils to an apparently subjective view of the medics working over him. These hospital scenes change to memories of his son and of his wife. The sense of Murphy moving away from the living world is given in a point-of-view shot of moving away from his wife and son at increasing speed.[8] These scenes give way to images of the team of medics trying shock Murphy's heart back to life. Each time he is shocked, there is another memory image of the group who shot him; at the final shock, there is only the image of Clarence Boddicker, the ringleader. In this extended sequence, as conventional medical technology fails to save the severely injured Murphy, the end of his life is signalled by a fade to black. This failure of conventional technology is counterposed with the success of unconventional technologies, ones that have the capacity not only to keep the body of Murphy alive, but also to radically transform the notion of being alive.

The reanimation of Murphy as RoboCop is visualised when the blank screen of Murphy's death is broken by white noise, white noise that is followed by a tuning-in effect as RoboCop's visual functions come on-line and are focused. That the images on the screen are the point of view of a technologically enhanced being is evident in the use of visual grid device placed over the field of vision. However, the physical nature of this technologically enhanced being is initially withheld. The stasis of the point-of-view shots echoes those of the previous hospital scene with its view of ceiling lights, heads peering down and disembodied off-screen voices. In the first set of images it was clear that Murphy's death was signalled, but in this second instance it is unclear what is being signalled, as the audience is only given a partial view. The knowledge that the technological being no longer has a human body is obvious through the stated intention of using a 'total body prosthesis'. And that something organic remains is indicated by the comment: 'we have the best of both worlds … fastest reactions technology can give and a life-time of on-the-street law enforcement programming'. This statement suggests that the point of view is not simply that of a machine, even though the shots are mediated through a technologised process of visualisation. When the audience is finally given glimpses of this being, it is initially only through mirror reflections, opaque glass and rear views. Such visual fragments provide the first views of RoboCop, an entity that is itself a set of fragments, and whose identity will remain in question throughout the remainder of the narrative.

Discussions of *RoboCop* often revolve around this question of fragmented identity, most often in terms of technology versus human, though also in terms of a hybrid technology-human.[9] Scott Bukatman has argued that the fictional constructions of technology in *RoboCop* represent a materialisation of the human experience of contemporary technologies. He states: 'it is the purpose of much recent science fiction to construct a new subject-position to interface with the global realms of data circulation, a subject that can occupy or intersect the cyberspaces of contemporary existence.'[10] Bukatman is here placing the 1980s cyborg films such as *RoboCop* in the context of contemporary 'invisible' technologies, especially that of the computer and more recently the Internet. His position is that the interface between human and technological bodies alters the subject positions of both, an alteration that enables a different experience of a technologised world. The question of an interface between a technologised body and human remains emerges within the narrative of *RoboCop* as RoboCop begins to function beyond the parameters of its technological programming. These parameters are first established in a parodic sequence of law enforcement in which the new hero saves shopkeepers from a robber, a woman from a violent assault, and the city mayor from a hostage situation. Whilst these sequences amply demonstrate its efficiency in policing, they also serve to indicate its lack of humanising qualities – RoboCop's pre-programmed response to the gratitude of the attacked woman makes her pull back in surprise. Such machinic displays of efficient law enforcement are contrasted with the re-emergence of something of Murphy. This re-emergence is most strongly articulated in the 'dream' sequence in which associative editing is used to create connections between visual cues and RoboCop's sensory reactions. RoboCop is shown 'experiencing' the visual cues through several different technological routes. Initially, the graph pens that make a visual record of RoboCop's neural activity go off the scale, and they are followed by the appearance on monitor screens of electronic noise, suggesting that the increased neural activity is associated with some kind of visual disturbance. Since these screens show RoboCop's visual field, the image must be being 'seen' by RoboCop, and what it sees is the same image of Clarence Boddicker that Murphy had remembered in the moment of his death. This connection is clarified for the viewer by a cut to a replay of Murphy's shooting. The convulsive physical reaction that RoboCop demonstrates to this sequence of images suggests a link between RoboCop's new titanium body and something akin to residual memories that can be attributed to Murphy.

Whilst these memories subsequently motivate RoboCop to behave outside of the parameters of its programming, what they actually mean to the hybrid being of *RoboCop* remains unclear. Samantha Holland suggests that because it can feel pain there is a 'genuine' mind, implying a human mind, in the cyborg.[11] Both Steve Best and Scott Bukatman also point out that RoboCop has a subjectivity that may be attributed to the remaining human parts of the cyborg; Bukatman suggests that keeping the 'meat' grounds the subjectivity of the character.[12] These positions rely on a connection between the organic flesh of the remaining neural network and subjectivity. But RoboCop's subjectivity cannot be simply allied with its organic parts; it has become different, altered by its intersection with technology. This difference is clear in RoboCop's statement about Murphy's family: 'I can feel them, but I can't remember them.' And even though the closure of *RoboCop* seems to want to suggest that RoboCop is fully humanised through its reclamation of the name Murphy, RoboCop is a shot-up piece of sophisticated machinery, one that exists in an interdependent relationship with organic parts derived from a human. It is possible to say that it embodies certain characteristics of traditional masculinities, and that it has something like memories, that it experiences something like pain, and that it is motivated by something that seems to be revenge. But the difficulty in saying anything more about the identity of this hybrid being, more than that it has 'something like' human traits and emotions, reveals the difficulty of speaking about the difference of technology in fictions of technoscience.[13]

Genetic uncertainty

The images of technologies within *Wargames*, *Edward Scissorhands* and *RoboCop* all feature a physical object – a box-like machine, an android or a cyborg – and the narrative concerns revolve around the relationship formed between these technological objects and the human figures in the text. *GATTACA* is unlike these texts in that it does not feature a specific embodied technology through which the definition of humanness and technologies are negotiated. Instead, it features a discourse that is derived from technoscientific knowledge; furthermore, just as the film's title is derived from scientific nomenclature, so too are the definitions of humanness in *GATTACA* derived from technoscientific discourse.[14] In this reading of *GATTACA*, I focus on the technoscientific discourse central to the film, that of the gene, and consider how the narrative of the film explores the limits of the operations of that discourse. My particular emphasis is on the certainty and uncertainty of the outcomes predicted by the genetic discourse that informs the narrative of the film. In a similar way to my discussion of technologies, this approach reveals the gaps and limitations of any attempt to contain the meanings of human and non-human objects in the world. Just as the terms of humanness prove unable to contain those of technologies, the technoscientific discourse of GATTACA proves unable to contain the meaning of humanness.

Briefly, GATTACA is set in a future where in-vitro genetic manipulation is more common than not. The children born in this 'not too far distant future' are manipulated to have as high an intelligence as is possible and a low susceptibility to illnesses, both psychological and physical. A non-manipulated human, Vincent Freedom, is denied access to a good education and job because his genetic profile is inferior – it still contains all the genetic material which might cause him to die an early death from heart failure. According to the world-view of GATTACA, all human potential can be absolutely predicted on the basis of a genetic profile, and any problems revealed in this profile cause an individual to be excluded. Although designated as an 'in-valid', Vincent sets out to prove the prediction of his profile wrong, as he attempts to achieve his dreams of becoming a member of the elite, a navigator for the Gattaca Corporation. To do so he takes on the genetic persona of Jerome Morrow, a near-perfect manipulated human who has refused to live his life according to the predictions based on his genome. Through the two characters of Vincent and Jerome, GATTACA is explicitly concerned with the limits of prediction, and especially with the predicative capacity of the technoscientific discourse around the gene.

Throughout GATTACA, the technoscientific discourse of the gene is the primary site through which the definition of the human is constructed. A human is represented as the expression of a series of genetic determinants, and their line of genetic code is of more consequence than anything else. Each individual is inserted into the discourse of the gene immediately after birth – a blood sample is translated into a statistical analysis that provides the probabilities of a disposition towards genetically quantifiable conditions. This quantification of predispositions refers not only to disease but also to behaviour and intelligence, creating an individual whose identity is constructed primarily from genetic information. The human subject as an individual with interiority is of little consequence, as the limits of their endeavour are predetermined, down to the decimal place. This relationship between corporeality and identity is constantly in play in *GATTACA*. As the material reality of the body is predicated on genetic discourse, the reliance on the genetic body as the only source of knowledge about the individual becomes the major site of contestation within the narrative of the film. Individuals are validated or invalidated solely on the basis of their statistics, their place on the percentile ranges of predicted outcomes of genetic events. An individual's social, economic and cultural progression is based on the gene, a somatic-technocracy taken to the extreme. As the character German, a seller of genetic profiles, comments to Vincent, the character who wishes to invest in a better genetic constitution, 'you could go anywhere with his [Jerome's] helix tucked under your arm'. The primacy of the helix is also suggested in the frequency with which it appears. It is visible as a letter sequence (GATA and so on) beneath the human faces that show up on the various detection technologies of the film. In the flat where the protagonists live, the spiral staircase echoes the twist of a helix, albeit a single one, that frequently dominates the background to the actions occurring within the flat.

The emphasis on the genetic body in *GATTACA* is revealed not only through the ways in which it predominates in questions of identity, but also through the means by which the state controls the individual. Although the state as a distinct set of institutions remains relatively opaque within *GATTACA*, the presence of an organisational structure is implicit in the operations of the police, whose practice of law enforcement resides in the collection of body swabs and fluids for the surveillance of the genetic body. Gone are the stark interrogation scenes; when a needle is produced, it is to take an intravenous blood sample, not to give drugs. Such operations ensure that the enforcement of the law amongst the citizens is mediated through the body. But the body in question here is not one defined by words and actions that manifest as contentious events which threaten the structures of the social. Instead, it is a body that materialises through its trails of dead skin and hair, its smears of sweat and saliva, things that are constantly monitored throughout the lives of the citizens of the story-world of *GATTACA*. In this context, the threatening body is one that is out of its genetic place. The

prominence of this body is evident in *GATTACA* even in the opening credits, where it is introduced through its detritus – nails, hair,
and dry skin. These constituents become objects of attention as,
magnified, they fill the screen, falling onto a surface in slow motion
to the sounds of the Michael Nyman score. These spectacularised
images of fragmented bodily detritus, each of which contains more
than enough genetic material to identify an individual, give way to
the source of these components, a human body. Not only, then, is the
body the site through which identity is constituted, the body and its
secretions are also the site of surveillance, enabling it to become an
object of the state. In the futuristic period of *GATTACA*, surveillance
has shifted from the macro to the micro, and the words and actions
of the individual become subservient to the traces of the body. An
individual can pass unnoticed in the movements of the group, but is
revealed on the basis of their genetic code. The normally unnoticed,
or invisible, takes precedence over the seen, to the extent that the
visible human ceases to matter.

Vincent Freedom and Jerome Morrow are the characters within
GATTACA through whom these operations of power, and specifically
the predictive power of the genetic code, are interrogated. 'Jerome' is
the near genetically perfect human specimen with 'an expiration date
approaching infinity', and 'he' becomes the means through which
Vincent launches his bid to be a member of the elite Gattaca Corporation, as he masquerades as 'Jerome' by using his genetic-body. (I
designate this figure as Vincent/Jerome.) 'Jerome', however, is not
equivalent to Jerome Morrow, 'he' is instead an idealisation, an idea
of perfection that Vincent and many other characters think Jerome
Morrow, or Jerome/Eugene, embodies. This distinction is played with
in *GATTACA* in the scene in which Vincent changes his hairstyle to
echo Jerome's appearance, and as he does so the image moves
between Vincent, Jerome and a photograph of 'Jerome'. The photograph of 'Jerome', which is the same image as that on the official
records, sits between both of the men, yet they each have a very
different connection to it.[15] For Jerome/Eugene, 'Jerome' is someone
he should have been, in terms of his genes, but who is also someone
he chooses not to be. For Vincent/Jerome, 'Jerome' is the means by
which he can become an astronaut. The different perspectives offered
by these two figures illustrate limits of the genetic discourse that operates within the story-world of *GATTACA*. Interestingly, these two
characters represent two very different forms of critique.

As the apparent hero of *GATTACA*, Vincent is, of course, more than his genetic printout would suggest. His possession of the 'will' to get into Gattaca Corporation, to become one of the elite, marks his difference; it is something that was not predicted by his profile. Vincent's strength of mind and purpose overcomes the weaknesses of his body, as he ignores his high probability of heart failure, makes up for his lack of good education and pushes himself to achieve. To put it rather crudely, as indeed *GATTACA* does, unlike the over-bred humans with whom he associates, Vincent relies on his will to overcome the perceived limitations of his body. And, since the character of Vincent/Jerome takes up the role and narrative space of the central protagonist, this character might be expected to function as the figure with which a spectator might identify. Through this emphasis, *GATTACA* presents the will-full Vincent/Jerome as a better human – he does not acquiesce to the predictive technoscientific discourse that controls the lives of many of the others in the Gattaca Corporation. As such, Vincent/Jerome operates within the narrative as the hero who exposes the limits of the technoscientific discourse of the gene, and the closed assumptions of the genetic discourse are broken open by the unpredicted element that he represents.

But *GATTACA* is something of a contradictory text. Through the figure of Vincent, the narrative plays out a resistance to the predictability of the technoscientific discourse, but really this resistance only operates as something on the outside trying to get in. After all, Vincent the 'hero' simply wants to be a corporate man. The contradictions of the text are also apparent in its depictions of fit and unfit bodies. Whilst it seems to recuperate Vincent because of his will to overcome the potential weaknesses of his genetic-body, his possession of a fit body is central to this endeavour. Whilst Vincent makes use of 'Jerome's' genetic-body, he also disciplines his own. He is seen creating his own bodily perfection, doing body curls weighted symbolically with the navigator's 'bible', and he ritually cleanses his body each morning, scrubbing away the evidence of his in-valid genetic-self. Of course, within the terms of the narrative Vincent needs to have a fit body to be Vincent/Jerome, an elite member of the Gattaca Corporation. But these images of the fit body seem to signify more than is necessary for the narrative coherence of *GATTACA*. As Vincent scrubs himself and does his body curls the camera lingers, displaying the muscularity of his body. Such displays reveal that the fit body matters, and this is a revelation that sits

uneasily with the eradication of Jerome's disabled body in the resolution of the film.

A further set of contradictions emerges in the cinematography and
mise-en-scène of the film. Whilst Vincent/Jerome's fit (genetic-)body
matters, *GATTACA* also frequently displaces the individual body
from the centre of visual attention, a displacement underlined by the
cinematography and *mise-en-scène*. The inhabitants of *GATTACA*
are often seen neatly in place, so in place that they become an aspect
of the symmetry of the set. Lines of figures ride the escalator into the
Gattaca Corporation, they walk along the corridors and sit in neatly
ordered rows at their neatly ordered workstations. The lack of any
spontaneity and energy amongst these genetically superior humans
is echoed in the colour range of the images. The film is imbued with
indistinct tones of colour; the interior sequences often have a green-
ish look, whilst the exterior sequences are shot in a diffuse yellow
haze. In keeping with the absence of depth and breadth of tonal
range, direct sunlight is never seen. Even when, in the heterosexual
romantic subplot of the film, Vincent and his potential girlfriend,
Irene, experience the romance of the sunrise together, the sun is only
seen as a slightly dissipated reflection on the solar panels. Despite
the lines of perspective frequently used to create symmetries within
the framing of images, such a use of colour has a flattening effect.
The tendency towards symmetries in relation to the architecture and
internal fittings also has the effect of diminishing the human figures.
The central placing of the escalators and stairwells of the Gattaca
Building, the high-angle shots of the corridors, the arrays of dull
metal workstations of the elite, overwhelm the human figures. Even
in the scenes when Vincent and Irene begin to build a relationship
they are dominated by the architecture. Standing outside on the concrete concourse bathed in a yellowish light, they are shown beneath
a hollow-cube concrete formation. Their black suits, rather than
making the central romantic couple of the film more distinct against
the yellow-bathed concrete, foreground how diminutive they are.
Despite his status within *GATTACA* as the rebel and the male half of
the heterosexual romance thread, this diminution of the human also
undermines Vincent/Jerome. He may have the will to overcome
the genetic discourse, but to what end? One of the paradoxes of
GATTACA is that its hero really only wants to be a part of the elite
that has excluded him. In his desire to be an astronaut he simply puts
the power circuits of the Gattaca Corporation into use. Vincent/

Jerome's actions within the narrative of *GATTACA*, whilst apparently operating as a critique of the genetic discourse in play in the film, ultimately become implicated in the maintenance of that discourse. The only way to 'freedom' is to follow the rules already in place, not to create anything new.

There is another way of reading *GATTACA*, a reading in which Vincent, the apparent hero of the film, does not really matter. Instead he is something of a ruse, a dodge which covers over the other story about technoscience that operates within the film. This other story, mediated through Jerome/Eugene, also engages with the question of the unpredictabilities of technoscientific discourse, but these unpredictabilities emerge from inside that discourse, and are an unexpected outcome of the correct operations of that discourse. Jerome is a man with a near-perfect genetic sequence; however, he refuses to be a part of the gene game and represents a different sort of limit to that suggested by the character of Vincent/Jerome. When he is first introduced within the plot, it is suggested that Jerome is unable to fulfil his genetic potential because of an accident. Jerome/Eugene later reveals to Vincent/Jerome that his accident was something that he wanted to occur. Jerome is as rebellious as Vincent, only his rebellion is to refuse to accept his perfection, and a place within the world-order of *GATTACA*. Jerome's initial role in the film is to provide the bodily traces that will aid Vincent's transgression of the genetic regime, something he does in return for his keep. By the end of the film, Jerome has choosen to go beyond the original parameters of the bargain. In an extension of his rebellion against his genetic profile, he offers something different to the corporate promise of Gattaca – he commits an unrequited act of kindness as he stores up supplies of his bodily traces, 'enough to last two-lifetimes'. Although never explicitly acknowledged, this would appear to be a gift of love, an interpretation suggested by Jerome's parting gesture to Vincent of a lock of his hair. This gesture could be read as a practicality of the on-going subterfuge, but this lock of hair is not given in a plastic pouch or tube, it is in a card, curled like a lover's keepsake.

At the end of *GATTACA* there is a shot of Vincent opening this card after he has been blasted into space, an event that coincides with Jerome's fiery suicide in the incinerator of their home, an act that is depicted intercut with the firing of the space-rocket engines. As Vincent contemplates his future amongst the stars, a triumphant hero unaware of Jerome's death, the contingent nature of his success recedes. Aside from the question of the kind of world that Vincent has willed his entry into, the narrative has revealed that Vincent's will alone was never enough. His success was ultimately dependent on the silence of Jerome, and also that of Lamar, the doctor who carried out all the Gattaca tests and had always known that Vincent was a fraud, but who had chosen not to reveal his knowledge. But this is a point only lightly touched on, quickly burnt out by the sight of the blasting rockets.

GATTACA, then, celebrates Vincent's will-power as a counterpoint to the genetic determinism of the Gattaca Corporation and presumably the power of the state, but this a muted and ambivalent rebellion that gives the film an uneasy resolution. Vincent represents a reassertion of human will and uncertainty against the closed predictions of the genetic discourse. But this reassertion of human will ultimately leads to conformity. In contrast, Jerome represents something unpredictable on the inside. Jerome was not simply an outsider, one whose existence called into question the operations of a dominant discourse. He is a fully incorporated and corporeal component of that discourse. As such, he reveals the limits of the power of a technoscientific discourse to encapsulate fully the meanings of its products. Like the technological beings of *Wargames* and *Edward Scissorhands* and the hybrid RoboCop, Jerome/Eugene represents a gap in the narrative, something unexpected by the genetic discourse. That Jerome dies in the resolution of *GATTACA* undercuts the film's celebration of Vincent as the symbol of human will and endeavour. It is as though Jerome's unexpected humanness, his love for Vincent and his refusal of perfection, are beyond the limits of uncertainty that the narrative of *GATTACA* is willing to allow.

Many fictions of technoscience create images of technology and technoscientific discourse by making use of constructions of humanness. *Wargames*, *Edward Scissorhands* and *RoboCop* feature technologies that are to some extent conceived in terms of humanness, either by the simple process of communication or through more complex questions of behaviour and gaining a position within a community. *GATTACA* represents a genetic discourse, one that is used in the prediction of humanness. However, it is important not to see images of technologies simply as the reproduction of particular versions of humanness. This is not to argue that images of technology can say nothing about constructions of gender, race, class or sexuality, but that we are losing something if we do not pay attention to the gap between humans and technologies that are evident within these and other fictions of technoscience. The images of technology and technoscience in *Wargames*, *Edward Scissorhands*, *RoboCop* and *GATTACA* are, finally, not only concerned with reproductions of humanness. In the unarticulated gap between the humanness in play within the text and the image of technology, they also attempt to say something about technology *as* technology. To some extent, these readings might be simply seen to reforeground a cultural uncertainty about technologies, an uncertainty in which technologies are either objects in the world that we can live with or objects that we should fear, set to one side, as in *Edward Scissorhands*. But there seems to be something else important going on in these texts. And what is important is precisely located in the gap that emerges between humans and technologies, when the technologies are not fully defined or managed by terms attributed to humanness. This gap keeps in place an openness in the relationship between the two terms, a conceptual openness that enables a provisionality in what is meant by human and what is meant by technology. Without this provisionality, the terms are caught in a circularity that seems destined to reduce rather than enhance our ways of thinking about changes in the world. To see technology only as a site through which constructions of gender are played out creates a closed circuit in that argument, a closed circuit that limits both the meaning of technology and the construction of gender. It is always tempting, however, to fill these gaps with those elements of difference which keep escaping the operations of the narrative – the difference of the android community in *Android*, the queerness of the relationship between Frankie and Ulysses, or Jerome and Vincent, or the difference of Jerome's disability. Filling these gaps would only result in another management of the technology, this time as a more generalised sign of difference. If these gaps are instead held open, they can be maintained as reminders or prompts about the contingency of the relationship between humanness and technologies. But such provisionality is at times uncomfortable. And perhaps this is the discomfort that resides in the gaps that opened up in my readings of *Wargames*, *Edward Scissorhands*, *RoboCop* and *GATTACA*. The discomfort is not in the uncertainty about what technology will or will not do to humans, but that the terms humanness, technologies or technoscientific discourse, however they are treated within the text, remain outside of our limits of prediction.

Notes

1 J.P. Telotte discusses the figures of the terminators as versions of human-ness, whilst other critics such as Claudia Springer, Susan Jeffords and Yvonne Tasker discuss the technological figures more in terms of gender. Susan Jeffords, *Hard Bodies: Holywood Masculinity in the Reagan Era* (Princeton, NJ: Rutgers University Press, 1994); Claudia Springer, *Electronic Eros: Bodies and Desire in the Postindustrial Age* (Austin: University of Texas, 1996); Yvonne Tasker, *Spectacular Bodies: Gender, Genre and the Action Cinema* (London and New York: Routledge, 1993); and J.P. Telotte, *Replications: A Robotic History of Science Fiction Film* (Urbana and Chicago: University of Illinois Press, 1995).
2 Paul Edwards, *The Closed World* (Cambridge, Mass.: MIT Press, 1996) p. 330.
3 Paul Edwards, *The Closed World* p. 330.
4 It is clear that Edward already knows something of the ways of humans, since he is able to communicate with Peg when they first meet, and like Max and Ulysses, he has been taught how to behave like a human being by his creator, but this source of his knowledge is not revealed until later in *Edward Scissorhands*.
5 *Edward Scissorhands* plays on the idea of gothic, partially through the 'Goth' look of dyed black har, a whitened face and black clothing, but also in terms of the gothic architecture of Edward's home. In an inversion of the tradition of gothic novels, the house may appear to be threatening but in fact it is Edward's sanctuary from the threats of the outside world. The film also inverts the *Frankenstein* construction of the mad creator. The creator in *Edward Scissorhands* rather than being megalomaniacal appears instead as a lonely and elderly man.
6 *The Cyborg Handbook* contains a series of essays on the figure of the cyborg as a cultural phenomenon as well as a fictional being. Chris Hables Gray (ed.), *The Cyborg Handbook* (London and New York: Routledge, 1995).
7 An interesting precedent for these films is *The Colossus of New York*. Made in 1958, the film features a scientist whose experiments could result in the expansion of the world's food resources. He dies in an accident but is brought back to life as a cyborg figure by his father, another scientist. The dilemma of *The Colossus of New York*, like that of *Robo-Cop*, *Universal Soldier* and *Running Delilah*, is the effect of a technologised body on the experience of being human.
8 The actual image used to give this sense of increasing distance is of a tree-

lined road moving away from the house where Murphy's wife and child stand waving. In the subsequent scenes where RoboCop attempts to go back to his life, it is this same road that he travels along, moving towards rather than away from the house.

9 The gendered construction of *RoboCop* has also been commented upon by Claudia Springer, *Electronic Eros* pp. 108–111; Yvonne Tasker, *Spectacular Bodies* pp. 150–151; and Susan Jeffords, *Hard Bodies* pp. 106–118.

10 Scott Bukatman, *Terminal Identity: The Virtual Subject in Postmodern Science Fiction* (Durham, NC: Duke University Press, 1993) pp. 8–9.

11 Samantha Holland, 'Descartes Goes to Hollywood: Mind, Body and Gender in Contemporary Cyborg Cinema', in Mike Featherstone and Roger Burrows, *Cyberspace/Cyberbodies/Cyberpunk: Cultures of Technological Embodiment* (London: Sage Publications, 1995) pp. 157–174; p. 160.

12 Steve Best, 'RoboCop: The Crisis of Subjectivity', *Canadian Journal of Political and Social Philosophy*, 13: 1–2 (1989) 44–55, and Bukatman, *Terminal Identity* p. 258.

13 An interesting comparison with *RoboCop* is the Japanese anime *Ghost in the Shell* (1995, Jap.). This cartoon takes the question of a hybrid being much further than *RoboCop*. The central character of the text is a female gendered cyborg, Major Kusanaga. In the resolution, she merges with a fully technological intelligence. And whilst the narrative of *Ghost in the Shell* cannot say what this new being is, it does make clear that it is neither fully human nor fully technological.

14 G, A, T and C are the single-letter codes used for the nucleotide bases that are understood to constitute DNA molecules, the information-carrying portion of the gene.

15 I use the combinations Vincent/Jerome and Jerome/Eugene to differentiate between the two characters who use the name Jerome.

Conclusion

Popular culture is a site through which cultural tensions are negotiated. These negotiations are never straightforward, encapsulating as they do multiple and competing positions. As a key element of popular culture, the cinema has generated many fictions of technoscience, and these serve as a cultural resource through which ideas about science and technology can be explored. My particular view in *Technoscience in Contemporary Films* is that many films present a complex narrative about science and technology. Through an emphasis on contemporary American films, I argue that these texts construct science and technology as a technoscience. That is, fictions of technoscience construct science and technology as systems of knowledge and institutions that are constituted within and through a specific social, economic and cultural context; they are *not* the product of a separate scientific domain. As science and technology come to be understood as technoscience, so it becomes clear that the meanings of these two terms are contingent and open to varying degrees of contestation. In the process of contesting the meanings of science and technology, ideas about the constructions of humanness also become evident. In the same way that technoscience is contingent on social context, so too are the meanings of humanness contingent on the technoscientific ones.

When I began this book I wanted to explore how contemporary films told stories about the relationships between humans, science and technology. This was primarily motivated by the films themselves, but also by my growing sense that many of the existing analyses left unturned a whole range of questions about images of science and technology. Taking science fiction as an example, as this is where many of the debates about science and technology occur, much of the emphasis of other critics has been on how this genre negotiates changing ideas about gender, and also how images of technologies are a more general commentary on changing ideas of humanness. My own thinking was initially also about humans, but as the book progressed I realised that I was equally interested in what films had to say about science and technology. This was not simply because I was interested in those ideas, but because many films were themselves making quite complex and thought-provoking explorations of the processes of science and technology.

Throughout *Technoscience in Contemporary Film* a central device has been to adapt ideas taken from technoscience studies. For me, a key concern has been to think about the different ways in which films depict humans and the processes of science and technology as elements that constantly interact with each other, since it is in these interactions that humans, science and technologies take on various sets of meanings and associations. Technoscience refuses to separate the social from the scientific. One of the meanings and associations that emerges in contemporary fictions of technoscience is that scientists are not the only source through which knowledge is produced, as the institution is also part of that production. As my analyses of *Lorenzo's Oil* and *Medicine Man* suggest, fictions of technoscience depict the emergence of knowledge as contingent on the structures of the institutions within which it is formed, as well as the individual or groups of scientists who operate within the institution. Another feature of fictions of technoscience made since the 1980s is their ongoing concern with the ways in which scientific knowledge exists through a negotiation between different sets of forces. These forces typically include the military, and various kinds of corporate groups, as well as the institutional practices of science and medicine, all of which display an interestedness towards the knowledge or object produced from within their sphere of influence. These interests, one might add, are frequently at cross-purposes with one another.

The argument that the processes and practices of science and technology are embedded within a social world appears to imply that the direction of influence is always one way, that social effects determine scientific and technological ones. However, that is only one aspect of the intersection. Science and technologies themselves impact on the social world, or more specifically the human inhabitants of that world. This aspect of the intersection between humans and technoscience is not only complex but frequently contradictory, indicating that fictions of technoscience are neither simply technophobic nor technophilic. Through the range of possibilities found in *12 Monkeys*,

D.A.R.Y.L., *Junior* and *sex, lies and videotape*, the positioning of humans as the objects of technoscientific processes emerges as a contested site. The struggles of these narratives reveal fictions of technoscience as revolving around the ways technoscience empowers, disempowers or erases particular constructions of humanness. Just as technoscience is contingent on the social world, so too is humanness contingent on technoscience.

The notion that technoscience is contingent on the social world need not only be seen as demonstrating that particular contexts have particular outcomes. Whilst the 2035 scientists of *12 Monkeys* represent a pessimistic version of technoscience, and those of *D.A.R.Y.L.* a more optimistic one, other films make more explicit the idea that the meanings of knowledges and objects are open to transformation, as they are accumulated and divested at one and the same time. Particular examples of these transformations are technological objects that have multiple social locations evoked through changing patterns of connection and reconnection. These patterns enable humans and technologies to be viewed as components within a network where technological objects gain their meanings not simply through their functionality, but also through their social location. Different social locations can contribute different social meanings to technological objects, leading to the view that technologies can exist as multiple social objects. The intersections between technologies and humans again becomes an active site of negotiation, and the outcome of this negotiation can never be fully certain as the intersections remain open to competing influences.

The fictions of technoscience that I have discussed have all been produced since 1980, and as such they explore cultural imaginings from the late twentieth century. But the idea of technoscience could also be fruitfully applied to other eras. Even the brief sketch of fictions of technoscience from different chronological periods provided in Chapter 1, suggests that concerns around science and technology change with different historical contexts. Vivian Sobchack suggests that 'the SF film gives concrete narrative shape and visible form to our changing historical imagination of social progress and disaster, and to the ambiguities of being human in a world where advanced technology has altered both the contours and meaning of personal and social existence'.[1] The specific historical contexts of images of technoscience are perhaps most written about in relation to the SF and horror genres of the 1950s. For example, Susan Sontag suggests

that the historical imagination of SF films from the 1950s is one that
is primarily concerned with the 'aesthetics of destruction', and John
Baxter suggests that 'SF cinema is ... the poetry of the atomic age ...
and heir to a strange hieratic beauty and cultural humour'.[2] Between
them, Sontag and Baxter view the SF films of the 1950s as a bringing
together of wonderment and terror, a view that again evokes an
ambivalent image of technoscience. Whilst these two critics do
indeed provide an insight into the particular historical context of the
genre, what they have to say about science and technology remains
primarily at the level of effect rather than process; that is, they both
treat science and technologies as objects which have an effect on the
world, rather than objects which are formed within that world.
Through the view of technoscience, the films of the 1950s have the
potential to make a range of comments about the processes of science
and technology, and as in the contemporary period, this is not confined to either the SF genre or the horror genre. Imaginings about
science and technology can equally be found in other genres of the
period, and so provide a rich resource of fictions of technoscience.

   Although the focus of this book has been on American texts, fictions of technoscience are not confined to this national cinema. Not
only has Hollywood been a dominating presence in the production
and distribution of science-fiction cinema, the images of technoscience which can be teased out from them represent an American-
based view of the processes of science and technology. There is,
however, more than one history of technoscience, and some alter-
natives can be found in cinematic contexts distinct from that of
Hollywood. Perhaps one of the most obvious examples of such cultural imaginings of technoscience can be found in Japanese cinema,
especially within mecha and cyber anime.[3] In a similar way to the
American texts discussed, these films provide a resource for thinking
about how images of science and technology tell stories about
technoscience as well as about constructions of humanness – in this
instance from the perspective of Japanese cultural and technoscientific traditions. *The Dish* (2000, Aus), *Ringu* (1998, Jap.) and
Xizao (1999, China) are other texts, recently on release in the UK,
which have the potential to be seen as fictions of technoscience. *The
Dish* could be seen as a film that explores the relationship between
Australian and American space-science expertise in the 1960s, possibly touching on concerns around globalisation; *Xizao* reflects on
ideas about the transforming effects of technology on traditional

communities in China; and *Ringu*, as an alternative to anime, inter-weaves ideas about story-telling and new technologies in Japan.

So far in this conclusion I have suggested ways in which the idea of fictions of technoscience could be expanded to include different chronological periods or different cultural contexts. In so doing I am not trying to impose a particular view of technoscience or human-ness on these different chronological periods or cultural contexts. Instead, it is the process of thinking about technoscience and humanness through networks and contingencies that can be usefully put to work. The outcome of that process is not a given; it will itself be contingent on historical contexts and cultural locations. This par-ticular point brings me to a reflection on the limits of *Technoscience in Contemporary Film*, and to turn some of the questions raised about the images of technoscience back on the book itself. There is always a danger of overreaching in a study like this, which seems to make generalising statements based on a small group of films. The texts chosen here do touch on issues that frequently appear in films made since the 1980s, but they are not generalisable in the sense that not all films come to the same conclusions as the ones discussed in this book. There are many things to be said about technoscience, and only some of them can be said here. My awareness that there are things left unsaid is not only a result of the selection of the texts; it is also an outcome of the mode of production of many of films. With the exception of the video-feature *Fresh Kill*, almost all of the films are produced within the contemporary American studio system. The final version of the film is the result of an interplay between writers, directors, producers, set designers, actors and, in some instances, the special-effects teams. The contingencies of these fictions of techno-science, then, are not only located in historical periods and cultural contexts, but also in their modes of production. Detailed questions about the mode of production of films lie beyond the scope of this study, but as the various influences on production change, so too will the kinds of stories told. One influence that has been evident throughout the history of filmmaking has been special effects. The last ten years have seen enormous advances in the use of comput-erised effects in films, and one outcome has been changes in how images of science and technology are visualised. The increasing spectacularity of such images is another element in the generation of fictions of technoscience. For instance, the layers of human and animal bodies seen in *Hollow Man*, as well as demonstrating the potential of computer graphics, are also a narrative of contemporary ideas about bodies. In addition, multiplex cinemas frequently have good surround-sound systems, an improvement that enhances the sound dimension of special effects.

One possible implication of much of what I have said is that a careful thinking through of the various influences present in any given context – whether chronological, cultural or mode of production – will produce a full account of that particular historical moment. There is, however, a danger in the notion of a network within which technological objects and humans intersect and generate a full set of meanings for each other. The danger lies in the assumption that *all* meanings of humanness or technologies can be understood to reside in that intersection. As a consequence, any potential sites of difference are glossed over as they are renegotiated to they fit within a network. In effect, this can amount to an assimilation of difference. An example of the process of this assimilation is evident in many fictions of technoscience where a technological being is managed through their acquisition of codes more usually associated with humanness. Through this device, technological beings – such as Max, Ulysses and Call in *Android*, *Making Mr Right* and *Alien: Resurrection* – are renegotiated as objects in the world through their similarities to humans rather than their differences from humans. Although on one level this appears to be an inherently conservative tactic, there is a potentially interesting side-effect. This side-effect appears because the devices through which the differences of technology are glossed over have the effect of demonstrating that humanness, rather than being a natural category, is instead constructed from a set of categories that are validated or invalidated according to the operations of an individual text. As the cultural, social and political workings of any given film become evident, so too does the work that goes into generating the apparently neutral constructions of humanness. In the same ways that scientific knowledge is contingent on institutional practices, the constructions of humanness are contingent on the workings of a given text.

In spite of this revealing side-effect, few of the films themselves operate as explicit reflections on the idea that humanness is a construction. Instead, they more simply seem to generate terms of humanness. The terms that are especially privileged in the American texts discussed here include a self-reflexive consciousness, a capacity for communication, caring, a rationality balanced by emotions, freedom of choice and the need for community. Following Scott

Bukatman's critique of the SF genre as a site where 'human definitions ... remained rooted in Western, masculine, heterosexist –
"neutral" – paradigms', these terms are most often constituted
through the male characters of the films.[4] Having said this, however,
there is some degree of heterogeneity in the figures that contribute
to the constructions of humanness. Although the racial profile does
predominantly remain white, the gendered heterogeneity of humanness is evident; for instance, Call operates in much the same way as
the male-gendered androids Max and Ulysses, when each draws
attention to the privileged constructions of humanness within their
respective films. But whilst it is possible to suggest that there is a
degree of heterogeneity in the constructions of humanness, some
categories do remain intact. One of the most evident of these is the
Western tradition of science and technology. It is unusual to find a
film produced from within the Hollywood context that suggests
there are alternative systems of scientific knowledge, such as those
of the Islamic or Chinese traditions. Of the films discussed in this
study, only *Medicine Man* invokes the possibility of other traditions
and knowledge systems. Overall, then, any heterogeneity of humanness still revolves primarily around American conventions and traditions, and all figures, whatever their race or ethnicity, operate
within these same conventions. If we are not careful to draw this
out, such traditions are liable to continue to retain a universal status,
when in fact these traditions have very distinct cultural histories.

My own use of the term 'humanness', although it has the potential to come close to losing the aspects of difference I briefly touch
on above, is an attempt to expose the tendency to universalise the
meanings of humanness. This tension between covering over and
exposing is most evident in my use of humanness to overarch gender
difference. It has often been pointed out that 'man' has stood in for
'human', but I use humanness here to indicate that *both* categories
of gender contribute to its construction. My intention is not to erase
the differences of gender; rather, it is to indicate that the term
humanness is not a monolithic category. Instead, humanness is a
multifaceted word, and what is included or excluded in its construction is as much as question of politics as anything else. Having
said this, it has always struck me as a paradox that categories of
gender are themselves most frequently used within fictions of
technoscience, both within the films themselves and also in the critical literature, to erase the difference of technology. This tendency

to manage or capture technology within the terms of a gendered humanness has problems. In using images of technology to say something about gendered constructions of humanness, there is a danger of stabilising such categories of humans. This is especially evident in those critical commentaries which claim that images of technologies simply reinscribe already existing categories of gender. This position is something of a double bind, as technology can only be perceived in terms of gender, and the gender categories invoked are often perceived as conservative ones. Instead of opening up new ways of thinking about either technologies or gender, such a construction leads to a reductive circularity.

To avoid this circularity, *Technoscience in Contemporary Film* ends with an emphasis on the difference between humans and technologies. This difference is located in the gaps that exist when technologies cannot be either fully defined or managed by the multiplicity of terms attributed to humanness. Although there is always a temptation to fill these gaps with meanings, keeping them open is essential to maintaining a provisional construction of both humanness and technologies so as to avoid displacing the meanings of technology into other categories. For instance, it would be easy to collapse the difference of technology into the other differences evident in the texts discussed in this book, but this tactic only leads to another reductive circularity. By keeping this in mind, it may also be possible to keep in place the provisional relationship between humanness and technologies. My insistence on a gap between humanness and technologies is essentially an optimistic tactic. Although such gaps are frequently problematic in fictions of technoscience, they have the potential to be productive sites where new meanings of humanness as well as technologies can be generated.

I recently watched the animated feature *Titan A.E.* (2000, US). In this film the planet Earth has been destroyed by the Drej, aliens who consist of 'pure energy'. Since this is a fantasy in which intergalactic travel has become commonplace, there turn out to be numerous survivors of this apocalypse. These survivors form a diaspora as they are spread across the galaxy, either in small enclaves or as dispossessed individuals eking out an existence, one entity amongst many different kinds of entities. The central struggle of *Titan A.E.* is around the attempt to re-establish a place for humans to live, and associated with this is an idea of restoring some sense of human identity. The success of this endeavour relies on the two key figures of the plot, Akima and Cale, being able to find a technological device. This device is a sophisticated machine containing vast amounts of genetic information, and its activation will lead to the generation of a new planet. In amongst the many chases and fights of this cartoon feature, there is a fiction of technoscience – a lost sense of community can potentially be restored by the workings of technoscience. Here is a machine powerful enough to hold the destiny of the whole of the human race in the outcome of one vast experiment: the ideal of a restorable human community is contingent on technoscience. All it takes is the flick of a switch and the place for human community and identity is reinstated. Of course, this is an extremely romantic ideal. A diasporic community is given back its sense of home, a place in which to belong all over again. And not only are humans given back their home, their representative heroes are transcendent, obliterating the threat of the alien Drej. But if *Titan A.E.* is really so conservative, why bother to mention it? I mention it because, whilst its plot is nostalgic in the sense that it aims to recover something lost, it nevertheless also offers something different. The version or versions of humanness that are re-established are as yet uncertain, since the outcome of machine's regeneration of the planet is beyond the scope of the plot. Furthermore, the two representatives of humanness, one female and one male, are from different ethnic backgrounds, and so move away from the tradition of white male heroes. Such an ending suggests there is room in American popular culture for a change in the definition of humanness. And if this turns out to be so, then maybe there are also new possibilities for images of technoscience.

Notes

1 Vivian Sobchack, 'Science Fiction', in Wes D. Gehring (ed.), *Handbook of American Film Genres* (New York: Greenwood Press, 1988) pp. 229–247; p. 231.

2 Susan Sontag, 'The Imagination of Disaster',*October*, 40 (1965) and John Baxter, *Science Fiction in the Cinema* (New York: Barnes, 1970) p. 13.

3 The mecha tradition of anime has tended to feature large robots (for instance *Kidô keisatsu patorebâ: the movie* (*Patlabor: the movie*) (1990, Jap.) and *Roujin Z* (1991, Jap.). I am using the term cyber to include anime which also feature cyborg characters (for instance, *Appurushîdo*

(*Appleseed*) (1988, Jap) and *Kokaku kidotai* (*Ghost in the Shell*) (1995, Jap.).

4 Scott Bukatman, *Terminal Identity: The Virtual Subject in Postmodern Science Fiction* (Durham, NC: Duke University Press, 1993) p. 17.

Filmography

Unless stated otherwise the films listed below are all features.

Alien (1979, Ridley Scott; US)
Alien: Resurrection (1997, Pierre Jeunot; US)
Amazing Transparent Man, The (1960, Edgar G. Ulmer; US)
Android (1982, Aaron Lipstadt; US)
Apollo 13 (1995, Ron Howard; US)
Appurushîdo (Appleseed) (1988, Kazuyoshi Katayama; Jap.)
Armageddon (1998, Michael Bay; US)
Batman and Robin (1997, Joel Schumacher; US)
Blade Runner (1982, Ridley Scott; US)
Bone Collector, The (1999, Phillip Noyce; US)
Brainstorm (1983, Douglas Trumball; US)
Brides of Fu Manchu, The (1966, Don Sharp; US)
Bringing Up Baby (1938, Howard Hawks; US)
Casino Royale (1967, Val Guest and Ken Hughes; UK)
Chain Reaction (1996, Andrew Davis; US)
China Syndrome, The (1978, James Bridges; US)
Citadel, The (1938, King Vidor; US/UK)
Cité des enfants perdue, La (*The City of Lost Children*) (1995, Pierre Jeunot
    and Marc Caro; Fr)
Cloak and Dagger (1946, Fritz Lang; US)
Colossus of New York, The (1958, Eugène Lourié; US)
Colossus: The Forbin Project (1969, Joseph Sargent; US)
Contact (1997, Robert Zemeckis; US)
Conversation, The (1974, Francis Ford Coppola; US)
Creature from the Black Lagoon, The (1954, Jack Arnold; US)
Cyborg 2: Glass Shadow (1993, Michael Schroeder; US)
Cyborg 3: The Recycler (1995, Michael Schroeder; US)
Dark Victory (1939, Edmund Goulding; US)
D.A.R.Y.L. (1985, Simon Wincer; UK/US)
Date with the Falcon, A (1941, Irving Reis; US)

Demon Seed (1977, Donald Cammell; US)
Devil in a Blue Dress (1995, Carl Franklin; US)
Dish, The (2000, Rob Sitch; Aus.)
Doctor X (1932, Michael Curtiz; US)
Dr Ehrlich's Magic Bullet (1940, William Dieterle; US)
Dr Jekyll and Mr Hyde (1932, Rouben Mamoulian; US)
Dr No (1962, Terence Young; UK)
Dr Strangelove: Or How I Learned to Stop Worrying and Love the Bomb
  (1963, Stanley Kubrick; UK/US)
Edison, the Man (1940, Clarence Brown; US)
Edward Scissorhands (1990, Tim Burton; US)
End of Days (1999, Peter Hyams; US)
Enemy of the State (1998, Tony Scott; US)
Eraser (1996, Chuck Russell; US)
Eve of Destruction (1991, Duncan Gibbins; US)
Extreme Measures (1996, Michael Apted; US)
Fail-Safe (1964, Sidney Lumet; US)
Fantastic Voyage (1966, Richard Fleischer; US)
Fargo (1996, Joel Coen; US)
Flubber (1997, Les Mayfield; US)
Frankenstein (1931, James Whale; US)
Fresh Kill (1995, Shu Lea Cheang; US)
GATTACA (1997, Andrew Niccol; US)
Gremlins (1984, Joe Dante; US)
Gremlins 2: The New Batch (1990, Joe Dante; US)
Hollow Man (2000, Paul Verhoeven; US)
House on 92nd Street, The (1945 docu-drama, Henry Hathaway; US)
Incredible Shrinking Man, The (1957, Jack Arnold; US)
Invasion of the Body Snatchers (1956, Don Siegel; US)
Ipcress Files, The (1965, Sidney J. Furie; UK)
Iron Giant, The (1999, Brad Bird; US)
It Came from Beneath the Sea (1953, Robert Gordon; US)
Jetée, La (1962, Chris Marker; Fr)
Jingle All the Way (1996, Brian Levant; US)
Junior (1994, Ivan Reitman; US)
Junior G-Men (1940 series, Ford Beebe and John Rawlins; US)
Jurassic Park (1992, Steven Spielberg; US)
Kidô keisatsu patorebâ: the movie (*Patlabor: the movie*) (1990, Mamoru
  Oshii; Jap)
Kindergarten Cop (1990, Ivan Reitman; US)
Kokaku kidotai (*Ghost in the Shell*) (1995, Mamoru Oshii; Jap)
Last Action Hero (1993, John McTiernan; US)
Lawnmower Man, The (1992, Brett Leonard; US)

Lawnmower Man 2: Beyond Cyberspace (1996, Farhad Mann; US)
Liquid Sky (1982, Slava Tsukerman; US)
Logan's Run (1976, Michael Anderson; US)
Lookers (1981, Michael Crichton; US)
Lorenzo's Oil (1992, George Miller; US)
Lost World: Jurassic Park, The (1997, Steven Spielberg; US)
Madame Curie (1943, Mervyn le Roy; US)
Making Mr Right (1987, Susan Seidelman; US)
Man Who Fell to Earth, The (1976, Nicholas Roeg; UK)
Matrix, The (1999, Andy Wachowski and Larry Wachowski; US)
Medicine Man (1992, John McTiernan; US)
Metropolis (1927, Fritz Lang, Ger)
Monkey Business (1952, Howard Hawks; US)
Monster that Challenged the World, The (1957, Arnold Laven; US)
Mrs Miniver (1942, William Wyler; US)
Nell (1994, Michael Apted; US)
Net, The (1995, Irwin Winkler; US)
Nightmare Before Christmas, The (1993, Henry Selick; US)
Notorious (1946, Alfred Hitchcock; US)
Nutty Professor, The (1996, Tom Shadyac; US)
Our Man Flint (1965, Daniel Mann; US)
Outbreak (1995, Wolfgang Petersen; US)
Panic in the Streets (1950, Elia Kazan; US)
People Will Talk (1951, Joseph L. Mankiewicz; US)
Perfect Woman, The (1949, Bernard Knowles; UK)
Relic, The (1997, Peter Hyams; US)
Ringu (1998, Hideo Nakata and Chisui Takigawa; Jap)
RoboCop (1987, Paul Verhoeven; US)
RoboCop 2 (1990, Irvin Kershner; US)
Roujin Z (1991, Hiroyuki Kitakubo; Jap)
Running Delilah (a.k.a. *Cyborg Agent*) (1994, Richard Franklin; US)
Saint, The (1997, Phillip Noyce; US)
Screamers (1995, Christian Duguay; Can./US)
sex, lies and videotape (1989, Steven Soderbergh; US)
Short Circuit (1986, John Badham; US)
Silent Running (1971, Douglas Trumball; US)
Sleepy Hollow (1998, Tim Burton; US)
Small Soldiers (1998, Joe Dante; US)
Soylent Green (1973, Richard Fleischer; US)
Species (1995, Roger Donaldson; US)
Stepford Wives, The (1975, Bryan Forbes; US)
Story of Louis Pasteur, The (1936, William Dieterle; US)
Strange Days (1995, Kathryn Bigelow; US)

Terminator, The (1984, James Cameron; US)
Terminator 2: Judgement Day (1991, James Cameron; US)
Them! (1954, Gordon Douglas; US)
Thing from Another World, The (1951, Christian Nyby; US)
Titan A.E. (2000, Don Bluth and Gary Goldman; US)
Torn Curtain, The (1966, Alfred Hitchcock; US)
Tron (1982, Steven Lisberger; US)
True Lies (1994, James Cameron; US)
Twins (1988, Ivan Reitman; US)
Universal Soldier (1992, Roland Emmerich; US)
Vertigo (1958, Alfred Hitchcock; US)
Vivacious Lady (1938, George Stevens; US)
Wargames (1983, John Badham; US)
Weird Science (1985, John Hughes; US)
Westworld (1973, Michael Crichton; US)
Xizao (1999, Yang Zhang; China)
12 Monkeys (1995, Terry Gilliam; US)
2001: A Space Odyssey (1968, Stanley Kubrick; UK/US)

Bibliography

Adams, Alison, *Artificial Knowing: Gender and the Thinking Machine*, London and New York, Routledge, 1998.

Aronowitz, Stanley, Barbara Martinsons and Michael Menser (eds.), *Technoscience and cyberculture: A Cultural Study*, London and New York, Routledge, 1996.

Balsamo, Anne, *Technologies of the Gendered Body: Reading Cyborg Women*, Durham, NC, Duke University Press, 1996.

Baxter, John, *Science Fiction in Film*, New York, Barnes, 1970.

Bergstrom, Janet, 'Androids and Androgeny,' in Constance Penley, Elisabeth Lyon, Lynn Spigeland and Janet Bergstrom, *Close Encounters: Film, Feminism and Science Fiction*, Minneapolis, University of Minnesota Press, 1991, pp. 33–60.

Best, Steve, 'RoboCop: The Crisis of Subjectivity,' *Canadian Journal of Political and Social Philosophy* 13:1–2 (1989) 44–55.

Biskind, Peter, *Seeing is Believing: How Hollywood Taught Us to Stop Worrying and Love the Fifties*, London, Pluto Press, 1984.

Broderick, Damien, *Reading by Starlight: Postmodern Science Fiction*, London and New York, Routledge, 1994.

Bukatman, Scott, *Terminal Identity: The Virtual Subject in Postmodern Science Fiction*, Durham, NC, Duke University Press, 1993.

Butler, Judith, *Gender Trouble: Feminism and the Subversion of Identity*, London and New York, Routledge, 1990.

Byers, Thomas B., 'Terminating the Postmodern: Masculinity and Pomophobia,' *Mfs* 41:1 (Spring 1995) 5–33.

Cartwright, Lisa, *Screening the Body: Tracing Medicine's Visual Culture*, Minneapolis, University of Minnesota Press, 1995.

Casper, Monica, 'Fetal Cyborgs and Technomoms on the Reproductive Frontier: Which Way to the Carnival?' in Chris Hables Gray (ed.), *The Cyborg Handbook*, London and New York, Routledge, 1995, pp. 183–202.

Chalmers, A. F., *What is This Thing Called Science? An Assessment of the Nature and Status of Science and its Methods*, 2nd edn, Milton Keynes, Open University Press, 1982.

Clute, John and Peter Nicholls (eds.), *The Dictionary of Science Fiction*, London, Orbit, 1993.

Cohan, Steve and Ina Rae Hark (eds.), *Screening the Male: Exploring Masculinities in Hollywood Cinema*, London and New York, Routledge, 1993.

Deleuze, Gilles, *Negotiations: 1972–1990*, New York, Columbia University Press, 1990.

Deleuze, Gilles and Félix Guattari, *A Thousand Plateaus: Capitalism and Schizophrenia*, London, The Athlone Press, 1988.

Doane, Mary Ann, 'Technophilia: Technology, Representation, and the Feminine,' in Mary Jacobus, Evelyn Fox Keller and Sally Shuttleworth (eds.), *Body/Politics: Women and the Discources of Science*, London and New York, Routledge, 1990, pp. 163–176.

Dyer, Richard, *The Matter of Images: Essays on Representation*, London and New York, Routledge, 1993.

——, *White*, London and New York, Routledge, 1997.

Dyer-Witheford, Nick, *Cyber-Marx: Cycles and Circuits of Struggles in High-Technology Capitalism*, Urbana and Chicago, University of Illinois Press, 1999.

Edwards, Paul, *The Closed World*, Cambridge, Mass., MIT Press, 1996.

Foucault, Michel, *The Order of Things: An Archaeology of the Human Sciences*, London, Tavistock, 1970.

——, *The Archaeology of Knowledge*, London, Tavistock, 1972.

——, *The History of Sexuality: An Introduction*, Volume 1, London, Penguin, 1976.

Fox Keller, Evelyn, *Reflections on Gender and Science*, New Haven, Yale University Press, 1985.

Fox Keller, Evelyn and Helen E. Longino (eds.), *Feminism and Science*, Oxford, Oxford University Press, 1996.

Fuchs, Cynthia, '"Death is Irrelevant": Cyborgs, Reproduction and the Future of Male Hysteria,' *Genders*, 18 (Winter 1993) 113–133.

Gibson, Andrew, *Towards a Postmodern Theory of Narrative*, Edinburgh, Edinburgh University Press, 1996.

Gunn, James, *Inside Science Fiction: Essays on Fantastic Literature*, San Bernardino, Calif., Borgo Press, 1992.

Halberstam, Judith, *Female Masculinity*, Durham, NC, Duke University Press, 1998.

Haraway, Donna J., *Simians, Cyborgs and Women: The Reinvention of Nature*, London, Free Association Books, 1991.

——, *Modest_Witness@Second_Millennium.FemaleMan©_Meets_Onco-Mouse,™:Feminism and Technoscience*, London and New York, Routledge, 1997.

Harding, Sandra, *Whose Science? Whose Knowledge? Thinking from*

Women's Lives, Milton Keynes, Open University Press, 1991.

Harding, Sandra (ed.), *The 'Racial' Economy of Science: Toward a Democratic Future*, London and New York, Routledge, 1993.

Haynes, Rosalyn, *From Faust to Strangelove: Representations of the Scientist in Western Literature*, Baltimore, Johns Hopkins University Press, 1994.

Hillier, Jim, *The New Hollywood*, London, Studio Vista, 1992.

Holland, Samantha, 'Descartes Goes to Hollywood: Mind, Body and Gender in Contemporary Cyborg Cinema,' in Mike Featherstone and Roger Burrows, *Cyberspace/Cyberbodies/Cyberpunk: Cultures of Technological Embodiment*, London, Sage Publications, 1995, pp. 157–174.

hooks, bell, *Black Looks: Race and Representation*, London, Turnaround Books, 1992.

——, *Reel to Real: Race, Sex and Class at the Movies*, London and New York, Routledge, 1996.

Hutten, Ernest, *The Origins of Science: An Inquiry into the Foundation of Western Thought*, London, Allen and Unwin, 1962.

Jacobus, Mary, Evelyn Fox Keller and Sally Shuttleworth (eds.), *Body/ Politics*, London and New York, Routledge, 1990.

James, Edward, *Science Fiction in the 20th Century*, Oxford, Oxford University Press, 1994.

Jancovich, Mark, *Rational Fears: American Horror in the 1950s*, Manchester, Manchester University Press, 1996.

Jeffords, Susan, *Hard Bodies: Hollywood Masculinity in the Reagan Era*, Princeton, NJ, Rutgers University Press, 1994.

Jordanova, Ludmilla, *Sexual Visions: Images of Gender in Science and Medicine between the Eighteenth and Twentieth Centuries*, New York, Harvester Wheatsheaf, 1989.

Kerman, Judith B. (ed.), *Retrofitting Blade Runner: Issues in Ridley Scott's Blade Runner and Philip K. Dick's Do Androids Dream of Electric Sheep*, 2nd edn, Bowling Green, Ohio, Bowling Green State University Popular Press, 1997.

Kuhn, Annette, *Alien Zone: Cultural Theory and Contemporary Science Fiction Cinema*, London, Verso, 1990.

——, *Alien Zone 2*, London, Verso, 1999.

Laqueur, Thomas, *Making Sex: Body and Gender from the Greeks to Freud*, Cambridge, Mass., Harvard University Press, 1990.

Latour, Bruno, *Science in Action: How to Follow Scientists and Engineers Through Society*, Milton Keynes, Open University Press, 1987.

Lauretis, Teresa de, 'Signs of Wa/onder,' in Teresa de Lauretis, Andreas Huyssen and Kathleen Woodward (eds.), *The Technological Imagination: Theories and Fictions*, Madison, Wisconsin Coda Press, Inc., 1980, pp. 159–174.

Law, John, 'Technology and Heterogeneous Engineering: The Case of Portuguese Expansion,' in Wiebe E. Bijker, Thomas P. Hughes and Trevor Pinch (eds.), *The Social Construction of Technological Systems: New Directions in the Sociology and History of Technology*, Cambridge, Mass., MIT Press, 1987, pp. 111–134.

—— (ed.), *A Sociology of Monsters: Essays on Power, Technology and Domination*, London and New York, Routledge, 1991.

Law, John and John Hassard (eds.), *Actor Network Theory and After*, Oxford, Blackwell Publishers, 1999.

Lewis, Jon (ed.), *The New American Cinema*, Durham, NC, Duke University Press, 1998.

Lloyd, Genevieve, *The Man of Reason: 'Male' and 'Female' in Western Philosophy*, 2nd edn, London and New York, Routledge, 1993.

Loose, John, *A Historical Introduction to the Philosophy of Science*, 2nd edn, Oxford, Oxford University Press, 1980.

Lucanio, Patrick, *Them or Us: Archetypal Interpretations of Fifties Alien Invasion Films*, Bloomington, Indiana University Press, 1987.

Lyotard, Jean-François, *The Postmodern Condition*, Manchester, Manchester University Press, 1984.

McGinn, Colin, *The Problem of Consciousness*, Oxford, Blackwell, 1991.

Maltby, Richard and Ian Craven, *Hollywood Cinema*, Oxford, Blackwell, 1995.

Marchessault, Janine and Kim Shawchuk (eds.), *Wild Science: Reading Feminism, Medicine and the Media*, London and New York, Routledge, 2000.

Matheson, T. J., 'Marcuse, Ellul, and the Science-Fiction Film,' *Science-Fiction Studies*, 19 (1992) 326–339.

Myers, Greg, 'Out of the Laboratory and Down to the Bay: Writing in Science and Technology Studies,' *Written Communication*, 13:1 (January 1996) 5–43.

Neale, Stephen, 'Issues of Difference: Alien and Blade Runner,' in James Donald (ed.), *Fantasy and the Cinema*, London, BFI, 1989, pp. 213–223.

Newman, Kim, *Sight and Sound*, 9:1 (January 1999) 45–46.

Newton-Smith, W. H., *The Rationality of Science*, London, Routledge and Kegan-Paul, 1981.

Nye, David E., *Narratives and Spaces: Technology and the Construction of American Culture*, Exeter, University of Exeter Press, 1997.

Penley, Constance, *The Future of an Illusion: Film, Feminism, and Psychoanalysis*, London and New York, Routledge, 1989.

——, 'Time Travel, Primal Scene and the Critical Dystopia,' in Annette Kuhn (ed.), *Alien Zone*, London, Verso, 1990, pp. 116–127.

——, *Feminism and Film Theory*, London and New York, Routledge, 1988.

Penley, Constance, Elisabeth Lyon and Janet Bergstrom (eds.), *Close*

Encounters: Film, Feminism, and Science Fiction, Minneapolis, University of Minnesota Press, 1991.

Putnam, Hilary, *The Many Faces of Realism*, LaSalle, Illinois, Open Court Publishing Company, 1987.

Rich, B. Ruby, 'The Party Line: Gender and Technology in the Home,' in Jennifer Terry and Melodie Calvert (eds.), *Processed Lives: Gender and Technology in Everyday Life*, London and New York, Routledge, 1997, pp. 198–208.

Roberts, Robin, *A New Species: Gender and Science in Science Fiction*, Urbana and Chicago, University of Illinois Press, 1993.

Rosario, Vernon A. (ed.), *Science and Homosexualities*, London and New York, Routledge, 1997.

Ross, Andrew, *Strange Weather: Culture, Science and Technology in the Age of Limits*, London, Verso, 1991.

Schiebinger, Londa, *The Mind Has No Sex? Women in the Origins of Modern Science*, Cambridge, Mass., Harvard University Press, 1989.

Schelde, Per, *Androids, Humanoids, and other Science Fiction Monsters: Science and Soul in Science Fiction Films*, New York, New York University Press, 1993.

Scholes, Robert, 'The Roots of Science Fiction,' in Mark Rose (ed.), *Science Fiction: A Collection of Critical Essays*, Englewood Cliffs, NJ, Prentice Hall, Inc., 1976, pp. 46–56.

——, *Fabulations and Metafiction*, Urbana and Chicago, University of Illinois Press, 1979.

Screen, The Sexual Subject: A Screen Reader in Sexuality, London and New York, Routledge, 1992.

Seed, David, *American Science Fiction and the Cold War*, Edinburgh, Edinburgh University Press, 1999.

Shortland, Michael, *Medicine and Film: A Checklist, Survey and Research Resource*, Oxford, Wellcome Unit for the History of Medicine, Research Publications Number IX, 1989.

Slusser, George and Tom Shippey (eds.), *Fiction 2000: Cyberpunk and the Future of Narrative*, Athens, University of Georgia Press, 1992.

Sobchack, Vivian, 'Science Fiction,' in Wes D. Gehring (ed.), *Handbook of American Film Genres*, New York, Greenwood Press, 1988, pp. 229–247.

——, *Screening Space: The American Science Fiction Film*, 2nd edn, New York, Ungar, 1991.

Solomon, Stanley, *Beyond Formula: American Film Genres*, New York and London, Harcourt Brace Jovanovich Publishers, 1976.

Sontag, Susan, 'The Imagination of Disaster,' *October*, 40 (1965) 42–48.

Springer, Claudia, 'Sex, Memories and Angry Women,' in Mark Dery (ed.), *Flame Wars: The Discourse of Cyberculture*, Durham, NC, Duke University Press, 1994, pp. 157–178.

——, *Electronic Eros: Bodies and Desire in the Postindustrial Age*, Austin, University of Texas, 1996.

Squier, Susan, 'Reproducing the Posthuman Body: Fetus, Surrogate Mother, Pregnant Man,' in Judith Halberstam and Ira Livingston, *Post Human Bodies*, Bloomington and Indianapolis, Indiana University Press, 1995, pp. 113–132.

Stevenson, Leslie and Henry Byerly, *The Many Faces of Science: An Introduction to Scientists, Values and Society*, Boulder, Col., Westview Press, 1995.

Straayer, Chris, *Deviant Eyes, Deviant Bodies: Sexual Re-orientations in Film and Video*, New York, Columbia University Press, 1996.

Tambiah, Stanley Jeyaraja, *Magic, Science, Religion, and the Scope of Rationality*, Cambridge, Cambridge University Press, 1990.

Tasker, Yvonne, *Spectacular Bodies: Gender, Genre and the Action Cinema*, London and New York, Routledge, 1993.

Telotte, J. P., 'The World of Tomorrow and the "Secret Goal" of Science Fiction,' *Journal of Film and Video*, 45:1 (1993) 27–39.

——, *Replications: A Robotic History of Science Fiction Film*, Urbana and Chicago, University of Illinois Press, 1995.

——, *A Distant Technology: Science Fiction Film and the Machine Age*, Hanover, NH, Wesleyan University Press, 1999.

Terry, Jennifer and Jacqueline Urla (eds.), *Deviant Bodies: Critical Perspectives on Difference in Science and Popular Culture*, Bloomington and Indianapolis, Indiana University Press, 1995.

Traweek, Sharon, 'An Introduction to Cultural and Social Studies of Sciences and Technologies,' *Culture, Medicine and Psychiatry*, 17 (1993) 3–25.

Tudor, Andrew, *Monsters and Mad Scientists: A Cultural History of the Horror Movie*, Oxford, Blackwell, 1989.

——, 'Unruly Bodies, Unquiet Minds,' *Bodies and Society*, 1:1 (1995) 25–41.

Wasko, Janet, *Hollywood in the Information Age: Beyond the Silver Screen*, Cambridge, Polity, 1994.

Watson, James D., *The Double Helix: A Personal Account of the Discovery of DNA*, London, Weidenfeld and Nicolson, 1968.

Wolmark, Jenny, *Aliens and Others: Science Fiction, Feminism and Postmodernism*, Iowa City, University of Iowa Press, 1994.

Young, Lola, *Fear of the Dark: 'Race', Gender and Sexuality in the Cinema*, London and New York, Routledge, 1996.

Index

Note: 'n.' after a page reference indicates a note number on that page.